STRESS
Remedies

Hundreds of Fast-Relief Tips to Relax Your Body,
Calm Your Mind—And Defuse the Number One Cause of
Everyday Health Problems and Chronic Disease

by Carl Sherman

and the Editors of **PREVENTION** Magazine
Medical Adviser: Paul J. Rosch, M.D.
President, The American Institute of Stress

Rodale Press, Inc.
Emmaus, Pennsylvania

Library of Congress Cataloging-in-Publication Data

Sherman, Carl.

    Stress remedies : hundreds of fast-relief tips to relax your body, calm your mind—and defuse the number one cause of everyday health problems and chronic disease / by Carl Sherman and the editors of Prevention Magazine.

          p.   cm.

    Includes index.

    ISBN 0–87596–308–0 hardcover

      1. Stress management. I. Prevention Magazine.

    II. Title.

    RA785.S524   1997

    155.9'042—dc21   97–4299

Distributed in the book trade by St. Martin's Press

2   4   6   8   10   9   7   5   3   hardcover

— **OUR PURPOSE** —

"We inspire and enable people to improve their lives and the world around them."

Editorial Staff for *Stress Remedies*

Senior Managing Editor: Edward Claflin
Editor: Steven Slon
Contributing Editors: Susan G. Berg, Julia VanTine
Assistant Research Manager: Anita C. Small
Editorial Researcher: Paris Muchanic
Copy Editor: Kathy D. Everleth
Associate Art Director: Faith Hague
Cover and Book Designer: Lynn N. Gano
Technical Artist: J. Andrew Brubaker
Manufacturing Coordinator: Melinda B. Rizzo
Office Manager: Roberta Mulliner
Office Staff: Julie Kehs, Bernadette Sauerwine

Rodale Health and Fitness Books

Vice-President and Editorial Director: Debora T. Yost
Design and Production Director: Michael Ward
Research Manager: Ann Gossy Yermish
Copy Manager: Lisa D. Andruscavage
Studio Manager: Stefano Carbini
Book Manufacturing Director: Helen Clogston

CONTENTS

C

Contents

Contents

FOREWORD

More than a decade ago, *Time* magazine ran a cover story that referred to *stress* as the epidemic of the 1980s, like it was some sort of new plague. The problem has progressively worsened since then. It's hard to go through a day without hearing or reading about stress.

Why all the sudden fuss and commotion? After all, stress has been around since Adam and Eve were in the Garden of Eden. Is it because there is so much more stress today? Is contemporary stress somehow different or more dangerous than the stress our ancestors experienced? Has interest grown because scientific studies have shown how stress can precipitate or aggravate so many different health problems?

There can be little doubt that stress has mushroomed over the past two decades. Surveys about job-related stress, for example, have shown a 20 percent increase over about 10 years in the number of Americans who say that they feel stressed daily or several days a week. Seventy-five percent of all American workers describe their jobs as stressful.

In addition to its harmful effects on health, job stress imposes a staggering financial burden. Soaring medical and legal expenses, increased absenteeism, employee turnover, and diminished productivity all take a toll that's tallied in dollars and cents. The price tag for job stress in corporate America is estimated to be between $200 billion and $300 billion annually. Put into perspective, that's more than 10 times the costs of all strikes combined and the total net profits of Fortune 500 companies.

What can we do to stop the upward spiral of stress in our lives? Before attempting to answer this, we need to understand and agree on what we are talking about. Just what is stress, anyway?

The term *stress*, as it is currently used, was originated by Hans

Selye around 60 years ago. He defined it as "the nonspecific response of the body to any demand for change." Later, he found it necessary to coin another word, *stressor*, to refer to the threatening stimuli that evoke the body's stress response.

In 1950, Selye published his magnum opus *Stress*, a massive treatise containing well over 1,000 pages of text, illustrations, and photos as well as more than 5,000 references. It generated so much interest and furor that it became necessary to produce a yearly update in order to report on numerous new studies by Selye and other researchers as well as to correct any confusion caused by the previous edition.

In helping Selye prepare the *1951 Annual Report on Stress*, I included the comments and conclusions of one critic to illustrate the existing state of consternation and chaos on the subject of stress. Based on verbatim citations from Selye's own lectures and publications, the critic concluded that apparently, "stress, in addition to being itself, and the result of itself, is also the cause of itself."

Certainly, we've learned a lot about stress since then. But we still can't explain it in a cut-and-dried way. For one thing, stress is such a highly personalized phenomenon. Situations that are distressful for some individuals may be pleasurable for others—or have little significance either way.

Consider the passengers on a roller-coaster ride. Some are crouched down in their seats with their eyes shut and jaws clenched, squeezing the retaining bar so hard that their knuckles turn white. Others—the wide-eyed thrill seekers—relish every steep plunge and can't wait to go around again. Still others seem to have an air of nonchalance, bordering on boredom. So: Is the roller-coaster ride stressful? It depends on which passenger you ask.

Our stress responses differ tremendously, too. Some people blush, while others become pale. Emotional reactions can range from anxiety and panic to anger and depression. There are numerous and diverse physical symptoms as well, including stomach pain, diarrhea, palpitations, hives, muscle spasms, and nervous twitches—and various combinations of all of these. As Selye admitted in his later years, "Everyone knows what stress is, but in reality, nobody really knows."

Stress is an unavoidable consequence of life. It arrives in the wake of traumatic life events such as the loss of a loved one, illness, poverty, retirement, and relocation. It can also be a by-product of deadlines, traffic jams, lost keys, and an assortment of other daily hassles.

There are some stressors you can do something about and others you can't hope to avoid or influence. The trick is in learning to distinguish between the two. Otherwise, you can be constantly frustrated—like Don Quixote, tilting at windmills—instead of applying your time, talent, and energy to situations where you can make a difference.

Stress is not necessarily bad. Increased stress results in increased productivity, up to a point. What that point is varies from one person to the next. It's something you must find out for yourself.

It's very much like the tension on a violin string. Not enough produces an annoying, raspy sound, while too much results in an irritating shrill—or causes the string to snap. But the correct degree of stress can create a beautiful tone. Similarly, we each have to find the right amount of stress that allows us to make pleasant music in our lives.

While stress is very much an individual experience, all of our research confirms at least one common thread: The feeling of having little control is always distressful. The diverse responses among those roller-coaster riders result from the sense of control they have over the event. While none of them has any more or less, their perceptions and expectations are quite different. Your sense of control is something you can learn to change for the better.

This book offers a selection of stress busters that have been found useful in re-establishing control in your life and in diminishing the damaging emotional and physical effects of stress. Every recommendation is based on interviews with doctors, researchers, and others in the field of stress management who have generously shared their expertise.

Of course, since stress is so very different for each of us, it should come as no surprise that no stress-reduction strategy works for everyone. By exploring the many options presented in this book, you'll find what works best for you and learn how stress can help you to become productive rather than self-destructive.

Paul J. Rosch, M.D.
President, The American Institute of Stress
Clinical professor of medicine and psychiatry, New York Medical College

PART I

STRESS AND YOU

INTRODUCTION

STRIKE BACK AT STRESS—STARTING NOW

Stress seems like a way of life these days. In fact, you often don't even realize just how tense and anxious you've been feeling until you have one of those all-too-rare opportunities to relax. Then suddenly you notice that your head isn't throbbing. Your stomach isn't churning. You're thinking more clearly. And you don't feel so run-down and exhausted.

Clearly, stress is one thing you can live without. And the less of it you have, the better off you are, health-wise.

Now if it's any consolation, stress is nothing new—not by a long shot. It has been around since our cavemen ancestors first battled with dinosaurs over who was going to have whom for lunch. But it's made a whole lot worse nowadays by all of the trappings of modern life.

Of course, we have a big advantage over all of the stressed-out generations that preceded us. We know the enemy. And we know how to fight back.

YOUR BUILT-IN SELF-DEFENSE SYSTEM

We tend to view stress as something that happens to us. In reality, it happens within us. Our perception of a particular situation is what makes it stressful.

At the first sign that there's trouble brewing, your brain releases

Introduction

a cascade of chemicals that raise your blood pressure, speed your heart rate, and make your breathing more rapid and shallow. These physical changes make up what is known as the fight-or-flight response. They give you the strength and energy you need to either take on the "attacker" or get out of harm's way.

This power surge had obvious advantages in the days when humans had woolly mammoths and saber-toothed tigers for neighbors. But it isn't very useful against stressors such as an interminable car alarm, a slow-moving checkout line, a spat with a spouse, or a corporate memo that hints ominously of downsizing.

Unfortunately, your brain doesn't make the distinction between a physical threat and an emotional one. It instructs your body to go through the same self-protective motions, no matter what.

When your body goes on red alert time and again, it eventually takes a tremendous toll on your health. Research has linked stress to a host of physical ills, including colds, bowel problems, headaches, backaches, high blood pressure, and heart disease. As many as 90 percent of all doctor visits are for stress-related symptoms.

The emotional wear and tear of chronic stress can be just as debilitating. Allowing your body to simmer in a stew of stress chemicals can produce low-level anxiety that just won't quit. It may also contribute to depression.

REAL RELIEF

The good news is that you can take steps to protect yourself against the toxic effects of stress. No, you don't have to quit your job, say so long to your family, and head for the seclusion of some uncharted Caribbean isle. (If that's what you had in mind . . . well, sorry to disappoint.) It's much less complicated than that.

Part Two of this book is filled with techniques that will help you manage the stress in your life more effectively. You'll learn how to:

Build supportive relationships. Stress can't bring you down when you're surrounded by caring family members and loyal, dependable friends. You may have the same day-to-day hassles in your life, or an unavoidable crisis like the death of a loved one, but they don't seem

4

quite so daunting when you have loved ones in your corner.

Think positive. Remember: It's how you view a situation, not the situation itself, that triggers your body's stress response. Learning to identify patterns of negative self-talk—that is, words and phrases you unconsciously use to sabotage your self-esteem—and substituting more positive language can go a long way toward stopping stress in its tracks.

Express yourself. Everyone experiences strong negative emotions from time to time. Anger, jealousy, shame—such feelings are just part of being human. Trying to keep them bottled up inside you demands psychological energy and only makes matters worse.

Control your thoughts. Many stress experts believe that the mastery of attention is essential to stress relief. When you can keep your thoughts in the here and now, you stop yourself from rehashing the past and fretting about the future—neither of which you can change anyway.

Simplify your day-to-day routine. It doesn't take something as serious as losing a job to trigger your body's stress response. Losing your car keys can do it just as easily. Getting your life in order with better organizational and time-management skills can whittle away at stress, too.

Master your body. You can actually switch off your body's stress response after it has begun with relaxation techniques such as meditation, deep breathing, and yoga. In fact, just knowing that you have these techniques at your disposal can give you a heightened sense of control, which experts say is crucial to effective stress management.

Keep yourself healthy. Stress delivers a double whammy to your body by sabotaging your eating habits and exercise routine. You'll find out what you need to do to keep yourself in fighting trim, so you can head off stress-related illness.

TAKING IT PERSONALLY

Ultimately, stress is a highly individual matter—as unique to you as your appearance and your personality. Only you can say whether a particular situation is stressful. And only you can decide whether a particular stress-reducing strategy works for you.

As you read through the rest of this book, consider the vast array of stress-fighting tools that you have at your disposal. Learn how each works and what it requires from you. Think about whether it suits your needs and lifestyle.

Then you have two options. You can pick and choose your remedies on an as-needed basis, or you can plan ahead and create your very own stress-management program. No matter which road you take, you'll be well on your way to a lifetime of less stress and better health.

THE TOP 10 STRESSORS
TAKE ON LIFE'S BIGGEST CHALLENGES

Most of us are creatures of habit. We don't like it when something upsets the applecart, so to speak. That's why events that cause sudden or drastic change in our lives are often the most stressful.

Most of the stressors that are listed as the top 10 will come as no surprise to you. There's no question that the death of a loved one, a divorce, or the loss of a job can cause tremendous turmoil. But you might be surprised to discover that positive as well as negative events can cause stress. Good stuff like marriage, the birth of a child, and buying a new house can be just as stressful as events that we dread.

For better or worse, change is a part of life. So your best bet is to learn how to cope with it and the stress that it can cause.

Following are the life events that experts have identified as the most stressful, along with some very practical advice on what to do if one of them happens to you.

DIVORCE

You've been betrayed. You're furious. You're humiliated. Your life has fallen apart, and you can't see any way of putting it back together again.

Such feelings are by no means uncommon in the wake of divorce. And they do fade away with time. But they're also one reason that divorce ranks among life's top stressors. In fact, experts say, only the death of a spouse is more stressful.

The trauma of divorce hits you physically—like a ton of bricks. In a study at Ohio State University in Columbus, men who were separated or divorced showed decreases in immune function and reported significantly more illness than married men. Other research has shown that divorced people of all ages are at greater risk of premature death than married people.

"Digestive problems, skin problems, hair loss—all can be associated with divorce," says Emily Stein, Ph.D., director of Human Resources at Mount Sinai Medical Center in New York City. "Many people lose their appetites, while others gain a lot of weight."

As you might expect, the emotional fallout is every bit as extreme. "People get depressed or anxious or paranoid," says Dr. Stein. "You may be weeping all the time, or you may feel lethargic. You may have difficulty remembering things and walk around in a daze."

It may take two years or more from the time of real separation before the dust settles and a person gets his life truly back on track. The first six to eight months are the worst, according to Dr. Stein. That's when stress can have you reeling.

Account for your losses. Take time out to acknowledge and assess the extent of the emotional damage that has been done. "You have to understand that this trauma is serious business," Dr. Stein says. "Even if you're the person who did the leaving, it can be very hard."

Exercise your coping skills. You've been through difficult times before. What did you do to cope? "Meditation, relaxation—anything like that is helpful," says Dr. Stein.

Treat your body right. It's important to pay particular attention to your physical health at this time, Dr. Stein notes. Make a point of eating a balanced diet, maintaining an exercise schedule, and getting enough sleep. All of these things are surprisingly helpful in keeping you on an even keel.

Divide and conquer. Once you've re-established your healthy habits, it's time for some reflection. Get some paper and a pencil and list all of the emotional and practical issues that you face, suggests Michael Broder, Ph.D., a clinical psychologist in Philadelphia and co-author of *Living Single*. In the practical area, for example, there are legal matters, financial commitments, child-care concerns, and so forth. "When you break down the situation into units, it starts to feel a lot more manageable," he says.

Take a giant step forward. The newly divorced can feel like they're living in transition, with one foot in the failed marriage and the other poised at the crevasse of the unknown. You must move on, urges Dr. Broder. "If you've left no stone unturned in your efforts to save your relationship, then you have to start thinking of yourself as living in a totally new phase of your life," he says.

Do something new. To break free of a relationship, try a little exploration and experimentation. It's time to change your routine, find new friends, and develop new interests. "If you've never gone to the ballet because it bored your husband, now you can go," says Dr. Broder. "If you've never played tennis but always wanted to try, now's the time. Take up something new that won't be a reminder of the past."

Expect a few bad days. Even if you're coping beautifully, it's perfectly normal to occasionally wish that things were the way they used to be. Think of those pangs of regret, twinges of loneliness, and longings for what you've lost as cravings, nothing more. And like all cravings, they will pass.

It's far better to experience the feelings and then let go of them than it is to act on them. "If you act on them, you can make serious mistakes—phone calls you'll regret later and so forth," says Dr. Broder. "Better to find someone to talk to who will ease your feelings."

Consider outside help. Divorce is one situation in which a trained counselor, a therapist, or a clergyperson can be extremely helpful, Dr. Stein says. "Sure, you'll eventually get over your divorce on your own," she says. "But no one should underestimate how horrifying, humiliating, and overwhelming it can be at the time."

Group therapy sessions can be particularly helpful, she adds. Just being in the same room with others who are dealing with the exact same problems that you are helps you see that you're not alone.

The YMCA and other community organizations frequently

sponsor support groups for the newly divorced. Or check with your place of worship for any services that it may provide.

DEATH IN THE FAMILY

Death is inevitable—the biological destiny from which no creature is exempt. All religions and spiritual traditions exist in part to help us come to terms with this frightening fact of life. And yet when someone close to us passes on, we're seldom prepared for the force of the blow.

The loss of a spouse or child is the most stressful of all human experiences, experts say. When a spouse dies, the risks of death appear to rise rapidly among the bereaved. The recently widowed often develop dangerous heart rhythm irregularities, and their immune systems are well under par.

The effects of the death of someone close to you are felt for a long time. The acute phase of adjustment can last for three years, says Camille Lloyd, Ph.D., professor of psychiatry and behavioral sciences at the University of Texas-Houston Health Science Center. And you may have lingering sadness for a decade or more.

The following suggestions may help you better cope with this devastating experience.

Accept your grief. The depth of your desolation may shock you, but it's important to realize how normal such feelings are. "You have to know that it's okay to cry for hours, to feel empty," says Dr. Lloyd. "To avoid the feelings or push them off takes a lot of energy. And they come back anyway."

Allow yourself to mourn. One thing that can help you through the grieving process is the mourning ritual provided by your religion. "Grief is the inner experience of loss, while mourning is the public expression and sharing of that loss. There's a healing quality to mourning," says Daniel Dworkin, Ph.D., a psychologist in private practice in Fort Collins, Colorado. "It intensifies the expression of your feelings and reduces your sense of isolation."

Traditional mourning gives you permission to spend time grieving. The Jewish faith, for example, provides for a seven-day period known as shivah, during which no work is done by the mourners, and friends and family pay condolence calls. If your religion is meaningful to you, accept the consolation that it offers, Dr. Dworkin urges.

Stay in touch. Death robs you of an important human connection. Maintaining contact with family and friends "reminds you of the connections that you still have," says Dr. Dworkin.

"It's important to rally your sources of social support," agrees Dr. Lloyd.

Help others to help you. Those closest to you can escort you through the grieving and healing process—if you let them. But you have to be clear about what you want from them. "People often want to help but don't know how," Dr. Lloyd explains. "So you have to take responsibility for cueing them to your needs and asking them for help without feeling embarrassed about it." Your loved ones will appreciate it when you say, "I'm feeling kind of lonely tonight. Can we get together?"

Be up-front on the job. While your boss and co-workers are likely to sympathize with your loss, you can't assume they understand that your ability to function may be substantially reduced for months. "You have to talk to them about how you feel, what you can and can't do right now, and how they can help you," Dr. Dworkin says. "Tell them if you're finding it hard to concentrate and need to lighten the load."

Enlist some support. Support groups often have much to offer the bereaved, particularly those whose social circle isn't wide. You gain great comfort from others who truly know what you're going through because they're coping with a similar loss. Friendships often form that extend outside the group and last a lifetime.

In addition, participants in a support group have the opportunity to give as well as receive assistance. Knowing that you've helped someone else gives your spirits a much-needed lift.

Find time to be alone. As vital as social support may be, you also need time by yourself, says Dr. Dworkin. "Grief is such a personal process. You need to get away from everyone from time to time," he explains.

Find time to exercise. When the initial intense phase of bereavement begins to subside, it's important to resume moderate physical activity, Dr. Dworkin says. "It gives you back some sense of control. You know that you're doing something positive."

Take care of yourself. Often we're not prepared for the sheer physical impact of grief, says Dr. Dworkin. "For a time, most people simply don't have the energy to do much of anything," he says. "You'll feel tired, your appetite may be impaired, and you may be unable to follow any routine. It's important to accept this as a normal part of the process and to not fight it."

ILLNESS

You already know that stress can make you sick. It has been linked to ailments ranging from the common cold to cancer. But on the flip side of the coin, becoming sick can actually contribute to stress.

Change is the big agitator here, says Roderick Borrie, Ph.D., a psychologist at South Oaks Hospital in Amityville, New York. "Chronic illness in particular means accepting a lot of changes in your relationships at home and on the job—not to mention in your identity," he says. "You may need help with things that you used to be able to do on your own. And you may have to do a lot of new things for your health—take medications, see doctors."

When the illness is severe, the underlying fear of death can compound suffering. And with some conditions, such as cancer, irrational beliefs make things even worse. "Many of us grew up learning that cancer is a death sentence. This isn't necessarily true, but the fears persist," says Andrew Baum, Ph.D., professor of psychiatry and psychology at the University of Pittsburgh and director of behavioral medicine and oncology at the University of Pittsburgh Cancer Institute.

Managing stress is especially important when you're sick because there's plenty of evidence to suggest that doing so can affect the course of your illness. Although it hasn't been definitively proven, stress may impair the efficiency of the immune system, Dr. Baum points out. This can have a serious impact on your ability to fight off the disease. It may lead to the growth of tumors and the spread of infection. And it may promote the blood clots, narrowed arteries, and high cholesterol that are characteristic of heart disease.

11

Here's how you can minimize the stressfulness of illness.

Accept that you're scared. The first step is recognizing how natural your reaction is, says Dr. Baum. It's perfectly normal to experience anxiety attacks and depression after a diagnosis of cancer, diabetes, or even high blood pressure.

Understand your condition. Uncertainty is stressful. Learning what you can about your illness can greatly reduce your fear of the unknown. "If you wake up after surgery with pain in your gut, knowing that it's normal and that it's nothing to worry about makes the experience less traumatic," says Dr. Baum.

Talk it out. You need to recruit some sympathetic listeners with whom you can share your worries and concerns. One study of people with chronic fatigue syndrome found that antibodies to the Epstein-Barr virus, the suspected cause of the condition, increased when the patients were allowed to communicate the stress and trauma of being sick. "It suggests that talking about the problems associated with an illness increases your ability to fight it," Dr. Borrie says.

Seek out support. Family and friends tend to be most sympathetic when you first get sick, but their capacity for empathic listening tends to wane with the passage of time. "This is one real advantage of a support group," Dr. Borrie says. "The group members will always be there for you."

Help yourself. If no one is around to listen, or if you simply don't feel comfortable opening up to another person, you might want to put pen to paper and write about your physical and emotional suffering. Or you may prefer the comfort of prayer.

Learn to relax. Techniques that induce relaxation, such as meditation, can be indispensable when you're dealing with the stress of illness. "After a diagnosis of breast cancer, for example, your worry can escalate to an anxiety attack," says Dr. Baum. "Having a way to turn off the worry and calm your mind and body can be especially useful."

There's a healthful bonus that goes with learning to relax. "When tension builds up in your body, pain feels more severe," says Dr. Borrie. Techniques that reduce tension can also ease pain.

Dr. Borrie prescribes flotation tank sessions to his patients. He has found that floating in water helps people relax quickly, and it doesn't require any skill to master. "In an hour, you'll probably feel very different. You'll feel less tense, and you may notice a decrease in symptoms," he says. (Refer to the chapter on flotation tanks on page 95 for more information.)

GETTING MARRIED

A marriage may be made in heaven—but all of the planning falls into the hands of us mere mortals. The big day is preceded by months of frenzied preparation that can be aggravated by friction between families that don't yet know each other. And that's only the beginning. The newlyweds soon discover that being Mr. and Mrs. is a whole other ballgame.

Stress can take its toll in the months leading up to a wedding and in the period of adjustment that follows it. Some marriages don't survive. In fact, the first two years of married life is one of the two times when a couple is most likely to divorce.

The wedding itself is "a field day for stress," says Matti Gershenfeld, Ed.D., a psychologist and president of Couples Learning Center in Jenkintown, Pennsylvania. "Families have to work together. One may want something big and elegant; the other, something small and simple. Disputes arise: Should the groom's family pay for the band and the photographer? Should the bride's family pay for everything? Should the bride and groom pay?" And that's before you even walk down the aisle.

To help ease the transition to married life, heed the advice of experts who have helped others through this stressful phase.

Speak up. When you're planning your wedding, good communication is vital. "You should first sit down and talk about what you want, then discuss who will pay for it," Dr. Gershenfeld suggests. If conflicts develop, each of you should broach the subject with your respective parents.

Mind your money matters. When the honeymoon is over and you're settling into life as husband and wife, financial issues are usually the ones that most need working out. Before you were married, even if you lived together, you probably had a clear sense of "his" and "hers" as far as income and expenses. Now, most likely, money will be pooled and shared. This frequently causes conflict.

"A woman may dream of buying a house and want to put money away for a down payment, while her husband may prefer spending on travel while they are young and have no children," Dr. Gershenfeld says. "You have to sit down and agree on how you're going to handle money jointly—not just for today but for the future."

Master the art of compromise. "The real reason for marriage is commitment and companionship," says Dr. Gershenfeld. "You should be supportive of each other's interests. If he loves hockey games and wants her along, she should go. In return, she can expect his companionship at the opera. It's a matter not just of being there but of going with good grace."

Establish roles. The very texture of a marriage must be negotiated in its early months, according to Suzanne Pope, Ph.D., clinical director of the Colorado Institute for Marriage and the Family in Boulder. "There's a stage of jockeying for position—who takes charge in different situations, who does what," Dr. Pope says.

Without traditional expectations to guide you, "everything is up for negotiation," she adds. For one couple, it became clear that the bride was much better with numbers and organization. Although it went against the groom's traditional upbringing, she ended up taking care of the bills. And he, it turned out, had a largely unexplored talent for cooking.

Expect dissension. During this negotiation phase of a marriage, some strife is inevitable. "One thing that relieves the stress is realizing how normal conflict is," Dr. Pope says. "Having an argument doesn't mean that you're ready to divorce." In fact, she says, couples really need to have some serious struggles in the early days of marriage. If you don't confront your conflicts, "they'll go underground, and you'll swallow one frustration and resentment after another," she explains. "That's really deadly for a marriage."

Be extra-cautious with family matters. In-law problems are notorious for putting strain on a marriage. It's best not to get embroiled in arguments between your spouse and his or her family. Just be there to listen and to lend support as he or she works through the inevitable rough spots between parents and brothers and sisters, Dr. Pope says.

14

Remember the reason. When your spouse's zany sense of humor, absentmindedness, or extreme disorganization starts getting on your nerves, you may be able to defuse the escalating tension by reminding yourself of the qualities that made you fall in love in the first place.

UNEMPLOYMENT

Corporate honchos euphemistically refer to it as downsizing. In plain English, it means that you're out of a job. And there's no question that job loss can send you into a tailspin as you come to terms with the fact that your financial security has been suddenly and unceremoniously snatched away. Often, your sense of self-worth gets snatched away too.

That unemployment is a hard-hitting stressor is beyond question. The mere threat of a layoff significantly increases blood cholesterol, according to a Swedish study of middle-age shipyard workers. Unemployment also increases the risks of premature death: The *British Medical Journal* has reported that for middle-age unemployed men, the risk of premature death is double the risk of those who are employed.

Being out of work sets the stage for a smorgasbord of practical and emotional stressors, according to Barry Lubetkin, Ph.D., clinical director of the Institute for Behavioral Therapy in New York City. Besides creating financial hardship and insecurity, unemployment can severely strain family relationships. But the most intense pressure is often highly personal: Losing your job can strip you of your sense of who you are.

Here are some tips to help you survive the loss of a job.

Rethink your values. "All too many people—particularly men—are totally ego-involved in their work," Dr. Lubetkin says. "They define their values, their mission in life, and their worth to themselves, their families, and their communities by their success on the job."

But the fact is, you are many, many things besides what you do for a living. "Ask yourself: If being a success at work rates as a 10, how much is it worth to be a good parent? A loving spouse?" says Dr. Lubetkin. "Keep in mind the other things you do that show

15

your value to the world—such as being a good citizen or contributing to charity."

Quiet the negative self-talk. If your inner voice is saying, "I'll never find another job again" or "I can't stand the pain I'm going through," then challenge the message, advises Dr. Lubetkin. "Being unemployed is uncomfortable, but it's not like a nuclear war. And while it may be difficult to find a new job, it's highly likely that you will be working again in the near future."

Banish shame. Many unemployed people feel embarrassed and humiliated and become convinced that something must be wrong with them. That creates unnecessary stress. "Identify just what it is that makes you feel ashamed," Dr. Lubetkin says. Think about it realistically. Will your spouse really think less of you? Will your children really view you as a loser? They won't if you don't.

Open up. Discussing the problems that you are about to face goes a long way toward relieving stress. "Talk about the economic and psychological issues that are likely to arise—for example, how everyone in the family is going to have to control expenditures," Dr. Lubetkin says. "Get family members to discuss how they're going to feel about having Mom or Dad home all day."

Get in the hunt. If you haven't been in job-hunting mode for a while, your skills are probably a little rusty. It's worth the investment to take a short course in résumé writing or to hire someone to troubleshoot your résumé. And when you snag your first interview, sit down with a good friend or a family member beforehand and do a role-play of the anticipated exchange.

Establish a routine. However you spend your days, make sure you fill them. "After a couple of weeks of healing, you have to approach each day as if you had a job," says Dr. Lubetkin. "Develop an hour-by-hour plan the night before. Get up at 8:00 A.M. and know where you're going to go and what you're going to do. Structure each day."

You may spend three hours on your job search, two hours on a hobby, and a few more hours on volunteer work. If you don't find time for something that's on your list, make sure you get to it the next day. You might want to enlist a family member or friend to monitor your schedule and make sure you stick to it.

Safeguard your health. Good nutrition and regular exercise are essential to stave off stress-related illness and keep your energy level high. Likewise, relaxation techniques can defuse any tension and anxiety that you're feeling and give a much-needed boost to your mood and your spirits.

Shore up your social contacts. "Losing a job is like bereavement. When you're unemployed, some people don't want to get too close to you," says Marilyn Puder-York, Ph.D., a psychologist in private practice in New York City. "They don't like to be reminded of their own vulnerability."

When phone calls aren't returned by friends who were best buddies after your last promotion, you have to realize that it's not you but them. On the other hand, says Dr. Puder-York, a little reaching out to family, friends, and neighbors will help you discover people who are genuinely sympathetic and supportive.

Get in a group. Plenty of support groups exist to provide emotional comfort as well as practical advice for your job search. It's a good idea to get involved in a group like this—but choose carefully. "Sometimes there are a lot of negative people who can drag you down," Dr. Puder-York says. "Avoid a group where members do nothing but vent their frustration and despair."

And if you're having serious problems coping with unemployment, she adds, don't hesitate to seek professional counseling or therapy.

RETIREMENT

You dream of retirement for decades. You can't wait to be free of the demands of the daily grind. You can do what you want when you want to, and you don't have to answer to anyone.

But then the big day comes. You say good-bye to the people who for years have been like family. And then it occurs to you: What, precisely, are you supposed to do with yourself now?

"Retirement may undermine your self-worth in many ways," says Allen Elkin, Ph.D., program director of the Stress Management and Counseling Center in New York City. You no longer have a title, a staff, or people to stroke your ego.

"No one says on his deathbed, 'I wish I had spent more time at the office,'" Dr. Elkin continues. "But when people finally have time to relax, they find that they miss their work."

Retirement often requires you to clarify your value system. You'll have to answer questions that you've probably put on hold for years, such as: Who am I? What really matters to me?

It's not what you retire from but what you retire to that's important. "You have to prepare for retirement," Dr. Elkin says. This means appreciating who you are. "You can't fit a type A personality into a type B retirement," he notes. "The ideal for you may not be lying on the beach or playing golf all day. You may need to be really active."

To make your retirement rich and fulfilling:

Find a hobby. You can prepare yourself for retirement by developing interests outside your work. Serious leisure pursuits—hobbies and activities such as singing in a chorus or studying astronomy—are enriching at any time of life, but they become absolutely essential when you're retired.

In one study of older adults, those who were happiest in their retirement were spending 40 percent or more of their time engaged in hobbies or similar pursuits that represented something of a challenge and gave them a sense of competence. "People who fell below that level were much less happy with their lives," says Roger Mannell, Ph.D., professor and chair of recreation and leisure studies at the University of Waterloo in Ontario.

Share your skills. An even more rewarding use of your now-abundant leisure time is volunteer work. You can put a lifetime of experience to good use by helping others. In some communities, for instance, there are volunteer corps of retired executives who give guidance to neophytes who are just starting out in business.

Examine your union. Retirement can test the most stable of marriages. "Many marriages will tolerate almost anything except both spouses being at home 24 hours a day," says Dr. Elkin. At mid-career, the average husband and wife spend as little as 10 minutes a day talking with each other. And now they're face-to-face full-time.

To smooth the transition, some preparation is in order. "Before you retire, spend some weekends together. Take some trips together," Dr. Elkin suggests. If you explore activities that you enjoy doing together, you'll whet your appetite for that extra time you have in retirement.

Don't pack up right away. For many people, retirement means relocation. Often they migrate to a place where the weather is hospitable and the pace is slow.

It may seem like a great idea, but it's not something to rush into. Moving in itself requires lots of adjustment, so "moving right away when you retire means double the stress," says Dr. Elkin. "If you can separate the two events, it's a lot easier. Let yourself recover from the initial stress of retirement. Wait six months to a year, and use this time to plan for the move and the changes that it will bring."

Do some legwork. When the dust has settled from retirement and you're ready to relocate, consider your options carefully. "It's easy to say, 'Let's move to Hawaii,' " observes Dr. Elkin. "But you need to do some research to put the fantasy in perspective."

Before you pack up for a new area, ask residents what they consider the local problems and difficulties. And get to know the locals themselves a bit better. What are they really like? After all, they're going to be your new neighbors and friends.

NEW BABY

The birth of a child is such a joyous occasion that even in the jaded world we live in we refer to it as a blessed event. Yet as parents everywhere can attest, the changes and demands that accompany the arrival of a baby can prove unexpectedly stressful.

"Uncertainty and ambiguity are always grounds for stress—particularly if you're the kind of person who prides yourself on being in control," says Jeanne T. Grace, Ph.D., associate professor in the School of Nursing at the University of Rochester in New York. No matter how many books you read, no matter how many classes you attend, no matter how many other parents you talk to, you're never quite as prepared for baby as you think you are.

The period of greatest adjustment—and stress—is typically the first three months after a baby is born. But it can take a good eight months or longer to completely integrate the new family member into the rest of your life. In the meantime, here's how to ease your transition into parenthood.

Expect changes in the family dynamic. All of your familial relationships have to be adjusted during this critical time. Your life roles—spouse, friend, son or daughter—must be adjusted to accommodate a new human being, says Dr. Grace.

Get some shut-eye. Or at least try to. Sleep deprivation is almost a cliché among new parents. But the more snooze time you can squeeze in, the better you'll be able to deal with the demands and responsibilities that parenthood has in store.

Make a conscious effort to grab some Zzz's whenever you can. Also, create a schedule that encourages regular sleep for your baby. "If your baby doesn't sleep well, you don't sleep well," Dr. Grace says. "And your whole life seems more difficult."

Expect some bad feelings. The reality of new parenthood may be very different from what you expected. There may be some anger and disappointment mixed in with the joy. Your feelings about your baby and your new life may be surprising—and distressing—but these emotions come with the territory, says Dr. Grace. Accepting them is the first step toward getting over them.

Don't be afraid to ask for help. "Most of us don't have the family support that was available generations ago," Dr. Grace says. So you should make the most of whatever assistance is offered. If a friend says, "Let me know what I can do," tell her what you really need—whether it's picking up an older child from soccer practice or doing the grocery shopping.

"Not everyone is comfortable accepting help. Some new parents may feel that it shows failure," Dr. Grace says. "Just remember the West African proverb: 'It takes a whole village to raise a child.' "

Avoid guilt trips. Mothers who must return to work while their babies are still small often feel tremendous guilt and anxiety. Some of this can be allayed by making the transition gradual: If at all possible, go back part-time at first.

Don't fall prey to perfectionism. Child-rearing is an imprecise science at best. So don't convince yourself that you have to get it exactly right all the time. Instead, try to be what modern psychologists call a good-enough parent: Understand your baby's needs and try

BABY BLUES

Ups and downs in mood are a natural response to parenthood. But 10 to 20 percent of new mothers develop serious depression that may require professional help.

If you have prolonged periods when nothing—not even the baby—brings you joy, or if intense sadness and weepiness just don't go away, talk to your doctor or nurse practitioner without delay, urges Jeanne T. Grace, Ph.D., associate professor in the School of Nursing at the University of Rochester in New York.

Above all, if you start having feelings that you want to hurt your baby or yourself, you must seek help immediately. Post the number for the local crisis hotline, along with the number for your local poison control center and other emergency services, near your telephone. Don't hesitate to call if your feelings frighten you. There's no need to be ashamed: These folks are professionals, and they're trained to help you.

your best to fulfill them. Your baby will sense this, Dr. Grace says.

It may help you to realize that a child whose parents responded to his every cue and satisfied his every demand would be ill-equipped to go out into the world and tolerate delay and frustration. "Don't beat yourself up about being less than perfect," says Dr. Grace.

CHANGE IN FINANCIAL STATUS

Feelings about money can get so mixed up with feelings about life that any significant change in your financial status requires emotional adjustment. And that, of course, means stress.

Money provides a psychological cushion of safety and security, explains Michael Cunningham, Ph.D., professor of psychology at the University of Louisville in Kentucky. "When money is tight, you feel the rocks of life more," he says. "As your wealth goes down, so do your status and self-esteem."

Having less cash also means a decline in your standard of living. Maybe you can't replace an ailing car even though you'd like to. Or you have to make the very difficult decision to move to a smaller house in a less pleasant neighborhood. And you might have to give up a number of things that you enjoy, like dining out frequently. Each of these can just add to your stress.

Here's how to keep your head until you get back on your feet.

Re-evaluate your needs. You can take some of the sting out of negative financial change by adopting a realistic attitude. "A lot of things associated with the upper-middle-class lifestyle are dispensible," says Dr. Cunningham. It's probably not necessary to continue leasing a brand-new car every two years, for example, when a five-year-old vehicle can serve you just as well.

Learn from your mistakes. Instead of reacting to serious debt or even bankruptcy with denial ("It's all the economy's fault") or runaway guilt and self-blame ("I'm a horrible, terrible person"), view your situation as an error in judgment that you can learn from. What will you do differently from now on? With the help of a budget and honest introspection, you can regain control of your financial picture.

Join the crowd. You're not the only one going through financial hardship right now. Chances are that mingling with others in similar straits will make you feel better. Consider joining a support group that can help you cope with your crisis creatively and modify your habits constructively.

Be cautious with newfound wealth. It's not just being broke that can cause stress. An unexpected inheritance, lottery winnings, or a substantial increase in salary can throw a person off-kilter, too.

"Don't spend a windfall until you make a plan that you feel comfortable with, perhaps with the help of a financial adviser," Dr. Cunningham suggests. He warns against spending in the first flush of excitement. "Research has shown that people become much more spendthrifty when they're in an elated mood," he says.

CAREER CHANGE

No matter what the circumstances, career change is an excursion into the unknown. And that can have major psychological repercussions. Whether you're an accountant who moves into sales or a nurse who moves from one hospital to another, you're in for a certain amount of readjustment, says Larney R. Gump, Ed.D., psychotherapist and adjunct professor of psychology at American University in Washington, D.C.

"Security comes from knowing what the future holds," says Dr. Gump. "Uncertainty is stressful. If you're just a little pessimistic, you can build up some pretty big fears."

Dr. Gump's advice: Whatever kind of change you may be going through, be prepared. Recognize that some emotional turmoil is inevitable, and do your best to separate rational concerns from needless anxiety. Here are some other ways to help keep a lid on stress.

Keep negativism in check. Are you telling yourself things like, "I'll never be able to learn those new tasks" or "I just can't handle new situations"? That's negative self-talk, and it's of no benefit to you or your career.

Acknowledge your doubts. Many of us forget how stressful it is to start a new job, says Dr. Gump. A career change may be bedeviled by the same self-imposed stresses as a second marriage. "There's tremendous anxiety about failing," says Dr. Lubetkin. And that can breed insecurity about your abilities and self-worth.

But instead of trying to bury your self-doubts, acknowledge them. Afraid that you made the wrong choice? "Recognize that the information you had led you to your decision," Dr. Lubetkin says. "It wasn't foolhardy or impulsive, but reasonable in light of what you knew at the time."

Reframe your thoughts. Still having doubts? Try casting them in a new light. "We use the term *anxious* in two different ways," Dr. Gump points out. "It can mean worried, but it can also mean excited and eager. Look at your reaction to the prospect of a new career as the arousal of adventure."

Give yourself a pat on the back. When you're feeling overwhelmed, remind yourself of your basic talents. Listing skills that you've mastered in your previous job can help take some of the newness out of your new position, Dr. Gump says. Managing, writing, researching, and organizing are just some skills that are transferable. And if you've been honing them for years in a small manufacturing business, for example, you have a head start on your new duties in the field of communications.

Get a second opinion. "A friend, a relative, or anyone you know who has made a career change can give you the ins and outs of what to expect and lead you around stumbling blocks," Dr. Lubetkin says. A role model of this sort can tell you what it feels like to start over again. He will sympathize with your anxieties and provide an encouraging example of how it all works out.

"In fact, I advise people who are making career changes to practice acting like role models," Dr. Lubetkin adds. "One day a week, just pretend that you're a person who has made the transition successfully. This is how we learn new skills and new attitudes."

MOVING

Moving into a new home is usually a time of great anticipation and excitement. But if you aren't careful, you just might set yourself up for a truckload of stress. "Any time you leave a comfortable environment, any time when demands will be made on you that are out of the ordinary—that's stressful," says Charlotte Kahn, Ed.D., a psychotherapist in private practice in New York City.

"There are two major types of stress in moving," adds Dr. Elkin. "There are what I call logistical stressors: finding and buying a house, getting a mortgage, choosing a mover, getting the kids in school. Then there are the emotional stressors—the feelings of uncertainty and being uprooted that naturally arise when you move."

To de-stress your moving experience, try these tips.

Make a list. Do as much preplanning as you possibly can, urges Dr. Elkin. "Get a piece of paper and list all of the possible stressors, from finding a mover to signing a mortgage. Expect everything to be just a little more of a hassle than it seems."

"Do your homework," agrees Dr. Baum. "The more you know, the less stress you'll experience."

Visualize the move. Try using a little imagination to acclimate to your new surroundings. "I advise people to do a time-projection exercise," Dr. Elkin says. "Imagine what it will be like living in your new home after you've begun to settle in. Describe what it will be like in six months, then a year down the road. Emphasize the positive aspects—the new friends, the wonderful experiences that your kids will be having in school."

Draw on past experience. If you're like most adults, you've moved before. Make a conscious effort to remember how nervous and scared you felt when you made those relocations—and how everything worked out just fine.

Ease the transition. "Spend as much time as possible in the area you're moving to," says Dr. Elkin. If you can, get the name of someone—say, a friend of a friend—who lives in the vicinity. "It's someone you can contact when you get there, so you don't feel completely lost," Dr. Elkin explains.

Reach out. It's often a good idea to ring a few doorbells and meet the neighbors in advance, just to tell them you're moving in. "It forms an emotional climate that's less alien," says Dr. Elkin.

Keep relationships intact. One of the biggest sources of stress is being uprooted from your established social network. Take steps to ensure that ties won't be totally severed. Plan to keep in regular telephone contact, and arrange to exchange photos or videotapes, suggests Dr. Kahn.

You may even want to set dates for relatives and friends to come and visit your new home. "I knew a young man who had to go away to a foreign university at a young age," Dr. Kahn recalls. "Six weeks after his departure, his grandmother took a vacation and went to visit him. Some months after that, his mother went to see him during a holiday break. And his father visited later."

Get involved. Take steps to create some continuity between your old and new locations. Joining a church or temple will help you maintain a vital sense of identity and also put you in touch with a whole network of supportive people. Likewise, if you've been doing volunteer work in a school or hospital, look for similar opportunities in your new community. This could be a good time to become active in your union or professional organization.

Decorate for comfort. Take along at least some things that represent the life that you're leaving behind. Even if you're replacing your furniture, hanging the same picture in the same place in the living room or using the same set of dinner dishes can be comforting, Dr. Elkin says.

Talk it over. Everyone in your family—adults and children alike—should have an opportunity to express their concerns about the move. Communication is essential, Dr. Elkin says. "Before resentment and anger build, talk about why the move is necessary and what options may be considered," he suggests. "Recognize that everyone may not have the same agenda."

Negotiate. If you have more to gain from the move than your spouse, some trade-offs may be in order. Suppose you're relocating because of your job. Your spouse deserves the final say on where you should live. Getting the kitchen, the backyard, or the neighborhood of his or her dreams can ease some of the distress of moving.

Comfort the kids. Likewise, you can help your children adjust to the move by emphasizing the positive aspects of it: "There's going to be a park just three blocks away," or "Your new school has a great computer program." Make a point of using whatever contacts you have in your new community to set up play dates for the youngest family members, so they can make new friends. Maintaining ties to old friends through telephone contact and planned visits is just as important.

PART II

EVERYDAY STRESS SOLUTIONS

ACCEPTANCE

ROLL WITH LIFE'S PUNCHES

Suppose you spotted a burglar trying to break into your house. You wouldn't loan the guy a ladder, would you?

Yet this is exactly how stress often operates. It has no problem finding its way into our lives without any help from us. Then we unwittingly give it a leg up by allowing ourselves to become agitated about situations over which we have little or no control.

We could do ourselves a world of good by coming to terms with the fact that some things in life simply won't go the way we want them to, no matter what we do to influence them. It's the lesson of the well-known Serenity Prayer, which asks for "the serenity to accept the things I cannot change, courage to change the things I can, and wisdom to know the difference."

The simple act of acceptance fights stress by relieving the pressure of perfection. It frees us from what the late noted New York City psychiatrist Karen Horney dubbed the tyranny of the shoulds, which are handed to us in childhood and become guideposts for how we lead our lives: "You should do better in school," "You should be a neater person," "You should have more respect for your elders," to name a few. These are wonderful ideals to live by, but taken together, they can overwhelm us with the demands that they place on us.

"Constantly talking to yourself as a judge, an evaluator, can be a source of tremendous anxiety," says Richard Sackett, Ph.D., director of Integrative Psychotherapy Services in New York City.

LETTING GO CAN BE LIBERATING

When we stop trying so hard to be perfect and instead allow ourselves to be human, life suddenly settles down, says Allen Elkin, Ph.D., program director of the Stress Management and Counseling Center in New York City. Among the stress-busting benefits you may notice:

Greater tranquillity. Abandoning unreasonable expectations leads to inner peace. As Dr. Elkin puts it, "Acceptance is saying, 'This is the way I am; this is the way you are; this is the way the situation is.' You aren't moralizing, judging harshly, or demanding that yourself, another person, or life be different."

Protection from failure. When you stop judging yourself, failure is simply out of the question. That's because nothing about you is bad, and your mistakes only make you human. "It's important to understand that you have a choice in how you see yourself," Dr. Sackett says.

Less shame. Shame is the reason why we refuse to accept many of our inner feelings and impulses, according to Rebecca Curtis, Ph.D., professor of psychology at Adelphi University in Garden City, New York, and a psychologist in New York City. We expend vast amounts of energy attempting to squelch internal cues that we judge as bad. But they have a way of bubbling up to the surface despite our efforts: We can't sleep, we develop indigestion, we get headaches, or we feel just plain miserable. Accepting ourselves the way we are melts shame away.

A path toward self-improvement. When you're constantly judging your own thoughts and behavior, you become so mired in self-criticism that change seems impossible. Acceptance is the first step in breaking out of unhealthy patterns and habits, says Dr. Sackett.

AWARDING YOURSELF THE STAMP OF APPROVAL

As good as acceptance can make you feel, it won't necessarily come easy. After all, you're going to be challenging and changing thought patterns that were instilled in you as a child. These strategies should help.

Recognize your response. You can increase your capacity for acceptance by being aware of how you're reacting to a stressful event. Dr. Sackett suggests getting into the habit of asking yourself, "What am I doing right now? How am I treating this moment?" periodically over the course of a day.

Look through someone else's eyes. "Imagine another person—perhaps a good friend—in a situation that you're finding hard to accept," says Dr. Elkin. "What would you say to that person to help him feel better? Sometimes it's much easier to give advice to someone besides yourself."

Give yourself a pep talk. Dr. Elkin also recommends what he calls the double-chair technique: Sit quietly, close your eyes, and visualize an alter ego—a wise, nonjudgmental self. Imagine that this person is in a chair opposite you. Tell your alter ego how you feel as honestly as you can, then listen to what your accepting self has to say.

Be honest. Stress often builds up when we suppress thoughts and feelings that we believe to be improper or unacceptable. Recognizing that everyone possesses angry, aggressive impulses is the first step toward accepting them in yourself. "When a psychologist is trying to help an anxious patient, she may start out by searching for the angry feelings that lie buried beneath the surface," says Dr. Curtis.

But keep in mind that while it's healthy to recognize and acknowledge emotions such as anger, it's not okay to act on them. You might feel like throttling the co-worker who steals your idea or the driver who cuts into your lane, but that doesn't give you license to act on those impulses. Fantasizing about revenge and acting on it are two entirely different things.

Go easier on those around you. Suppose you have a friend who chronically shows up late when the two of you have plans. Don't moralize about it by thinking, "How dare she do this; she has no right to act this way," says Dr. Elkin. You're better off if you address the problem directly. "Accept the way she is," Dr. Elkin suggests. "But once you've done that, you can try to influence her behavior. Talk to her about it and make your feelings known."

Plan ahead. Most people try to avoid thinking about upcoming events that make them tense or uncomfortable. The fact is, simply acknowledging that the event is really going to happen can help take the edge off it—no matter if you're seeing your doctor for your annual physical, making a presentation to co-workers, or entertaining your in-laws for a four-day weekend. "Picture how it's going to be, in as relaxed a situation as you can," Dr. Curtis suggests. "Go through all of the worst-case scenarios while safe at home with your family and friends."

AROMATHERAPY

SCENT-UOUS STRESS RELIEF

These days, we'd all like to take a little more time in our lives to stop and smell the roses. Now there's scientific proof that we should: Rose is one of many fragrances that research has shown to be an antidote to the body's stress response. Just a couple of whiffs of this and other special scents can tame tension and restore calm when we're feeling frazzled.

"We all know that pleasant smells can make us feel good," says Alan Hirsch, M.D., neurological director of the Smell and Taste Treatment and Research Foundation in Chicago. But his studies suggest that the link between scent and mood is actually part of our biological makeup. "The section of the brain that registers smells is part of the primitive area that also generates emotions," he explains.

The practice of using aromatic plants for therapeutic purposes has been around for thousands of years. Its present-day incarnation has roots in the eleventh century, when middle eastern healers began experimenting with highly volatile plant extracts called essential oils. This is what we know today as aromatherapy.

Researchers such as Dr. Hirsch are working to understand just how aromatherapy works. One theory is that certain scents affect the brain directly, just as certain drugs do. For example, experiments have shown that lavender increases the brain's alpha waves, which are associated with relaxation, while jasmine increases beta waves, which are connected to alertness.

Aromatherapy may also play off the power of association, says Dr. Hirsch. Smells that evoke pleasant childhood memories, such as vanilla and floral fragrances, could bring about the relaxed mood that comes from nostalgia. "Consider how easy it is for a whiff of baking bread to transport us back to our youth or for the salty smell of sea air to remind us of the beach," says Dr. Hirsch.

AMAZING AROMAS

Studies of the effects of aromatherapy on body and mind have yielded some surprising results. Besides helping us relax and recharge, the right scent can:

Improve mental clarity. Many of us find it difficult to think clearly and objectively when we're under stress. Sniffing the appropriate aroma can help keep our thought processes calm and rational. In one study, for example, people assigned to do math problems under pressure showed fewer mental and physical signs of stress when they first smelled the scent of green apple. "Their anxiety went up, but not as much," says Dr. Hirsch.

Peel off pounds. In a study of more than 3,000 people, those who took a whiff of green apple, peppermint, or banana whenever they felt like eating ended up losing as much as 2.1 percent of their body weight per month. "It could be that these scents reduce the anxiety that triggers appetite," Dr. Hirsch speculates.

Counteract claustrophobia. At Memorial-Sloan Kettering Hospital in New York City, patients sniffed vanilla prior to undergoing magnetic resonance imaging (MRI), a highly sophisticated diagnostic procedure that may require spending a half-hour or more confined inside a narrow, tubelike chamber. The scent appeared to significantly lower the anxiety that the people felt during this claustrophobic experience.

FINDING YOUR FRAGRANCE

Of course, not everyone will respond to a particular scent in the same way. So how do you know which one is right for you?

YOU SMELL PO-TAY-TO, I SMELL PO-TAH-TO

Smell, like taste, is highly individual. Personal experience can make all the difference in how each of us responds to a particular scent. The smell of the ocean, for example, produces a wave of relaxation in most adults. But it just might make you green at the gills if your principal memory of the ocean is a doozy of a bout with seasickness.

It also appears that when and where you grew up can influence your reaction to certain fragrances, says Alan Hirsch, M.D., neurological director of the Smell and Taste Treatment and Research Foundation in Chicago. Those of us who were born in the 1930s are likely to feel at home with natural scents, while children of the 1960s tend to find more comfort in artificial odors such as Play-Doh. Likewise, people who were raised on the East Coast usually react favorably to floral scents, while the smell of farm animals does the job for Midwesterners.

You can start by asking yourself which fragrances you enjoy the most. As a general rule, "the more you like a smell, the more likely it is to work for you," says Dr. Hirsch. In his research, Dr. Hirsch has found that vanilla, sea breeze, green apple, banana, cucumber, and floral fragrances seem to work especially well in promoting general relaxation and well-being.

For a specific stress symptom, you might want to try one of the following remedies, recommended by John Steele, an aromatic consultant with Lifetree Aromatix in Sherman Oaks, California. You can find these essential oils in health food stores and specialty boutiques.

- For insomnia, put four to five drops of lavender on your pillowcase just before going to sleep.
- To prevent panic attacks, apply a few drops of lavender to your handkerchief, then inhale when anxiety builds.

- For depression, rose, jasmine, neroli, and ylang-ylang are often helpful. You can simply inhale one of the scents directly from the bottle, but for no more than 5 to 10 seconds, five or six times a day, says Steele.

JUST FOLLOW YOUR NOSE

You can get more from your aromatherapeutic experience, Dr. Hirsch says, by developing a strong subconscious association between a scent and the stress-free emotional state that it produces. To do this, he suggests that you first learn a relaxation technique such as biofeedback or meditation. Once you're comfortable with the technique you've chosen, introduce the stress-relieving scent to your practice sessions. After a few sessions, you'll automatically associate the scent with a relaxed state. So when stress threatens to overwhelm you, a couple of whiffs of the scent—a few drops of vanilla on a handkerchief, for example—should evoke relaxation on the spot.

Of course, while direct inhalation may be the most obvious way to use aromatic essential oils, aromatherapy takes advantage of other methods of application as well. Here's a handful for you to try.

Soak it up. Add six to eight drops of essential oil in your bath and immerse yourself in fragrance. Lavender, geranium, ylang-ylang, and bergamot are all wonderfully suited for this purpose. If you want to try another scent, be sure that it's not a skin irritant such as cinnamon or lemon, cautions Steele.

Vaporize it. An electric aromatic diffuser can fill the air in your home or office with the scent of your choice. Prices for these devices can vary, but you should be able to find one for between $35 and $100. You can also use a candle diffuser.

Rub it in. Add 10 drops of essential oil to ½ ounce of almond, olive, or sesame oil (called carrier oils), and you have the recipe for a soothing aromatherapeutic massage or moisturizer. But don't apply undiluted essential oil directly to your skin, as it can cause irritation and even an allergic reaction in some people.

Before you try aromatherapy on your own, Steele says, consult a trained aromatherapist or at least read up on the subject. The fact is that despite their soft, soothing scents, essential oils are quite strong,

35

and they can cause problems if you use them improperly. Also, they should never be ingested without the guidance of an aromatherapist.

Pregnant women, in particular, must exercise caution when using essential oils. Some of these oils, including calamus, mugwort, pennyroyal, sage, and wintergreen, can actually induce miscarriages if they're taken internally—and inhalation and topical application are also strongly discouraged.

For assistance in locating a professional aromatherapist in your area, contact the National Association for Holistic Aromatherapy at P.O. Box 17622, Boulder, CO 80308-7622 or the American Phyto Aromatherapy Association at 7436 SW 117 Avenue, Suite 188, Miami, FL 33183.

See also Meditation

ASSERTIVENESS
HAVE IT YOUR WAY

How do you react when something doesn't quite go the way you expected it to? If you're the type to lose your cool, you might feel better after you've vented—but the people around you are probably ready to hang you in effigy. On the other hand, if you're the type to swallow your tongue and squelch your true feelings, you're suffocating your natural stress response—and your body may be suffering for it.

Between these two extremes lies a more healthful middle ground. It's called assertiveness, which Richard Blue, Ph.D., a clinical psychologist at the Behavioral Institute of Atlanta, describes as "knowing you have the right to speak up . . . in a tactful, diplomatic, respectful way."

Assertiveness has developed a slightly tarnished reputation over the years, maybe because folks tend to equate it with aggression. It has even been fodder for cartoons, like the one depicting a door with a sign that reads "Assertiveness Workshop—Don't Bother to Knock."

In fact, true assertiveness is not selfish or insensitive or rude. Instead, it gives you the satisfaction of making your needs heard while sending those around you the message that you respect their opinions and value your relationships with them.

SPEAK UP FOR LESS STRESS

If the idea is to keep your interactions with others positive and productive, then what's the matter with simply letting a problem slide? While you may be keeping everyone else happy, you're really not doing yourself any favors. "People who don't know how to assert themselves allow frustration and anger to build over time," says Dr. Blue. The more issues that are unresolved, he explains, the stronger these emotions become.

And while you may forget about a problem, your body doesn't. Passively swallowing your irritation is like keeping a fire smoldering in your insides. "From a physical perspective, you're bottling up all of the arousal of the fight-or-flight response," says Mitchell Clionsky, Ph.D., a clinical psychologist at Neuro-Psychology Associates in Springfield, Massachusetts. Repeatedly sending your body into this red-alert stage—which produces rapid, shallow breathing, an accelerated pulse, and increased blood pressure—can lead to serious health problems unless you take action to counterbalance it.

BE FRANK, BE FIRM, BE FAIR

Assertiveness allows you to respond to a difficult situation in a way that's beneficial to everyone involved—including yourself. It can take some getting used to, especially if your style has been to lose your cool easily or to avoid saying what's on your mind. These tips should help.

Remember: "We both count." The most important element of true assertiveness is fairness. It's saying that you value the needs and feelings of the other person just as much as you value your own. It helps to keep in mind the simple phrase, "we both count." It will guide you toward the assertive way to behave in almost any situation, Dr. Clionsky says.

Here's an example of how this works: Suppose you're waiting in line at a deli counter when someone cuts in front of you. She says that she's in a hurry and she needs just one item. The aggressive response to this situation would be "No. I was here first, and you'll just have to wait your turn." The passive response would be to give in, then stew about it later. The "we both count" response would involve a quick assessment and then a choice. If you have the time, you might well let the woman go ahead of you. If you truly don't have time, you could politely say, "I'd sure like to, but unfortunately I'm really pressed for time myself."

Take the high road. Approach a situation from a positive rather than a negative point of view, suggests Dr. Clionsky. If you're a woman who does most of the household chores and your spouse is constantly doing less than his share, you might be tempted to think the worst—that he's a selfish or lazy man. Instead, suggests Dr. Clionsky, start with the assumption that it's a simple misunderstanding. Then have a conversation with your husband about it.

You might begin by saying, "Let's talk about something. You may not realize that it's a problem and how it affects me." In other words, you're making a request that he understand your problem and help you solve it. It's an approach that is unlikely to be met with confrontation or a refusal to cooperate.

Then continue with something like, "I understand that you have a tough job, and that you don't always realize how much housework needs to be done." This demonstrates your awareness and appreciation of his position. You can finish by emphasizing the need to work out the problem together: "Maybe we can figure out a way to divide things up, so that both of us have regular tasks and I won't always have to remind you. That way we can avoid this situation in the future."

Delay if necessary. It's better to postpone a confrontation if you're already boiling over. For instance, maybe your mother is never on time when you have to take her to a doctor's appointment.

One day you decide that you've had enough. "Choose a later time—not the heat of the moment—to talk about it," Dr. Clionsky suggests.

When you do discuss the problem, remember that the goal is to reduce your stress, not to make your mom admit the error of her ways. Tell her how much it upsets you to wait for her and how important it is that she get to her appointments on time. Then ask questions that show her you're willing to help effect change: "What can we do differently? Should I call you before I leave the house to make sure that you're ready? Let's make a plan for next time."

Be a broken record. Sometimes it helps to repeat your position—politely but firmly—over and over again until the listener gets the message. For example:

YOU: "I'd like my money back. This pen doesn't work."
SALES CLERK: "Do you have the receipt?"
YOU: "No, but you can see that I bought it here. It has your label. It doesn't work, and I'd like a refund."
CLERK: "You need a receipt. It says so right there on the sign."
YOU: "Yes, I read the sign. But the pen doesn't work, and I want my money back."
CLERK: "But we have our rules."
YOU: "The pen doesn't work, and I'd like a refund."

The broken record technique really works. Eventually, your message penetrates the barrier raised by the other person. In the end, he has no choice but to agree to your request.

Roll out the fog. If you've made a mistake, a technique called fogging allows you to own up to it without letting the other person drag you down and make you feel inferior. It obscures the negative value judgment that the other person is placing on your behavior.

Suppose you're late arriving at a friend's house for a night out on the town, and he's furious. Here's how the exchange might go: "Yes, I'm late, and I'm sorry you had to wait . . . .Yes, I agree with you entirely. I was late, and you had to wait 20 minutes . . . .Yes, I'll try hard to be on time the next time we get together. But there's nothing we can do about what has already happened . . . .I've apologized. I regret your inconvenience. Now shall we go and enjoy the movie?"

Fogging takes patience. But it gets results.

Remember to listen. Whether you're confronting a curfew-breaking teenager or a photo-shop clerk who seems to have lost your vacation pictures, don't let your need to be heard interfere with your ability to listen. "Being fair means paying attention to the other person's reasons," says Dr. Clionsky. "Give him a chance to speak. Basically, it's a variation on the golden rule: Deal with others the way you'd want to be dealt with yourself."

Like anything else, assertiveness develops with practice. You shouldn't have to look too hard for situations in which you can hone your skills. "Eventually, you'll get to a point where you won't have to think constantly about how to respond to a problem," Dr. Clionsky says. "It will come naturally." And that, he adds, will make for a lot less stress.

AUTOGENICS
SPEAK, AND YOUR BODY LISTENS

The next time stress gets the best of you, try using a little body language. No, don't kick your boss in the shins because he wants you to work late—again. As rewarding as that may seem, you'll feel even better if you just instruct your body not to get hot and bothered by the aggravating turn of events.

That's right: If you tell your body to stay calm, it will pay attention. It's a technique called autogenics. First introduced in the early twentieth century by German psychiatrists Johannes Heinrich Schultz, M.D., and Wolfgang Luthe, M.D., autogenics is practiced throughout the world today.

Autogenics literally means "self-regulation." "Essentially, it opens a new channel of communication within the body," says Steven Fahrion, Ph.D., director of research at the Life Sciences Institute of Mind-Body Health in Topeka, Kansas.

The principle behind autogenics is simple: Your body already knows how to relax itself. All it needs is for the conscious mind to supply the proper cues. These cues—imagining that your hands and feet are growing warm, for example—produce physical changes that are the exact opposite of those induced by stress. Most notably, your pulse and breathing rates slow down, your muscles relax, and your blood vessels open up.

"To me, autogenic training is the most effective technique for activating the body's natural ability to bring about stress relief," says Micah R. Sadigh, Ph.D., director of psychology and behavioral medicine at the Gateway Institute in Bethlehem, Pennsylvania.

STRESS RELIEF? JUST SAY THE WORD

Autogenics benefits the body in much the same way that meditation and yoga do. Some experts have even suggested that it may be just as effective as certain anti-anxiety medications. Specifically, autogenics can:

Improve mood. In a study at the University of Bologna in Italy, autogenic training was given to 40 people who complained of "minor psychological problems of an anxious nature." These people described themselves with words such as "uneasy," "gloomy," "tense," and "spiteful."

After three months, the study participants demonstrated a measurable improvement in mood compared with a control group of 39 people that did not receive autogenic training. They also experienced a reduction in the physical symptoms that often go along with anxiety: sweating, rapid heartbeat, and frequent urination.

Head off headaches. Dutch researchers assigned 46 people who experienced chronic tension headaches to one of two groups. One group received autogenic training, while the other group learned a complicated self-hypnosis procedure.

Both groups reported experiencing less pain, but the people who felt they were in control of their pain showed the greatest reduction. The researchers concluded that techniques like autogenics worked better because it gave the participants a feeling of control over their bodies.

Keep asthma at bay. Stress often aggravates the labored breathing associated with asthma. In a Spanish study 24 patients with chronic asthma were divided into two groups. One group learned autogenics, while the other group met with a therapist for counseling but did not receive autogenic training.

By the end of the trial, lung function in the members of the autogenic group had improved significantly—they could breathe more deeply and easily. There was no change in lung function in the people who did not practice autogenics.

COMMANDS THAT CALM

It's easy to do autogenics on your own. "People quickly develop a sense of how it feels when their blood vessels open up—often within a single session," says Dr. Fahrion.

He suggests trying a simple hand-warming exercise to get a taste of how autogenics works. (For something a little more advanced, see "Keeping the Peace.") To begin, sit or lie in a comfortable position with your eyes closed. Place your fingertips together so that the index finger of one hand touches the pinkie of the other. Then curl your fingers together so that one hand clutches the other.

With your hands in this position, repeat to yourself, "My hands are warm." "Pay attention to the sensations in your hands—particularly in the fingertips, which have a rich blood supply," says Dr. Fahrion. Do you notice any tingling or pulsing? That's a sign that your hands are heating up.

Simple as autogenics is, some psychologists say that you should learn the technique from an expert. "Autogenics is powerful and extremely effective, but it's not just relaxation training," Dr. Sadigh explains. "You have to know what it entails."

People doing autogenics should be prepared for some uncomfortable reactions as the body and mind unload their accumulated stress and trauma. For example, they might experience "autogenic discharges" such as muscle twitches—the kind that many folks have just before they fall asleep.

KEEPING THE PEACE

When you use autogenics, spoken cues help guide you into a state of deep relaxation. If you'd like to give it a try, you can follow these steps recommended by Martin Shaffer, Ph.D., executive director of the Stress Management Institute in San Francisco.

Begin by sitting in a firm, comfortable chair—it should be upright but not rigid—in a quiet, darkened room. (If you prefer, you can lie down with your hands at your sides.) Close your eyes and let your breathing become slow and even. Then say each of the following cues to yourself, always as you exhale.

- "My hands and arms are heavy and warm." (Repeat five times.)
- "My feet and legs are heavy and warm." (Repeat five times.)
- "My abdomen is warm and comfortable." (Repeat five times.) *Note:* Skip this step if you have ulcers.
- "My breathing is deep and even." (Repeat ten times.)
- "My heartbeat is calm and regular." (Repeat ten times.)
- "My forehead is cool." (Repeat five times.)
- "When I open my eyes, I will remain relaxed and refreshed." (Repeat three times.)

Finish the exercise slowly. Gently move your hands and arms, then your feet and legs, before you open your eyes and get up. The entire session should last about 15 minutes.

With autogenics, "you need to be patient and to suspend judgment," Dr. Shaffer emphasizes. "An attitude of passive observation—you're watching what happens without rating your performance—is best. If people can do that, 95 percent of them will be successful."

Don't let such reactions alarm you. "They simply signal the release of pent-up energy," says Martin Shaffer, Ph.D., executive director of the Stress Management Institute in San Francisco. "If you just go along with them, they should disappear over time."

B

BACH FLOWER REMEDIES
NIP TENSION IN THE BUD

Nothing can brighten your day like a bouquet of fresh flowers. With their bright, rich colors and intoxicating fragrances, these beautiful blooms envelop your senses and buoy your spirits above everyday aggravations.

While they're pretty to look at and marvelous to smell, flowers may harbor more potent therapeutic benefits within their delicate petals. More than 60 years ago, a British physician, Edward Bach, M.D., began experimenting with distilled floral essences. He placed blossoms in bowls of spring water, set the bowls outdoors for about four hours to soak up the sun, then combined the water with equal parts brandy. Using this method, he eventually developed 38 distinct flower remedies, along with a system that pairs the remedies with specific emotional and psychological sources of distress.

No one can quite explain how or why the Bach flower remedies work. But those who use them say that these floral formulas have indeed helped many people overcome emotional problems of all kinds, particularly stress.

A MEDICINAL MYSTERY

Dr. Bach developed his remedies in the homeopathic tradition, according to J. Herbert Fill, M.D., a general practitioner in New York City who prescribes flower remedies for his patients. Homeopathy is a 200-year-old medical system that's based on the principle of "like cures like." Homeopathic remedies contain minute amounts of substances that, in greater amounts, would actually cause the symptoms that they're being used to treat. As a simple example, the homeopathic remedy for a turpentine rash would be a highly diluted, processed preparation based on turpentine.

Despite the similarity between homeopathic and Bach flower remedies, "Dr. Bach had an intuitive instinct for the effects of flowers. He didn't follow a theory," Dr. Fill says. "The reason these remedies work, in my opinion, goes beyond the simple existence of flowers. A plant has roots, a stem, leaves, and blooms—each imbued with life energy."

Indeed, the concept of life energy, or some variation of it, comes up in many theories that attempt to explain the medicinal effects of flower remedies. The remedies have been described as containing "the etheric imprint of plant energy" and "the life force essence" of the flower. While many people swear by these remedies, research so far has produced little, if any, hard data to document their effectiveness.

PETALS WITH METTLE

Unlike traditional medicine, which treats the physical symptoms of disease, flower therapy targets the emotional and psychological distress that underlies the disease. Let's say you have a headache. In traditional medicine you'd most likely reach for a bottle of aspirin. But in flower therapy you'd need to figure out the specific emotional and psychological state that is contributing to your headache.

This methodology applies to stress-related conditions as well. "If a patient is experiencing anxiety, for example, I take the components of his anxiety into consideration," Dr. Fill says. "Anger, fear, resentment, and hostility are often dominant." The presence of one, several, or all of these emotions will influence which remedy he prescribes.

The typical dosage for a Bach flower remedy is a few drops four times a day, diluted in pure spring water and sipped. Here are four ways the remedy can help you.

Reduce worry. The tendency toward excessive worry is usually influenced by a person's life history. It represents a stress-producing pattern that originated in childhood. "When this is the case, I use a flower like that of the walnut tree, which breaks up the link to past conditioning and gets rid of the deeper sources of worrying," Dr. Fill says.

Alleviate fear and anxiety. Since these emotions often contribute to stress, Dr. Fill prescribes the Rescue Remedy. This mixture of five flower essences is one of the most popular of the Bach flower remedies. You can find this product in health food stores.

Overcome fear of flying. One of Dr. Fill's patients was phobic about airplanes. Because he was a businessman who needed to travel often, this presented a serious problem. "I gave him extracts of rockrose, for panic, and mimulus, for fear of known things. After that, he had no problems," Dr. Fill says.

Cool down anger. Flower remedies sometimes relieve emotional turmoil in a paradoxical way. Holly, for example, is "a very aggressive plant," says Dr. Fill. "The spines at the tip of every leaf and the hard red berries say 'Don't touch me, or you'll get hurt.'"

"By the homeopathic process, we can reverse the nature of holly and transform it into its opposite," Dr. Fill says. He has seen anger vanish within minutes after administering holly essence.

BUYING BACH

If you want to give the Bach flower remedies a try, look for those with the Nelson Bach USA label. They're widely available in health food stores and some drugstores.

Ellon, which used to be the American distributor of the Bach flower remedies, now manufactures its own line of floral essences based on the system developed by Dr. Bach. For supply catalogs, questionnaires, and information on the use of Ellon products, you can write to the company at 644 Merrick Road, Lynbrook, NY 11563-2332.

Note: Both the Bach remedies and the Ellon floral essences are regulated as homeopathic remedies by the Food and Drug Administration. This means that they're genuine flower products, but the suppliers cannot make claims about their therapeutic benefits.

BIOCIRCUITS
REBALANCE YOUR BODY'S ENERGY

We all want balance in our lives—especially when we've been through a string of stressful events. Of course, we can't maintain perfect harmony between joy and sorrow, work and leisure, high energy and blissful calm. But proponents of a relaxation technique known as biocircuits say that we can correct these imbalances from inside our bodies.

The theory behind biocircuits, also known as polarity screens, first surfaced in the early twentieth century. Believers ranging from spiritual guides to psychologists proposed that within the human body flows an imperceptible current of energy that is easily disrupted. A simple tool can stop the disruptions and restore a state of harmony and relaxation, according to Terry Patten, co-author of *Biocircuits: Amazing New Tools for Energy Health.*

The biocircuit device described by Patten is extremely low-tech. A couple of mesh screens made of copper or silk are each connected to a wire, and a copper handle is attached to each wire. To use the device, you simply lie on your back with one screen under your head and the other under your tailbone and hold a handle in each hand. Then you wait for your muscle tension to release and your heart rate to drop. Patten says that your mind slows until you feel as if you're entering a twilight state.

Sound strange? Perhaps. But some people say that it really works.

A LEAP OF FAITH, A LARGE REWARD

Practitioners who advocate biocircuits say that the subtle energy conducted by these devices can't be measured by scientific means. Actually, Patten admits, "the principle behind biocircuits is a mystery."

But patients who have benefited from biocircuits don't need any proof other than their own experience. "For whatever reason, the device stimulates the relaxation response," says George Fritz,

Ph.D., a psychologist in private practice in Bethlehem, Pennsylvania. "You can actually feel it." Fritz prescribes biocircuits to some of his patients who suffer from chronic pain or stress-related conditions like migraine or bad backs, and he says the devices produce good results.

On the research side, one small study suggests that biocircuits do have positive results. In the study 12 volunteers underwent successive sessions with biocircuits, followed by sessions with dummy devices. The participants showed a significant decline in muscle tension when they used the biocircuits, while the dummy device had no effect.

As further evidence, electroencephalogram (EEG) tests of the volunteers' brain waves showed that the biocircuits produced more theta episodes, meaning that they produced the brain waves associated with deep, trancelike states of relaxation. Ten of the 12 participants rated their experience with the biocircuit device as more relaxing and more beneficial than with the dummy device, while 9 of the 12 reported greater sensations of warmth, which often correlates with feelings of relaxation.

These findings demonstrated that biocircuits are a "very natural way to induce a deep movement into the relaxation response," according to the conductor of the study, Julian Isaacs, Ph.D., professor in the Graduate School of Holistic Studies at John F. Kennedy University in Orinda, California, and president of Marin Biofeedback Associates in San Rafael, California.

LEARNING TO LET GO

If you want to try biocircuits for yourself, you can buy them with either copper or silk screens. Copper offers a more powerful experience, says Patten, while silk produces a gentler, subtler, and longer-lasting effect. For beginners, Patten recommends copper, unless you're highly allergic to the metal or unusually sensitive to the effects of biocircuitry. (If you're overly sensitive, you might experience irritation rather than relaxation.)

You can use the biocircuits for stress reduction "any time you're hyped up and overly aroused," says Patten. To get the most benefit from this device, keep these tips in mind.

Use it before snoozing. Just before bedtime, a 10- to 12-minute biocircuit session is usually enough to discharge accumulated muscle tension and help avoid insomnia, Dr. Fritz says. And you don't have to worry about overdosing. "In an inexplicable way, the device is its own timer," explains Dr. Isaacs. "You go into a deeply relaxed state, and 30 minutes later you'll come back up spontaneously. It's totally passive."

Don't tackle problems. For best results, you must cooperate with the device, says Dr. Fritz. "It's not like sticking your finger into a wall socket. If you lie there and try to balance your checkbook, you'll get up just as tense as when you started."

Combine it with other easers. To make the most of biocircuits, let your mind ease into neutral by starting out with another stress-relief technique, suggests Dr. Fritz. Among his recommendations: meditation, progressive muscle relaxation and imagery. Dr. Isaacs also recommends relaxation tapes. Once you're settling into a relaxed frame of mind, "biocircuits will take you the rest of the way," he says.

See also Imagery, Meditation, Progressive Muscle Relaxation, Relaxation Response, Relaxation Tapes

C

CHILDREN

DE-STRESSED BY THE YOUNG

Kids. They can bring you so much joy with their tender smiles, their loving spirits, their boundless, puppylike energy. And they can bring you so much aggravation with their endless demands, their whining, their unlimited capacity for . . . well, just plain trouble.

When experts analyze the conflicts and pressures of family life, they usually focus on the relationship between husband and wife. But for families with children—whether babies, grade-schoolers, or teens—the presence of the young has a definite effect on stress levels. In fact, one study of men found that their relationships with their children influenced their physical health even more than job-related stress.

In this study conducted at the Center for Research on Women at Wellesley College in Massachusetts, researchers looked closely at the lives of 300 men from families in which both husband and wife worked. They tracked specific physical symptoms that the men reported, such as headache, aching muscles, fatigue, and upset stomach.

So how did these symptoms reflect the stress and satisfaction that the men experienced at work, in their marriages, and with their children? The researchers' conclusion was that there's a clear link between fatherhood concerns and symptoms of stress.

The men who worried about problems or conflicts with their offspring were more likely to be reaching for the Tums or Tylenol than the fathers who were stressed-out by work. On the other hand, the men who found fatherhood highly rewarding seemed less vulnerable to the ravages of stress outside the home. Even when they had trouble at work, these happy dads were less likely to show stress symptoms.

Having good relationships with their children seemed to help these fathers meet the natural challenges they encountered at work, the researchers theorized. In other words, loving parents have an extra advantage on more than one stress front.

RELIEF IS JUST A CARESS AWAY

Many of us overlook children's ability to soothe our stress because we assume that parent-child nurturing is only supposed to go one way: "from parent to child," says Marvin Sussman, Ph.D., Unidel professor emeritus of human behavior at the University of Delaware in Newark and a faculty member of the Union Institute in Cinncinati. Here are some ways that you can get stress relief from your child as well.

Be huggable. "If a child can see your tension, he often wants to do something to alleviate it," Dr. Sussman says. "Hugging, stroking, just affectionate touching between parent and child can do a lot to relieve stress."

Play it up. Sharing time with your children and getting involved in their games and activities is a distraction. Any game can help neutralize stress by gently but firmly taking your mind elsewhere. Concentrating on a game of checkers and playing video games together are simple things that shift your concentration, notes Dr. Sussman.

Keep rituals. When the whole family has to weather times of stress, family rituals can be particularly helpful, Dr. Sussman points out. Any shared, regular experiences can help create and maintain supportive bonds. "I'd hypothesize that the more rituals a family has, the better family members will be able to cope with stress," says Dr. Sussman.

Lighting candles or saying prayers together, gathering for a family dinner every night to share the day's experiences, taking family vacations or holidays—all of these produce a sense of secure, pre-dictable stability. It's something for everyone in the family to look forward to, and it enforces the stress-taming certainty that "we're in this together," says Dr. Sussman.

Share some blues. Sharing some of your worries with your children can help with stress relief, says Dr. Sussman. Being open and talking about your feelings makes it possible for everyone to pull together when the going gets rough.

For example, if the loss of a job means that you'll have to cut back on family vacations for a while, share the truth and your feelings about it with your children, Dr. Sussman urges. It may not be easy, but the bigger mistake would be trying to act as if everything were just fine. Children know that you're upset any-way, and talking about your concerns gives them the rewarding opportunity to help you feel better.

See also Family

COMMUNICATION
MAKE THE CONNECTION

We humans are by nature social. Whether we're sitting down to dinner with our families, playing cards with friends, or partying with co-workers at the company picnic, we relish the sense of community that spending time with others provides.

Communication lies at the core of this connectedness. Through the simple act of talking—and listening—to each other, we are able to give and receive understanding, comfort, encouragement, and strength. It's a powerful means of defusing stress that might otherwise build to harmful levels.

But just as communication can heal, it can also harm. We all know how an angry exchange with a spouse or a demeaning dress-ing-down by a boss can leave us agitated, humiliated, and en-raged—and send stress through the roof.

Clearly, the spoken word can be a double-edged sword. That's why it's so important to learn the basics of good communication: how to convey what we mean, what we want, and who we are in a way that increases closeness and overcomes discord.

RULE #1: LISTEN UP

Experts say we can take a giant step toward improved communication just by closing our mouths and opening our ears. "If there is one thing I try to teach people, it's good listening skills," says J. Gibson Henderson, Jr., Ph.D., a psychologist in private practice in St. Louis who often works with couples. "When you speak, you want someone to listen and to let you know that you're being heard." If you want to become more aurally agile, give these tips a try.

Take turns. For starters, be sure to allow the other person ample opportunity to speak. Both of you should receive adequate "airtime" without having to struggle for it. Good communication involves balance.

Come to attention. Though we tend to think of good listening as nothing more than paying attention, it's actually something you do actively and physically. You show that you're listening with your whole self, using eye contact and gestures such as leaning forward slightly and nodding. If you're glancing at your watch or looking around the room while the other person is speaking, it's a clear indication that you're not listening—and that may undermine whatever sympathetic words you use.

Make like a mirror. A technique called reflective listening allows the other person to know that he has been heard. As taught by Don Gabor, an interpersonal communication skills trainer in New York City and author of *Speaking Your Mind in 101 Different Situations*, it involves periodically recapping what the other person has said.

For example, if a good friend tells you how her feelings were hurt at a dinner party, you might interject with, "You must have felt really left out when everyone started dinner before you arrived." Words like these acknowledge that you've heard her problem, and they open the door for further exchange.

Show understanding. People coping with a difficult situation usually want someone to acknowledge what they're going through, not to advise, Dr. Henderson says. "A word that comes up a good deal is *validation*," he says. "People in turmoil want to be assured by someone they love or respect that they're not crazy for feeling the way they do." If you feel overwhelmed by your 16-hour work-day, for example, while everyone in your company acts as if it's a normal part of life, there's a tremendous sense of relief in hearing a friend outside the office say, "That must be very hard on you."

Ask before you offer. Good listening also means refraining from making suggestions until the time is right. It may take some patience, but you need to find out what the other person is saying before you offer your own solutions. "Is there anything I can do to help?" is almost always more appreciated than, "Well, why don't you just . . . ," says Dr. Henderson.

RULE #2: FOCUS ON PROBLEMS, NOT ON PEOPLE

Effective communication also requires equal measures of honesty, fairness, and tact. It's the golden rule of any interaction: You can't expect another person to respect and respond to your needs unless you do the same for him.

This is especially important when you want to approach someone about a problem that has surfaced between the two of you. Above all else, you must keep in mind that you're attempting to change the situation, not the person. "When someone is attacked personally, it creates tremendous stress," says Gabor. And that can put a lot of unnecessary strain on your relationship.

Try these tips to keep any dialogue positive and productive.

Shed some light. When you bring up a problem, be clear about what it is that's bothering you, why it bothers you, what goal you hope to achieve, and what changes you will make to get you there. This game plan will help you avoid sounding negative and accusatory.

Consider how you would feel if your spouse said to you, "Why do you always slam the door when the baby is sleeping? Can't you ever think of anyone but yourself?" It's much better to focus on the problem and recommend a solution: "When you slam the door, it wakes the baby. I'd really appreciate it if you made a conscious effort to keep things quiet when he's sleeping."

Stick to the script. To ensure that you get your point across diplomatically but effectively, try scripting, suggests Gabor. Before you talk to someone about a problem, take some time to write down exactly what you want to say. "Select words that clearly express your thoughts and feelings," he says.

Scripting makes conflict much less likely and confrontation much less stressful. "You have more confidence when you know what you're going to say," he notes.

Choose the right time and place. Timing is everything when you're hoping to change the behavior pattern of someone who is causing you grief, whether it's a co-worker who habitually cuts you off in midsentence or a family member who consistently leaves the bathtub filthy. If you confront people at every little irritation, you may seem like a control freak. If you wait too long, on the other hand, you may get labeled as passive—and the pent-up anger could become explosive.

"As a rule of thumb, I become aware of a pattern if something happens two or three times. But I may not respond then," says Gabor. "After four to six repetitions, I'll let the other person know how his behavior is affecting me."

Meet anger with calmness. If the other person explodes with anger when you clearly state what you want and why, call for a brief time-out. You might say, for example, "I really want to resolve this issue, but we can't do it in this way. I want to talk about it calmly." That's the best strategy for getting the conversation back on track, notes Gabor. And once communication is flowing easily in both directions, it will drain the stress right out of the relationship.

RULE #3: DON'T POINT FINGERS

In his years of practice Dr. Henderson has noticed that when people experience a glitch in a relationship, they seem more concerned about finding out what caused the problem than about moving toward a solution. "It's as if they were diagnosing an illness," he says.

Unfortunately, this approach to problem solving often evolves into placing blame. And blame, Dr. Henderson points out, tends to polarize people and make them build little walls of defensiveness. Such circumstances are bound to short-circuit effective communication.

The following strategies should help you avoid this kind of interpersonal meltdown.

Set goals. Focus on concrete examples of what you want rather than endlessly analyzing what went wrong. Suppose you feel that you and your spouse haven't been spending enough time together. Don't call your spouse on the carpet for ignoring you. Instead, approach the problem by saying, "I really liked it last week when you stayed in the kitchen and we talked while I was making dinner."

Make up some miracles. It also helps to concentrate on your wish list—the changes that you'd like to see happen in a particular relationship, Dr. Henderson suggests. As a jumping-off point, each of you could share your answer to this question: If a miracle happened tonight and a problem was solved, what would be different tomorrow?

Try tact as a tactic. As Mary Poppins sang, "a spoonful of sugar helps the medicine go down." Discussing a problem with someone will go a lot easier, Gabor says, if you state your case assertively but sensitively. Make it known that you respect the other person's point of view.

Watch the clock. Good timing is also critical. It's best not to bring up sensitive issues first thing in the morning or right after work, nor do you want to compete with the television for attention. If either of you is already upset, wait until the tension subsides to talk. And of course, never air your dirty laundry—especially when it's very personal—in the presence of others.

If a problem is urgent but the timing is wrong, make an appointment with the other person, so you can say what's on your mind at a later date.

Ticked off by bad timing? Say so. If your spouse or a friend makes you uncomfortable because of poorly timed comments, let that person know what's wrong. "I know you're trying to help," you might say, "but when you contradict me in front of other people, I feel foolish." Then ask the person for feedback on why he contradicted you—and listen carefully to the response.

RULE #4: SAY WHAT YOU WANT

Ultimately, communication is successful when each person understands what the other wants out of the interaction. Is it just the opportunity to vent and get things off your chest? Or are you looking for constructive feedback and guidance? If you're expecting a specific kind of response, make that clear to the other person, experts suggest.

"There's a widespread fallacy that people shouldn't have to ask for what they want, especially in intimate relationships," says Dr. Henderson. "Many think that if an idea is not spontaneously forthcoming, it doesn't count."

But no matter how well people know each other, no matter how much they love each other, they can't read one another's minds. If you want your back scratched, you don't expect the scratcher to know where the itch is. You give specific instructions: "A little to the left . . . a little higher . . . a little harder." A similar kind of guidance is needed in communication.

See also Children, Family, Friendship

COUNSELING

FIRST-AID FOR THE SOUL

Stuff happens. We all feel a little overwhelmed by life from time to time. Usually, we're able to work through the tension until it subsides on its own. But not always.

Once in a while it just keeps on simmering below the surface, never really going away. Maybe all of those day-to-day aggravations are piling up. Or maybe we're facing a personal crisis, such as a serious illness in the family or the loss of a job. Whatever the reason, we start to feel that instead of running our lives, our lives are running us.

There's a price to be paid health-wise when things get out of control. We may develop persistent headaches or backaches or find that we're unable to sleep at night. And as we get wrapped up in our seemingly unsolvable troubles, we may find ourselves avoiding people—or is it that they're avoiding us?

While there's a lot that we can do to combat and control stress on our own, everyone has his limit. "When you're experiencing persistent or disabling distress in your life, despite your best efforts, it's important to get professional help," says Richard Sackett, Ph.D., director of Integrative Psychotherapy Services in New York City.

Such help can be effective, according to Kenneth Matheny, Ph.D., director of the counseling psychology doctoral program at Georgia State University in Atlanta. In an analysis of pooled data from many different studies, Dr. Matheny and colleagues found that people who sought help for stress disorders were better off at the conclusion of treatment than 72 percent of those who didn't seek help.

You Are Not Alone

Counseling aims to restore balance to our lives when things seem to be careening out of control. It intervenes when our own efforts to reduce our stress levels come up short.

Why does stress build to such toxic levels in the first place? "The stress response is triggered when you feel that the demands you're facing outstrip the resources you have to deal with them," explains Dr. Matheny. Whether you have an exaggerated sense of what you're up against or a diminished sense of yourself, it eventually leads to the same kind of stress overload.

These perceptions tend to have roots in basic assumptions that we all carry around inside ourselves. These assumptions are often untrue, yet they can be so deeply ingrained that we don't even know to question them. We might harbor a subconscious belief that "I have to please everyone," that "I'm not a successful person," or that "the world is a very dangerous place," for example. Do any of these sound familiar?

"Assumptions that we've made over and over again seem so right, so natural to us, that we can't see them," Dr. Matheny says. It's a lot easier for someone who is perceptive and committed to our welfare to spot them from the outside.

What's more, a good therapist can provide an objective perspective and help correct the excesses of self-blame. "Folks are extremely hard on themselves," says Dr. Matheny. "They're their own worst critics. If a therapist listens to them and plays back the kernel of what they've said about themselves, it touches their attention, and they may begin to run a reality check."

SOMEBODY TO LEAN ON

Regular sessions with a counselor or therapist can provide a supportive relationship just when you need it most. "Many clients are demoralized, beaten up by stressors, when they come into therapy," says Dr. Matheny. "Just having someone close the door, get quiet, and use good listening skills gives them the feeling that help is on the way. It's very comforting to realize that there is someone who knows more than the average person about the way the mind works, someone who is committed to their welfare."

While some people may worry about becoming too dependent on this assistance, the goal of counseling is to help you find your own way. "For a while you may lean on the therapist's resources," Dr. Matheny says. "That gives you the energy to acknowledge and develop your own strengths. You'll progress to a point where you want to please the therapist. Ultimately, you'll become self-supporting. Then you can celebrate together."

You can receive counseling from one of several health professionals. The type of counseling that therapists offer varies with their level of education and training. Here's an overview of the different professions and the services that they're qualified to provide.

Psychiatrists. As medical doctors, or M.D.'s, psychiatrists can prescribe medication to their patients. Their training after medical school focuses on mental disorders. They may use talk therapy, medication, or both in their practices.

Psychologists. Unlike medical doctors, psychologists can't prescribe medication, so they rely on talk therapy. They have earned an advanced degree—such as a Ph.D.—that reflects their education in mental health. They must be state-licensed before they can practice.

Social workers. These professionals usually have two years of graduate training that includes supervised internships in clinical settings. Most states require them to be licensed. Like psychologists, social workers use talk therapy.

It pays to check out a person's credentials before signing on for counseling. The fact is, anyone can call himself a therapist since no degree, training, or licensing is required. A few nonlicensed therapists have great instinctive healing skills, but most experts recommend that you seek therapy from someone who is licensed and certified.

Whom Do You Need?

If you decide to seek counseling, it shouldn't be too hard to find the right professional to assist you. Here are some guidelines to keep in mind.

Get some help from friends. Seek out a recommendation from someone you know who can personally vouch for the qualities and skills of a therapist, says Cory Newman, Ph.D., clinical director of the Center for Cognitive Therapy at the University of Pennsylvania in Philadelphia. "Word of mouth is the best guide," he says.

Just call. If no recommendations are forthcoming—or if you hesitate to ask around—try contacting a nearby university to get leads. Ask for the names of members of their psychology and psychiatry departments who do clinical work.

Check out community services. Most therapists in private practice charge between $50 and $150 for an hour-long session. (A small number of therapists-to-the-stars charge much, much more.)

If money is a limiting factor, consider going to a community mental health center, Dr. Matheny suggests.

Most of these centers have professionals who provide services on a sliding scale that's based on your income. The fee can range from a few dollars per session to nothing at all.

Screen your therapist. Many therapists offer a free or inexpensive get-acquainted session, which is extremely valuable. "Before you commit to anyone's services, feel free to ask lots of questions," says Dr. Matheny. For example, you might want to find out the following:

- "What kind of training do you have?"
- "How much experience do you have?"
- "What's your philosophy?"

Also, respect the personal chemistry factor. Will you feel secure revealing your deepest confidences to this person?

Remember, you can split. If you're not happy, don't feel that you're locked in, even after you've been to several sessions, notes Dr. Newman. "If you don't feel comfortable, go elsewhere," he urges.

AN INNY OR AN OUTEY?

Perhaps most important, make sure that you understand what the therapist intends to accomplish and how long he expects it to take. While counseling sessions are endlessly varied, it's useful to know from the outset whether the therapist believes in changing the inner you (your personality) or the outer you (your behavior). Let's look at these two different therapeutic styles more closely.

Inner change. During analytical or insight-oriented therapy, you'll delve into your past to discover the origin of feelings and attitudes that make it difficult for you to handle present-day stresses. The aim of this therapy is to effect change at the very deepest roots of your personality. The classic example is Freudian psychoanalysis, which requires daily sessions.

Outer change. Behavioral and cognitive therapies stay focused on events, actions, and thoughts as they're taking place in the present. In effect, you set out to change your behavior patterns rather than the deeply ingrained emotions underlying those patterns. By and large, these kinds of therapies achieve results more rapidly. Some are geared toward finishing the work in just a few sessions.

Selecting the right therapeutic style for you depends on what you're hoping to change, how quickly you want results, and how much time and money you're willing to invest. "If you're dealing with something that's happening in your life right now—such as a job transition or a divorce—it's important to have a therapist who is good at dealing with practical issues in the here and now," says Dr. Newman. "You don't have the luxury of spending a few months rehashing the past. On the other hand, if you're not in a crisis and you do have the time, you may want to deal with the issues and background factors that make you vulnerable to stress."

The goal of any therapy is to make you stronger and better able to use your own resources. The bottom-line question is: What does that mean to you? "Most people are looking for a tune-up, not a complete overhaul," Dr. Matheny says.

The most important thing to remember about counseling is that it's there. If ever you feel truly lost in a sea of emotional pain, remember that there are skilled, professional hands to help you make it back to shore.

See also Support Groups, 12-Step Groups

D

DANCING

FIND YOUR RHYTHM AND END YOUR BLUES

If the last time you did the cha-cha was at your senior prom or your nephew's wedding, you're missing out on one of the most enjoyable stress reducers around: dance.

"When you walk into a ballroom dance studio, you're already smiling. Everyone's happy," says Leah Davidson, M.D., a New York City psychoanalyst in private practice.

True, Dr. Davidson may be a little biased. A passionate ballroom dance enthusiast, she has won gold medals in major competitions. But there's plenty of evidence that big benefits are available to just about anyone who is willing to move with the music.

A PRESCRIPTION FOR PLEASURE

On the most basic level, dancing—whether ballroom, ballet, folk, or tap—is simply great exercise, and the stress-busting rewards of exercise are beyond question. But dance is a particularly effective kind of exercise.

In a study at Reed College in Portland, Oregon, undergraduates were asked to assess how they felt before and after a dance class, a gym class, or an academic class. Overall, the students in the dance class reported significantly greater increases in their feelings of well-being than the students in the other two classes. Compared with those who played sports, "the dancers felt significantly more creative, confident, relaxed, excited, motivated, intelligent, and energetic" at the end of their session, researchers concluded.

"Without any jerky, disruptive movements or strain on the joints, dancing is the best stimulator of endorphins I know," Dr. Davidson says. Endorphins are the body's feel-good hormones that give mood a natural lift.

Dr. Davidson prescribes dancing in liberal doses for patients who are experiencing emotional problems such as anxiety and depression. "I've seen people snap out of depression with the help of dancing," she says. "It can also counter insomnia and a host of stress-related symptoms such as stomach cramps and headaches."

MOVING MEDITATION

What's the magic ingredient that makes dance a natural antidote to stress? For one thing, says Dr. Davidson, dance is a meditation that takes your mind off whatever worries you have. "It leads you to focus on the task at hand," she explains.

Dance also provides an opportunity for release. "You can express your unique feelings and get in touch with your true self. This is essentially stress-reducing," Dr. Davidson says. "It's the opposite of sitting at a desk or working at a computer."

You get to know your body better, too, points out Bunny Dickerman, a psychotherapist and dance therapist in Bethlehem, Pennsylvania. "You become more aware of how you feel in different situations, and you begin to know better whether you're stressed or relaxed," she explains. "If you're tuned in to your body, you realize that your muscles are tightening well before aches and pains set in. Then you can do something to intervene."

Dickerman's own experience with dance has led her to increased self-awareness. She has found, for example, that she tends to move very rapidly when stressed. "Now, if I'm feeling frazzled, I deliberately try to move more slowly, easing into a relaxed mode," she says.

Dance is an especially appropriate form of therapy for couples.

"It's a collaboration—something they can do together that relaxes and connects them," says Dr. Davidson. "They sense each other's bodies, each other's energy. Dancing is another form of communication."

In fact, that's what makes it ideal for shy people, who may find it hard to express themselves verbally. "It's a beginning, a social activity they can feel comfortable with," says Dr. Davidson. "I've married off a few people this way."

FROM BALLET TO BALLROOM: CHOOSING YOUR STEPS

Ballroom dancing isn't the only style that gets high marks for improving emotional well-being. Country dancing can be perfect "for people who want to do interactive things," notes Dickerman. She also recommends square dancing or folk dancing. It's a matter of taste, she adds.

Whether you prefer the tango or the twist, tap or the Texas two-step, you'll experience the same "exuberance in movement, the kind of pleasure that kids take in playing hopscotch," Dickerman says. "Dancing is one of the few opportunities we have as adults to experience such joy."

Not sure which dance style suits you best? These tips should point you in the right direction.

Free yourself. For those with no dance experience, Dickerman frequently recommends so-called free-form, spontaneous movement, or creative movement classes. Here, the emphasis is on going with the flow and expressing yourself naturally. There are no steps to learn, no leader to follow. It's all about connecting the music to the rhythm within.

Get primed for pirouettes. At the opposite end of the skill spectrum is ballet, which involves very precise, choreographed movements. Many folks find the precision, discipline, and sense of physical achievement extremely stress-reducing, says Dr. Davidson.

Of course, some of us are, well, rhythmically challenged. Ballet beginners are faced with difficult, and possibly frustrating, physical tasks. "Ballet can be too much for some people. If you find that you still can't do it 'right' after a while, it can actually increase stress," cautions Dr. Davidson.

Have a ball. Midway between free-form dancing and ballet lies ballroom dancing. This style is easily mastered and can always be enjoyable. Not only does it relieve stress and build communication skills, it also benefits from its association with happy occasions, such as weddings and other celebrations.

And the moves in ballroom dancing are entirely natural, Dr. Davidson points out. They're all a variation on the most instinctive movement in the world: walking.

KICK UP YOUR HEELS AND GIVE STRESS THE BOOT

Most of us already know a little something about waltzes and polkas from family get-togethers and social functions. But if you want to learn more about dance, you can try these strategies for making the most of this rhythmic stress buster.

Show up for class. Ballroom dance classes are offered at dance studios and in many adult education programs. You can also find classes in jazz, square dancing, and bebop at many high schools, colleges, and community recreation centers such as the YMCA. You don't even have to go with a partner: Dance teachers are used to pairing up singles who like to dance.

Look for a booster. Pleasure should be your bottom line. "Look for a teacher who isn't a martinet," advises Dickerman. "He should be more encouraging than discouraging. He shouldn't insist that everyone dance in an identical way."

Demand a good time. You should find a class where all of the participants—teacher included—seem to be enjoying themselves, adds Dickerman. If you try to dance in a performance-oriented, judgmental atmosphere, you'll get more stress than stress relief.

Goof off. The perfectionists among us also need to be reminded that taking up dance is no time for self-inflicted pressure, says Dickerman. "Instead of insisting that you have to be good, try to just feel the joy in it," she advises.

Get into the habit. As with any other stress-reducing activity, you'll probably get more benefit from dance if you do it regularly. How often? "At least once a week, and if possible, twice," recommends Dr. Davidson. "Then go out on the weekend for a night of dancing."

Reap the rhythmic rewards. As your dance skills improve, expect to feel a profound increase in personal mastery and control that's rooted in a new sense of your body as an instrument. "And you take that with you wherever you go," says Dickerman.

See also Exercise, Music

DAYDREAMING
TAKE A FLIGHT OF FANCY FOR A LASTING LIFT

Been anywhere interesting today? Maybe you spent some time trekking across the Australian outback or the Alaskan wilderness. Or maybe you sat on the sofa where you received your first kiss . . . or on the throne of Queen Elizabeth at Buckingham Palace. The best part is, you did it without ever leaving your home or workplace.

That's the beauty of daydreams: They transport us out of the present and treat us to a few blissful moments of escape whenever and wherever we please. They're a remarkable testament to the range and agility of the human mind.

The average person spends as many as half of his waking hours daydreaming—that is, experiencing thoughts, images, and emotions unrelated to the task at hand, according to Eric Klinger, Ph.D., professor of psychology at the University of Minnesota in Morris. While a daydream can take the form of a detailed flight of fancy, he says, it's more likely to be a mundane reverie—something on the order of "Wonder what's for dinner?" And generally, we reenter reality after no more than five seconds.

At one time psychologists worked to help patients reduce the frequency of daydreams. Spending time in a fantasy world was deemed to be wasteful and pointless at best, harmful at worst. Some experts even suggested that it could lead to schizophrenia and other serious psychiatric disorders.

Not anymore. Today, it's widely accepted that daydreams benefit our mental health in several important ways. "They perform valuable functions, acting as a reminder mechanism and helping us organize our lives," points out Dr. Klinger. They're also a powerful coping mechanism when stress begins to build.

MELLOW VISIONS

Daydreams defuse stress in several ways. Their potential to induce relaxation has been well-documented. But they have another benefit that we tend to take for granted: They lift boredom. And boredom can definitely be a stressor, particularly in certain jobs. For instance, 80 percent of truck drivers use diverting daydreams as a way of dealing with the monotony of their work, according to Dr. Klinger.

Daydreams also fight fatigue, which contributes to stress if left unchecked. In a study at the University of Alabama at Birmingham, researchers questioned a group of 150 male and female runners about their thoughts while running. The study showed that those who let their minds wander felt less fatigued and more energetic after their workouts.

Try it the next time you want to liven up a dull, tiring task—cleaning the windows, for example. Envision your house on a Hawaiian beachfront. As you look out your window, you see nothing but palm trees, pure white sand, and clear blue water. Do you feel the warm sunshine on your skin? Do you smell the plumerias? Say, cleaning windows isn't so bad after all.

PICTURING THE POSSIBILITIES

Though we think of daydreams as random and uncontrollable, we can actually structure them to help us solve problems in the real world. "Daydreams are a channel for continuing information from the subconscious," says Dr. Klinger. "Many people who have had trouble making decisions report that they move closer to choices through deliberate daydreaming." Your desires and fears may seem like a confusing jumble that you can't make much sense of—until a daydream brings them clearly into focus.

"In daydreaming mode you think uncritically, without exerting control," Dr. Klinger suggests. The value lies in just watching a scenario unfold without judging or trying to manipulate the action. "You may discover things through this kind of spontaneous exploration that wouldn't occur to you if you tried to reason it out logically," he says.

Suppose you're playing with the idea of going back to school. But somehow, whenever you look over the course catalogs, you start feeling nervous and uneasy. It's quite a commitment of energy. Do you really want to do it? Will it take too much time away from your family, friends, and responsibilities?

Intentional daydreams can often help resolve just this kind of uncertainty. Want to see how?

Well, imagine you're actually back in school. It's September and classes are starting. You're sitting in class, notebook open. Now you're heading home to face your domestic duties. Daydream as much detail as possible, feeling yourself in your new role.

The satisfaction that you experience may emerge strongly enough to resolve all doubts. "Or as you explore the path, you may become aware of unforeseen problems that are more upsetting than you expected," Dr. Klinger says. For example, you might begin wondering how you will get the quiet you need to study for exams. Or you might start asking yourself whether your family will cooperate.

Another kind of reverie, known as empathic daydreaming, helps improve relationships. If you have been at odds with someone in your family or at work, try to imagine yourself in the other person's shoes. This can work wonders, Dr. Klinger notes. You'll quickly gain new insight into what the other person is feeling and how he sees the world.

Dr. Klinger acknowledges that there are no hard data on experimental attempts to increase empathy through daydreaming. But, he points out, "psychologists have observed that frequent daydreamers respond more sympathetically to others."

NOT TO WORRY

When we're faced with stressful situations, we often pledge to simply not think about them. We turn to daydreaming to divert our attention to other, more pleasant circumstances.

Unfortunately, no flight of fancy—no matter how vivid and intense—will completely shut out distressing thoughts. Trying to stop them through sheer force of will may add to our anxiety.

"Avoidance itself may be a problem," says Daniel Wegner, Ph.D., professor of psychology at the University of Virginia in Charlottesville. "When people try to control their thoughts in a laboratory setting, they can't. For example, they can't not think about a white bear on command. Just trying not to think of something can cause stress."

Suppose you're worried about the state of your bank account. You try to forget about it by focusing your mind elsewhere. But then you happen to spot a black square that, to you, looks just like a wallet. Before you know it, a chain of association has led you back to the stressor that you're trying to avoid.

Instead of resorting to daydreams to make you forget a problem, you might have more success by going the opposite route: Think about what's bothering you, and think about it hard.

One useful tactic is to set aside time—say, 25 minutes at the end of every day—to think nonstop about whatever is bugging you. Then when a problem comes up during the course of a day, remind yourself to set it aside for your special worry time.

"People who did this in an experiment found that they worried less over a three- to four-week period," says Dr. Wegner.

Airing your worries publicly can also free you from troublesome thoughts. "Discuss things with your spouse, a trusted friend, or a confidant," Dr. Wegner suggests. "It's often the things you're most embarrassed about that become major preoccupations. Opening up and talking is often all that's needed to make you feel better."

Mastering the Mind's Eye

Just as daydreaming can fill us with the warm fuzzies, it can also plague us with nagging doubts and troubling thoughts—not exactly conducive to stress relief. But you can turn even these vexing visions to your advantage with the right interpretation and perspective. These strategies should help.

Worry your way to relief. If you're nervous or fearful about a particular situation, exercising those emotions in your daydreams can help you work things through. "In studies of people who were facing surgery, those who were preoccupied with the details of the procedure—who spent some time imagining what might happen—adapted significantly better afterward than those who shut out all thoughts of what they were about to go through," Dr. Klinger notes.

Take notes. If you find yourself daydreaming about a troubling situation, write down the details of what you're envisioning. Then imagine your options for solving the problem and write those down, too. Once you have it all on paper, your mind is free to focus on other things. "It has a tremendous calming effect," Dr. Klinger says.

Count on a conclusion. If you're disturbed by your negative daydreams, realize that they usually don't last. "It seems that worry wears itself out after a time," says Dr. Klinger. If you have wheel-spinning worries that focus on your feelings, try using daydreams to analyze the situation. They may lead you to better understanding and constructive action.

Enjoy what comes to mind. No one has proven that you can actually increase your capacity to daydream. "But I'd speculate that you can change your style of daydreaming somewhat," Dr. Klinger says.

"A lot of people are embarrassed and inhibited about fanciful daydreams," he adds. "If they get the idea that it's okay and even potentially constructive, they'll give themselves permission to daydream. The result is that they learn to think more originally than they did before."

See also Imagery

DECISION MAKING

CHOOSE WITH CONFIDENCE

From the moment the alarm sounds in the morning, we're thrust into decision-making mode: "Do I get out of bed or hit the snooze button?" "What should I wear today?" "What do I want for breakfast?" "Should I take the usual route or try the shortcut?"

And that's just before we get to work.

We make a lot of fairly routine decisions over the course of a day. Then once in a while, life hits us with a real doozy. Like buying a house. Or changing jobs. Or starting—or ending—a relationship. Suddenly, our entire future seems to hang in the balance as we assess the situation, weigh our options, and struggle to make a choice that we can live with.

It's no wonder that the decision-making process can be so fraught with stress. "There's a tremendous fear that we all share: that we won't cope adequately with a situation, that we won't choose correctly," says William J. Knaus, Ed.D., adjunct professor of psychology at Springfield College and American International College, both in Springfield, Massachusetts, and co-author of *Overcoming Procrastination*.

Particularly when we face a tough decision, we may become stressed as we mull over what to do. This opens the door to self-doubt, fear, a sense of inadequacy or powerlessness—or all of the above. These feelings just compound the difficulty of making up our minds.

THE SOONER, THE BETTER

Often we try to postpone the inevitable, perhaps hoping that the situation will somehow resolve itself or that the right answer will suddenly become apparent. Here's the cold, hard truth: You truly won't feel better until you make up your mind.

It's true that you should never rush an important decision. But the longer you put it off, the more stress will build. Feeling edgy can blur the decision-making process, leading to confusion and poor reasoning.

"Good decision making is a logical activity. But when we get stressed, logic tends to shut down," says James Campbell Quick, Ph.D., professor of organizational behavior at the University of Texas at Arlington and editor of the *Journal of Occupational Health Psychology*. "It's easy to become emotional and irrational and to let feelings dominate. Emotions do have a part to play in decision making—but they shouldn't be a dominant force."

A study at North Carolina State University in Raleigh showed just how much stress can drain brainpower. Sixty-one college students filled out a questionnaire about their recent life experiences, took a test that measured their levels of anxiety, then completed a task that required astute decision-making skills. Those who had been through a number of difficult life events, such as a death or an illness in the family, tended to show poorer decision-making skills.

DE-STRESSING DECISIONS

When you notice stress getting in the way of clear, objective thinking, the first thing that you should do is relax using a technique such as meditation, yoga, or autogenics. "Momentary relaxation is the best intervention," says Dr. Quick.

He also recommends an exercise that he calls transcendant mind. It involves developing the ability to take a step backward and to see yourself, the situation, and the decision in a broader context. Things rarely have a life-or-death quality when observed in this way, he says.

Here's an example: Let's say that your living room sofa needs to be replaced. You can't decide whether to go with the no-nonsense functional style that you've always had or to take advantage of the opportunity for a full-scale professional redesign of your entire living room. An elegant room may be what you've always wanted, but is it worth the expense? Can you truly afford it now?

Take a step back. Just how important is this decision in the grand scheme of things? Will you even remember it five years from now? If not, maybe you don't need to get all worked up over it.

Respecting Your Right to Be Wrong

Certain behavior patterns can sabotage the decision-making process. The number one decision buster: perfectionism. If you expect to be right every time and regard every mistake as a disaster, you're setting yourself up for a lot of unnecessary stress.

The perfectionist, says Dr. Knaus, is burdened with the belief that he's worthless unless he does things exactly right—all the time. "Perfectionism is an impossible dream that leads to tension and, ultimately, poor judgment," Dr. Knaus says. "Human beings are mistake-making creatures. We have to learn as we go. If we don't take chances, we won't discover the possibilities. Human evolution simply doesn't work if we won't dare to do anything except when we're sure of success."

You should also become aware of any negative self-talk that may be loading the decision-making process with stress, Dr. Knaus counsels. If your internal messages run along the lines of "I always make mistakes," "I'm not really strong enough to deal with this situation," or "If I make the wrong decision the results will be horrible," you're generating doubts that can make the process downright excruciating. It's nearly impossible to choose wisely under such circumstances.

Plotting a Plan of Attack

Decision making becomes much less stressful when you have a plan to follow. This puts you in control of the situation and leads you step-by-step toward the solution that suits you best. What's more, you'll no longer feel the need to delay making up your mind. You'll have settled on a decision well before stress gets a foothold.

Here's a simple four-step decision-making strategy that's recommended by J. Edward Russo, Ph.D., professor of marketing and behavioral science in the Johnson Graduate School of Management at Cornell University in Ithaca, New York.

1. Know what you want. Decide how you'll know when you've found what you're looking for. If you need a contractor to do some house repairs, for example, the questions you must ask before you start your search are: "What am I looking for? How will I recognize the right person?" You need to consider whether honesty, reliability, and good construction skills are all equally important to you.

Thinking this through at the outset will keep you from making a spur-of-the-moment decision, such as hiring a contractor without checking out other jobs that he has done.

2. Shake the bushes. Now it's time for some intelligence gathering. If you need to contract someone's services, you'd check references. If you're about to make a large purchase, you'd do some shopping around. If you're considering changing doctors, you'd solicit recommendations from friends.

How long should this step take? "There's no fixed rule," says Dr. Russo. If you've asked enough people and followed a systematic process, after a certain point you'll discover a trend toward diminishing returns. No matter how much effort you put into your research, you're not learning much more. Just be sure that you consider negative information as well as positive.

3. Look at the facts. Dr. Russo calls this convergence: You bring together all of the information that you've gathered, then make your decision coolly and confidently. Whatever you do, don't rush it.

"You have to give convergence the same respect that you give the preceding steps," Dr. Russo says. "You've done a lot of legwork, used your intuition, spoken to people. Don't make your decision now on a fluke."

4. Evaluate for next time. Now you've chosen: You've hired a contractor. Or bought a ticket to the Bahamas. Or settled on a new doctor. You're done—almost.

"The last phase of decision making is learning from the experience," Dr. Russo says. "It's amazing how many decisions come up over and over." Almost always, there will be a "next time" when you're faced with a similar situation.

In fact, that's a good reason to stop agonizing over a choice you have to make now. Look at it this way: A mistake isn't really a mistake if it gives you insight that makes the next decision easier.

See also Autogenics, Meditation, Self-Talk, Yoga

DEEP BREATHING
TRAIN YOURSELF TO BLOW OUT TENSION

Breathing is essential to life. We can go for weeks without food, for days without water. But we'd last no more than a few minutes without air.

Of course, we have to make sure that our bodies are properly fed and hydrated. When it comes to breathing, though, they're pretty much on their own. Most of us don't think about it a whole lot. But perhaps we should. Monitoring our breathing can tell us when we're becoming stressed—and it's also one of the handiest and simplest relaxation techniques around.

When we're faced with a stressful situation, our bodies respond with shallow, rapid breathing as well as an accelerated pulse and increased blood pressure. These changes are part of the so-called fight-or-flight response with which our bodies instinctively meet real or imagined danger. It increases blood flow to our extremities, so we can either face down the danger or run for our lives if we need to.

This natural reaction was a boon to our ancestors when a Paleolithic predator was bearing down on them. But these days, it's triggered not by close encounters with furry carnivores but by demanding bosses, rush-hour traffic, and stacks of unpaid bills. Stressors like these can put our bodies on red alert several times throughout the day, and unless we do something to counterbalance this turbocharged state, it can weaken our immune systems and leave us vulnerable to diseases ranging from the common cold to cancer.

OUT WITH THE BAD AIR

Some doctors suggest that habitual rapid, shallow breathing isn't just a result of stress—it's a cause of it, too. They've found that routinely breathing this way can actually be responsible for many

PUT MORE WIND IN YOUR SAILS

Many experts counsel not only breathing more deeply but also breathing differently from the way most of us do. We commonly breathe using our chest muscles, drawing up our shoulders as we inhale to enlarge the chest cavity. The trouble is, this mechanism allows a limited amount of air and oxygen to enter the body. We can breathe more fully by lowering the diaphragm (the thin, broad muscle between the chest and abdomen) and letting the abdomen protrude as we inhale.

This technique is often called belly breathing, though no air actually enters the belly. Rather, pushing the abdomen out simply allows more space in the chest for air to inflate the lungs.

All of us started out by belly breathing. Just take a look at a toddler and watch that tummy expand as he inhales. You may have gotten out of the habit of breathing from your diaphragm over the years, but it still comes naturally.

To try belly breathing, here's an exercise recommended by Robert Fried, Ph.D., in his book *The Breath Connection*: Lie or sit down, placing one hand on your chest and the other on your abdomen. With shallower chest breathing, the hand on your chest will rise when you inhale and fall when you exhale. With belly breathing, the hand on your chest should remain fairly motionless, and the hand on your abdomen should rise when you inhale and fall when you exhale.

Concentrate on making your lower hand rise and fall with each breath. Don't overdo it: Like any muscle that has been underused for years, the diaphragm is vulnerable to fatigue and discomfort. Start with three minutes once a day and gradually work up to five minutes twice a day.

Regular practice will change the way you habitually breathe so that you'll use your diaphragm more and your chest less. The result will be a calmer, more in-control you.

symptoms that we often attribute to tension, such as anxiety, high blood pressure, headache, muscle pain, irritable bowel syndrome, and insomnia.

You've probably heard this breathing pattern referred to by another name: hyperventilation. What you may not know about hyperventilation is that it actually gets less oxygen into your body's tissues than breathing in a slow, measured way. When you breathe normally, your lungs function as kind of a stock exchange, trading oxygen on an equal basis for carbon dioxide. But when you breathe rapidly and shallowly, your body unloads too much carbon dioxide. Because a delicate balance has been disrupted, your blood loses some of its ability to deliver oxygen to your body tissues.

"When we looked at what symptom was most common among people with anxiety, it was rapid breathing," says Gary Grody, Ph.D., a clinical psychologist in private practice in Lawrence, New York. "If you can contain rapid breathing, it in turn reduces other components of stress like rapid heartbeat and dizziness. If you don't contain it, these other symptoms spiral out of control, leading to catastrophic thoughts and more anxiety. Controlling your breathing can stop the domino effect of anxiety."

IN WITH THE GOOD AIR

Fortunately, just as out-of-control breathing can contribute to stress, disciplined breathing can abort the stress cycle and activate the relaxation response. It's easy to train yourself to breathe in a more controlled way, so you can keep stress from taking its toll.

Many traditional methods of relaxation, such as meditation, tai chi, and yoga, emphasize proper breathing technique. Their practitioners believe that deep, controlled breathing calms body and mind and connects them to their inner or spiritual selves. In fact, the link between breath and spirit dates back to ancient times: In Greek and Hebrew, for example, one word refers to both "spirit" and "breath." (In Greek it's *pneuma*; in Hebrew it's *ruach*.)

To help you take advantage of the therapeutic benefits of deep breathing, Dr. Grody offers the following exercise, which he teaches to his patients.

1. Sit in a comfortable chair or lie on a couch, with your arms at your sides and your hands very loose.
2. Do a quick body scan—that is, become aware of any muscle tension in specific places (such as clenching your hands or curling your toes) and release it.
3. Close your eyes and let a pleasant image enter your mind. Don't force it, but allow yourself to imagine anything you like, such as an island beach with gently rolling waves or a grassy field of spring flowers.
4. Now breathe in deeply but slowly through your nose. Expand your lungs to hold as much air as you can without straining.
5. Slowly breathe the air out through your mouth, voicing a long, vowel-laden sound such as hooommm to help you extend the exhalation.
6. Feel the tension being released throughout your body.

Keep breathing in this way for 10 minutes the first time you try it. Gradually work your way to once-daily sessions lasting 15 to 20 minutes. By the end of a session, you should feel relaxed, even sleepy.

Note: If you start to feel dizzy, lightheaded, or more anxious, you may be breathing too deeply or too rapidly. If so, breathe normally until you feel better before resuming the exercise.

Practice deep breathing daily and add a session whenever you're particularly anxious or about to enter a high-stress situation. Also, many who have trouble sleeping find it useful to perform this exercise just before going to bed. A hidden benefit: Once your body has learned to connect this technique with relaxation, you may be able to discharge stress with just a few deep breaths. Try it when you're getting angry, or if a ringing phone makes you jumpy, or before you talk to your spouse about a troubling matter. In no time you'll find yourself breezing through life's most difficult situations.

See also Meditation, Mindfulness, Relaxation Response, Tai Chi, Yoga

E

EXERCISE
MOVE YOUR BODY, MEND YOUR MOOD

No one has to tell you about all of the wonderful health benefits of exercise. You know that it can trim extra pounds, fight disease, even add years to your life. But let's face it: When stress saps your energy, your strength, and your spirits, you just can't wait to get home, slip on some sweats—and curl up on the sofa in front of the boob tube. The last thing you want to do is hoist hand weights or rev up for a run.

But maybe you should. The fact is, exercise is one of the most effective stress busters around. No matter if you prefer cycling or stair-climbing, walking or water aerobics, working out can ease tension and anxiety and leave you feeling refreshed and invigorated. What's more, regular physical activity can improve your immune function, reduce your blood pressure, and slow your heart rate—almost the exact opposite of what stress does to your body.

"I prescribe exercise, along with medication or counseling, for just about all of my patients," says Robert S. Brown, M.D., clinical professor of psychiatric medicine at the University of Virginia in Charlottesville. "There's no question that it improves mood and decreases anxiety. And when you exercise, you actually end up with more energy. It boosts your self-concept to be doing something active for yourself."

You'll start noticing the therapeutic effects of exercise almost immediately, Dr. Brown adds. "If you're nervous or anxious, a brisk 20-minute walk-jog will make you feel better right away."

Easy Does It

The evidence is in: You don't need to run marathons to leave stress behind. In fact, moderation may make all the difference in whether exercise counteracts stress or contributes to it.

In a British study participants who regularly took brisk walks experienced reductions in anxiety, while those who enrolled in a more difficult exercise program did not. The researchers suggest that the fatigue and strain of fitting demanding workouts into an already hectic schedule negate the natural benefits of exercise and worsen mood.

Other research has shown that moderate exercise helps strengthen immune function, while too much can actually undermine the body's immune response. Marathoners, for instance, are more prone to infection than people who exercise less.

And in a study at Stanford University School of Medicine, middle-age people enjoyed the same stress-soothing effects of exercise whether they jogged or walked. The key, researchers concluded, was frequency rather than intensity: The people who devoted the most time to physical activity reaped the greatest rewards.

The bottom line: If stress reduction is your goal, choose any activity you enjoy—be it walking, running, cycling, swimming, weight training, or something else entirely—and make it a regular part of your life. But never let exercise become an additional burden. And, doctors caution, never push yourself to the point of pain and fatigue in order to fight stress.

Getting a Leg Up on Stress

The latest research seems to support Dr. Brown's view that exercise has significant stress-reducing benefits. In a major review of studies that examined the relationship between exercise and mood, researchers concluded that working out provides a significant mental and emotional lift—especially in people who are severely depressed or anxious.

One of the studies cited in the review showed that people who were hospitalized for depression felt significantly better when they followed an exercise program that increased their aerobic fitness by 15 percent or more. In another of the studies depression decreased immediately and remained improved for up to 12 months in patients who ran or lifted weights.

Even light exercise makes a difference, according to researchers. One study found that hospital patients greatly reduced their anxiety by walking or jogging. Another showed that subjects who exercised just a little—not enough to improve cardiovascular fitness—experienced reductions in anxiety, depression, and fatigue.

British researchers examined the effects of exercise on a particularly stress-prone group: police officers. The officers—all men—were assigned to one of three groups. The first group participated in a running program, the second lifted weights, and the third served as controls. After 10 weeks, those in both exercise groups reported substantial reductions in their overall feelings of stress, along with improvements in their health and their sense of well-being. They also indicated that they found their jobs less stressful than before.

"These data suggest that a fairly brief aerobic training program (running), and to a lesser extent an anaerobic program (weight training) of similar duration, offers substantial . . . benefits," the authors concluded.

BUILDING A BUFFER ZONE

As mentioned earlier, exercise protects you from the physical effects of stress as well. In fact, it may actually block the fight-or-flight response that generates so much wear and tear in your body.

In a British study researchers assigned 30 healthy men to solve complicated arithmetic problems while an audiotape played distracting noises at a disturbing volume. Twenty minutes before the test, some of the subjects pedaled a stationary bike set for either low or high resistance, while the others just sat quietly.

The men who worked out hard experienced virtually no rise in their blood pressure and, surprisingly, a drop in their heart rates while doing their math. Their nonexercising counterparts didn't fare nearly as well: Their blood pressure inched up, as did their heart rates—an average of 10 beats per minute.

It appears that exercise has the same positive effects in women as in men. Researchers at Wake Forest University in Winston-Salem, North Carolina, put 48 women in two separate stressful situations. First the women completed a difficult word test. Then a week later, they delivered a three-minute speech in front of a critical audience. A half-hour before one task, the women did 40 minutes of aerobic exercise; before the other, they just rested quietly.

Again, exercise significantly dampened the impact of stress. The women's blood pressure rose less when the stressful situation followed a workout. Also, the women reported significantly fewer anxious thoughts when they worked out prior to giving the speech.

All the Right Moves

Want to reap some of the feel-good rewards that accompany energetic exercise? Here's what you can do.

Work in workouts regularly. The stress-buffering effect of a single exercise session lasts a few hours. But when you make working out part of your lifestyle, you'll soon find that your body always stays cool under fire. One study, for example, showed that the heart rates of well-conditioned men slowed down faster than the heart rates of sedentary men following anxiety-producing events.

Pick up the pace. Gradually build up the time and intensity of your workout at a rate that feels comfortable, suggests Dr. Brown. "Most people don't know that they can push the limits of their bodies in a positive direction," he says. Just be sure to check with your doctor before you go overboard on running, lifting, weight training, or other high-exertion activities.

See also Dancing, Stretching, Walking

F

FAMILY

STRESS RELIEF? IT'S ALL RELATIVE

When it comes to the link between family and stress, most of us could probably throw out a few choice examples of how the former contributes to the latter. Like a spouse who doesn't pitch in enough with the household chores. Or a teenager who borrows the car and then leaves the gas tank empty. Or a parent who constantly criticizes.

Sure, family life has its foibles. But it also anchors us and gives us balance when the world around us has gone haywire. Indeed, while extended positive contact with any fellow human being can keep us healthy and help us live longer, those closest to us—spouses, children, parents, siblings—seem to have the most to offer.

"Both the quality and quantity of social relationships have a strong influence on physical health, but the family relationship is the most powerful factor," says Thomas Campbell, M.D., associate professor of family medicine and psychiatry at the University of Rochester School of Medicine and Dentistry in New York.

MATE TO LAST

Marriage, in particular, can have a lot to do with our sense of well-being. "Among my married patients, satisfaction with the union accounts for the bulk of their emotional health," says Dr. Campbell. "It's a much bigger determinant than work or friends."

The connection between marriage and emotional health may be rooted in the biology of our species. "The primary relationship is the one from which we receive the most emotional support and nurturance, and as a result, it has the most influence on our physical and emotional health," explains Dr. Campbell.

Husbands and wives buffer stress significantly better than friends do, according to Pamela Braboy Jackson, Ph.D., assistant professor of sociology at Duke University in Durham, North Carolina. In a study that she conducted, those who described their spouses as supportive reported less strain in the face of hard times and were less likely to become depressed when stress turned burdensome. "Spouses can address a wider range of stress-producing problems than friends can," Dr. Jackson observes.

The parent-child relationship can provide similar stress-blocking benefits. In fact, one of the strongest predictors of good emotional health in the elderly is contact with their adult offspring, Dr. Campbell says.

One study found that older folks coped better with the loss of their spouses—and were less likely to die in the years immediately after a spouse's death—if they had solid, affectionate bonds with their grown children. "Parents who feel emotionally close to their adult children are protected from the harmful stress of social loss because of heightened feelings of security," the study's authors observed.

FAMILY MATTERS

Close ties to our kin appear to protect us against stress in several specific ways. Here are some of the proven benefits.

Improved coping skills. People who have strong familial bonds can handle stressful events better than those who don't. Physically, their bodies don't react to stress as readily or intensely. This muting of the stress response may actually help lower the risk of heart disease, Dr. Campbell suggests. (Several studies have linked persistent unresolved stress to the development of heart disease.)

Stronger immune systems. Research has shown that people in harmonious marriages have better immune function than those who are divorced.

Healthier habits. A loving partner will naturally steer you away from stress-induced behaviors that contribute to an unhealthy lifestyle. "Married people are more likely to stop smoking," notes Dr. Campbell. "And they eat better foods."

Greater concern for personal well-being. People who become seriously ill are more likely to deal with it constructively when they have family members on their side. Symptoms are brought to the doctor's attention more quickly and medications are taken more faithfully with the gentle encouragement of loved ones.

WHEN THE BONDS BREAK

Clearly, family can give us the resilience and fortitude that we need to weather many of life's storms. But it can also invite stress into our lives when relationships become strained. "Some research suggests that the effects of negative family interactions have a much more powerful influence on us than the effects of positive family interactions," says Dr. Campbell.

One study, for example, found that a woman in a happy marriage is half as likely to develop depression as a single woman. A woman in a distressed relationship, however, is 25 times more likely to develop depression than a single woman.

In another study researchers videotaped and took blood samples of 90 newlywed couples engaged in half-hour discussions of two or three touchy relationship issues—things such as in-laws and finances. The couples whose discussions featured lots of criticism, interruption, disagreement, and other signs of conflict showed significant increases in their levels of stress-related hormones, along with a decline in immune function that lasted for as long as 24 hours. Comparatively, the more harmonious couples showed fewer biological signs of stress.

REKINDLING KINSHIP

So what makes for a harmonious family life? Well, there is no universal list of do's and don'ts. What works for one family may prove disastrous for another. It all depends on the personalities, needs, and interests of the people involved.

But most experts do agree that good communication is the foundation of any positive, productive relationship. With that in mind, the following tips should help take the knots out of your family ties and prevent future frays.

Hold a roundtable. Experts suggest that families make a point of holding weekly meetings. Every member, from oldest to youngest, should have a chance to express feelings, share concerns, and talk about what they like and don't like.

Be positive. Family members, especially spouses, should try to be aware of how they're responding to each other. Research has shown that couples who tend to pepper their conversations with disparaging comments are more likely to end up getting divorced, according to John Gottman, Ph.D., professor of psychology at the University of Washington in Seattle.

Positive, encouraging words should outnumber negative ones, experts advise. In fact, some say that you should make at least five positive statements for each negative one. When you voice more criticisms than that, marital dissatisfaction gets the upper hand.

Stick to the issues. When a disagreement arises, it's all too easy to lose sight of the problem and instead launch verbal missiles at the person involved. But that only leads to bad feelings—or worse, a permanent rift in the relationship.

"There's no way to avoid conflict all the time," says Dr. Campbell. "But there are lots of ways to deal with it." One way, he says, is to make sure that you keep your comments focused on the issue at hand.

Set ground rules. When you initiate a discussion, make it clear that you want to solve a problem rather than criticize the other person. That's a general principle for dealing with all family members, not just your spouse, say experts.

Be a team. Couples who tend to think in terms of "we" rather than "you" and "I" during the first year of their marriages have stronger, more satisfying relationships in their third year, according to a study by Linda Acitelli, Ph.D., associate professor of psychology at the University of Houston. Dr. Acitelli interviewed couples in their first year of marriage and then again two years later. She sees a big difference between saying, "You have a problem. You need to change" and "We have a problem. How can we make things better?" The first puts the blame on one partner, while the second conveys the idea that "we're working on this together . . . we're in it together."

Just say something. No matter what words you use, communication is better than silence. "Couples who talk more about their relationships tend to have stronger marriages," Dr. Acitelli says.

Men, in particular, seem to avoid talk until there's a specific problem to address. Their guiding principle is, "If it isn't broke, don't fix it." And in Dr. Acitelli's view, that's a mistake. Even when things are going well, it's worth commenting on the relationship just to convey that the harmony isn't being taken for granted.

Use regular discussion—with liberal use of "we," "us," and "our"—as preventive maintenance to keep your marriage and your family strong. If you're not comfortable with conversation, just remember that in the long run, it's a lot easier than trying to patch things up after there has been a break in communication.

See also Children, Communication, Intimacy

FINANCIAL PLANNING
MIND OVER MONEY

They say that the best things in life are free. Obviously, "they" have never gone to a grocery store, or bought a house, or paid a month's worth of utility bills.

The fact is, money—earning it, spending it, saving it—generates a whole lot of tension and anxiety for a whole lot of people. "It's rare to find a person whose self-concept has nothing to do with his assets," says Daniel Kegan, Ph.D., an organizational psychologist and attorney in Chicago. The green stuff colors the way we feel about ourselves, our work, even our loved ones.

Indeed, it often seems that money and worry go together like the proverbial horse and carriage. In a survey conducted by

GOING FOR BROKER

If you have a significant amount of money to invest, it's time to think about enlisting the help of a financial adviser. Not only is your bottom line likely to benefit, but you'll feel less stress when you know that your money is in good hands.

Honesty and competence can't be guaranteed in this area any more than in other professions. But you can safeguard your money to some degree by knowing what—and whom—to look for. These guidelines can help.

Tap a tutor. "A good adviser will help you become increasingly less dependent on him," says Daniel Kegan, Ph.D., an organizational psychologist and attorney in Chicago. The adviser should be able to explain to you investment concepts such as risk and return and to fill you in on important background knowledge such as standard rates of return on various investment options.

Be skeptical of "risk-free" investment. If an adviser uses this phrase, remember that there's no such thing. Risk can be reduced but not eliminated.

Also avoid any adviser who manipulates your decisions by playing on fears or greed. Alarms should go off if you hear, "This is the chance of a lifetime. You'll kick yourself if you miss it."

Expect good questions. An experienced adviser will know that no single investment strategy suits everyone. Before advising you, he should ask you questions that help him understand your personal attitudes, beliefs, and philosophy. Among these questions: How do you feel about risk? What are your present needs and future goals? Do you want to increase your current income or maximize long-term growth?

Plan to stay active. You should play a role in making and modifying investments, no matter how competent your adviser is. "You can't say, 'I just want someone to take care of me,'" says Dr. Kegan. "The more you know, the better you can judge what kind of job your adviser is doing."

Psychology Today, more than half of the respondents associated money with emotions such as anxiety, depression, and anger. It's no surprise, then, that disagreements about spending and saving are a principal source of family discord.

BALANCING NET WORTH WITH SELF-WORTH

Uncovering and understanding your feelings about money can go a long way toward de-stressing personal finances, Dr. Kegan says. "If you don't have access to your feelings about the stuff, it's like sailing a ship without a compass or a rudder," he adds.

As an example, Dr. Kegan poses this question: What meaning and importance does spending money have for you?

"A lot of people use money to relieve unpleasant moods," Dr. Kegan says. "They feel bad, so they go out and buy expensive clothing or eat in fancy restaurants. In the short term, it makes them feel good. In the long term, it creates nothing but debt.

"If you want to drown your sorrows in spending, that's a choice you can make," Dr. Kegan continues. "But once you're aware that this is what you're doing, you can ask yourself, 'Is the feeling worth what I'm going to spend?' "

Another question that only you can answer: How much money do you feel you really need? "The value of money is so subjective," says Dr. Kegan. "The minimally acceptable standard constantly shifts."

Is it important to you to have a higher standard of living than your parents had? To do as well as other members of your graduating class? To be richer than your neighbors? Try to put into words and numbers what amount of money would make you feel safe and successful.

You can't make intelligent decisions about your finances without looking closely at your whole sense of values. Where do free time, freedom, comfort, and the love of family members fit into the financial equation? Think of each of these as an asset, then re-evaluate how wealthy or poor you are.

Are you willing to trade your free time for more money by working longer hours or by making an effort to gain the information you need to invest wisely? How would you feel about living frugally now so that you could move to a bigger house 10 years down the road? When you balance the importance of all of your values, it often becomes clear that you're a lot better off than you may have thought.

SECURING YOUR FUTURE

Of course, guarding against financial woes also means planning ahead—whether for retirement, for a child's education, or just as a safety net. How you go about saving for the future depends heavily on your feelings toward risk.

Risk. The word itself can make many of us cringe. Essentially, it refers to how much money you'd be willing to lose in exchange for the opportunity to increase your wealth. A savings bond, for example, has virtually no risk: You put a certain amount in, you get a certain amount back. Stocks, on the other hand, have high risk: You could, say, double your investment or lose everything.

You should consider your level of comfort with taking risk in developing a financial plan. Think of it this way: Would you get more pain from losing $5,000 than pleasure from gaining $5,000? If the thought of losing money is abhorrent to you, then you know that you should make low-risk investments to keep your comfort level high and your stress level low.

Uncertainty about what lies ahead makes many people nervous about their financial plans. But the fact is, some uncertainty goes along with every investment. Neither you nor anyone else knows how economic conditions will change in the coming years, how much money you'll need to live comfortably, or how long you will live.

But while you can't predict what will happen in the future, Dr. Kegan says, you can clarify your goals for the future. Think about what you want your money for. If you want to live out your retirement in security and relative comfort, that requires one kind of financial plan. But if you feel strongly about leaving something behind for your children or for an important cause, you'll probably need a plan that's much more aggressive—one that will involve more risk and more attention on your part.

91

Savvy Spending and Saving Strategies

Most of the stress of managing our financial affairs comes not from long-range planning but from the money matters we deal with every day. We all know the feeling of having spent our entire week's paycheck before we even receive it. Or of starting the weekend with a wallet full of cash, then scrounging in the sofa for change Monday morning so that we have enough to buy lunch. And we can't help but wonder, "Where has all my money gone?"

The good news is, this kind of stress is completely avoidable. You just need to learn how to monitor and modify your spending and saving habits. The following strategies will help make you the master of your money.

Watch the ebb and flow. To get a realistic sense of where you are financially, first make a list all of your sources of income, then keep track of your expenses—large and small—for a month. Be sure to include spending for food, clothing, and other personal goods; rent or mortgage costs; and all insurance and automobile expenses.

Do you notice some surprises? Does more cash than you imagined disappear when you're shopping at the supermarket or picking up lunch at the corner sandwich shop? If so, it's time to make a budget.

Set aside your savings. The first step in your budget planning is to decide how much money you want to save in a month. Many experts recommend 10 percent of your net income as a good rule of thumb.

Subtract your fixed costs. Monthly payments on a mortgage or a car loan, for example, won't change. You can count on having to lay out this amount every month.

After you've accounted for your savings and set expenses, what you have left over will go toward miscellaneous expenses.

Consider cutbacks. Look for places where you can trim spending. Maybe you could take your lunch to work instead of going out to eat every day. Maybe you could join a carpool. Or maybe you could make a grocery list—and stick to it. Cost-cutting measures like these leave more money to put toward savings or entertainment—both vital cushions that help relieve money worries.

Watch the company you keep. If you hang out with people who are wealthier or less cost-conscious than you, you could pay for it in more ways than one. "A lot of times you end up going along with the people you associate with," says Dr. Kegan. It's not easy to be fiscally prudent if your friends are big spenders.

"If you want to save but you're in with a crowd that spends, perhaps you should search out people who enjoy sunsets and free concerts," Dr. Kegan notes. Keep your high-rolling friends, by all means, but be honest with them when they make plans that are too expensive for you to join in on.

WORRY LESS BY BUYING RIGHT

While gaining control of your day-to-day finances is important, it is those big-ticket purchases that can really make or break your budget. When you are contemplating buying a new car, house, or stereo system, bring solid decision-making skills into play, urges J. Edward Russo, Ph.D., professor of marketing and behavioral science in the Johnson Graduate School of Management at Cornell University in Ithaca, New York. Give these tricks of the trade a try.

Decide what matters. Is it more important to you to have a car that's flashy or a car with a superior repair record? It might make sense to pay more for greater durability rather than going for looks with less quality.

Gather intelligence. Take as much time as you need to get the facts about options. Educate yourself. Big items are not impulse buys, and the time you invest could produce a real payoff—saving you hundreds or thousands of dollars.

Look for trouble. Seek "disconfirming evidence"—the downside that you really don't want to know about. If the dramatic aerodynamic lines of a luxury car have all but swept you off your feet, make a real effort to investigate its fuel economy. How much will all that horsepower cost you over a year of use?

Similarly, you may be enraptured by a condo in an exquisitely charming old building, but have an expert check the plumbing before you make an offer.

Detect the subjective. When you're deliberating over a major purchase, be particularly alert to emotional issues. For instance, are you leaning toward the fully loaded high-end luxury car because the salesperson seems like such an earnest, trustworthy young man?

Many people who aren't particularly scrupulous are adept at generating the have-to-have-it feelings. Ask yourself: Is this transaction really part of an ongoing relationship? Your tax accountant wants to have your business every year, so he has every reason to serve your best interests in a way that will earn your trust. An automobile salesperson may not.

Seek the opinions of others. Someone who has previous experience with a similar purchase can be a big help. For instance, if you're a first-time home buyer, you might want to solicit the advice of a friend who has already been there and done that. In fact, you might want to have this person with you during negotiations—it can take a good deal of stress out of the process. "Sharing the experience is very soothing for some people," says Dr. Russo.

Also, a real friend will give you more than a rubber stamp. "You have to listen to a friend who tells you, 'Sure, the real estate agent has a lovely smile. But you're buying real estate, not the agent,'" Dr. Russo says.

Learn from mistakes. In the long run, wise spending decisions grow out of past experience. If you're not happy with a major purchase or another financial commitment, invest some time and energy in figuring out what you did wrong. Which stage in the decision process went awry? What could you have done differently? What will you do differently next time? Spending money, like making it, is a skill that improves with intelligent practice.

FLOTATION TANKS

LET YOUR CARES DRIFT AWAY

If you've ever whiled away a summer afternoon on the water—whether on a raft in a swimming pool or in an inner tube on a nearby creek—you know how utterly blissful the simple act of floating can be. Adrift on the water's surface, you tend to lose all sense of time and space and become immersed in the absolute calm and serenity of your surroundings.

A flotation tank operates on much the same principle. Basically, you lie in a body-temperature pool of water in which there has been enough salt dissolved to buoy you without the slightest effort on your part. The setting is dark and quiet, so nothing can stimulate your senses.

A half-hour session in a flotation tank—also known as restricted environment stimulation therapy—can relieve tension effortlessly by reducing the body's physical stress symptoms. The experience leads to "a marked reduction in the physical activity associated with stress," says Thomas Fine, associate professor in the Department of Psychiatry at the Medical College of Ohio in Toledo. In particular, muscle tension drops, heart rate slows, blood pressure declines, and stress hormones dwindle.

According to Fine, spending time in a flotation tank "is one of the most powerful ways of inducing the relaxation response"—the same mind-body antidote to stress that's triggered by practices such as meditation, breathing exercises, and autogenic training. "In fact, we tend to see a somewhat more marked response than with other techniques," he notes.

RELAXATION WITHOUT EFFORT

One reason flotation therapy works so well for stress reduction, proponents say, is that it gives your body permission to go into a state of deep rest. "Your body is totally supported," says Fine. "From a musculoskeletal standpoint, there's absolutely no need for effort."

Even your body's system of temperature regulation gets a break. The water in the tank is set at exactly skin temperature, 94°F, so your body has no need to produce or dissipate heat. Temperature regulation, Fine explains, is a major aspect of autonomic functions—the life-supporting body mechanisms that continue without our awareness, such as breathing and heartbeat. "In the tank no regulation is required," he says.

When the physical checks and balances go on holiday, the mind gets a break, too. The result is a closer link to our unconscious feelings. Normally, we inadvertently allow external stimulation to block out awareness of our feelings. When we do the dishes, for example, we concentrate on the task at hand, not on our mood. "Taking away all stimulation puts us back in contact with ourselves," Fine says.

In essence, flotation resembles other relaxation techniques such as meditation, says Roderick Borrie, Ph.D., a psychologist at South Oaks Hospital in Amityville, New York. Like these disciplines, it shifts your attention away from the outside environment and onto your inner thoughts and feelings. The difference is that "flotation requires no effort, training, or practice. It just happens," says Dr. Borrie.

What Flotation Therapy Can Do for You

Flotation tanks were something of a fad in the early 1980s, with facilities springing up everywhere. Their popularity has waned a bit since then, but they remain available in many cities and in clinics devoted to stress reduction. Research has shown that flotation therapy can help in some situations.

Relieve stress headaches. At the Medical College of Ohio, Fine and his colleagues have used flotation therapy to successfully treat stress-related conditions such as migraine and muscle tension headaches as well as lower back pain and anxiety disorders.

Lower high blood pressure. One study found that 20 flotation sessions reduced blood pressure as effectively as biofeedback. Moreover, the hormones associated with raised blood pressure, and those associated with stress itself, declined significantly.

Taking the Plunge

In the early 1980s you could have found a flotation tank almost anywhere. These days, however, you may have to do some searching. You can try looking under "stress-management systems" in the Yellow Pages.

Once you've found a flotation tank center, don't just jump in without checking it out first. "Make sure that the place is clean," advises Lee Perry, president of the Flotation Tank Association. As a general rule, the water is completely drained after each float session. "Also, the person who runs the tank should be knowledgeable and sensitive to your wants and needs," he says.

"Ask about the background of the people running the tank," agrees Thomas Fine, associate professor in the Department of Psychiatry at the Medical College of Ohio in Toledo. "Find out how much experience they have and what they know about flotation. Get a feel for whether they are just trying it out or if they really know something."

Improve mood. Another study showed that a flotation session gave vigor a boost while reducing feelings of anger, anxiety, depression, fatigue, and confusion.

Relieve chronic pain. Flotation tanks have proved particularly effective in helping patients control pain associated with autoimmune illnesses such as diabetes, rheumatoid arthritis, and lupus. "If we can help people relax deeply, we often see a dramatic improvement in their symptoms," says Dr. Borrie.

One patient with scleroderma, a disease characterized by swelling, joint pain, and thickening and scarring of the skin, was able to reduce her dose of steroid medication after starting a relaxation program that included flotation. Her skin became more supple, and she could sleep through the night. And after three months of regular sessions, she was able to return to work.

TANK TACTICS

If you want to give flotation therapy a try, here are a few things to keep in mind that can optimize your experience. (For information on selecting a reputable flotation tank center, see "Taking the Plunge" on page 97.)

Expect a few rough spots. Not everyone feels comfortable with total sensory deprivation right away. Some people experience a distressing spinning sensation the first time they find themselves floating in pitch-black silence, Fine says. Many places give you the option of soft music or soft lights.

But even people who tend to be claustrophobic often adapt to the tank surprisingly quickly, Fine adds. Realize that you are never trapped in the tank. You can get up, turn on the light, and easily get out at any time.

If at first you don't succeed, try again. Many people experience deep relaxation the first time they go into the tank, but generally, it takes several sessions before you can appreciate flotation therapy fully. "You need to give it 5 to 10 sessions, with no more than a week between sessions," says Fine.

Deepen the experience. Once you have adjusted to being in the tank, are comfortable with the darkness, and have accepted the idea that you really can float in this high-saline water without effort, you might want to try meditation, autogenics, or breathing exercises. Many people find these practices more powerful without the usual distractions of light and sound.

Take the lesson back to dry land. You'll find that it's easier to reach a state of deep relaxation in your day-to-day living once you've experienced it in the tank. "This is a classical conditioning response called pairing," explains Fine. "Any exercise you do in the tank can trigger the same deep relaxation outside the tank." If you've successfully practiced deep breathing in the tank, for example, try it at home by simulating the tank environment: Lie in bed in a darkened room with a pillow under your head and one under your knees. Then do your breathing exercises.

A final caution: While flotation is a nontoxic stress-reducing method, the extremely deep relaxation could conceivably trigger epileptic seizures in people who are susceptible to them. Check with your doctor. Also, never go in a flotation tank if you've been drinking or if you have taken sleeping pills or tranquilizers.

See also Autogenics, Deep Breathing, Hydrotherapy, Meditation

FRIENDSHIP
VITAL TIES FOR TROUBLED TIMES

Friendship is undeniably one of life's most basic pleasures. A friend can help make bad times bearable and good times even better.

Studies have found that the bond between friends has therapeutic benefits, too. In fact, in a major review of the research, Thomas Campbell, M.D., associate professor of family medicine and psychiatry at the University of Rochester School of Medicine and Dentistry in New York, concluded that the emotional ties associated with friendship have as strong a positive effect on health as cigarette smoking has a negative one.

Friendly contact with fellow humans satisfies a natural, nonnegotiable need, according to Linda Sapadin, Ph.D., director of the Biofeedback and Stress Reduction Center in Valley Stream, New York. "We are by nature social beings," she explains. "We need companionship and intimacy."

BENEFITS OF THE BUDDY SYSTEM

It's nice to have someone to commiserate with after a crummy day at work, to confide in about a personal problem, or just to hang out with when taking in a movie or a ballgame. But friendship does a whole lot more for us, too. For example, studies have shown that it:

Keeps anxiety levels down. The power of friendship to lift people above stressful situations was documented in a study of 56 students who were taking the Medical College Aptitude Test, an event with great implications for their future. The students who had a lot of social contact with friends reported slight increases in anxiety in the days before and after the test, while loners became significantly more anxious.

But it's not just having a support network that provides a stress shield. The physical presence of a friend has immediate stress-lowering benefits. In another study, researchers monitored the heart rates and blood pressure levels of 60 college women as they performed stressful tasks such as making complicated mathematical calculations. Their blood pressure levels rose nearly twice as much when they were working alone as when a good friend was present in the room.

It's safe to conclude that having a friend around can soften the body's reactions to stress, comments researcher Stephen Lepore, Ph.D., associate professor of psychology at Carnegie Mellon University in Pittsburgh.

Increases life span. A 17-year study of nearly 7,000 adults found that women who had few friendships were at "significantly elevated risk" of dying from all kinds of cancer. Friendships, in this study, had more of a protective effect than marriage. And in another study that monitored more than 1,000 patients with coronary heart disease, those who neither were married nor had a close friend in whom they could confide were significantly more likely to die in a given 5-year period than those who had a spouse, a confidant, or both.

Boosts immune function. Researchers have also examined the physical changes caused by stress and the ways that friendship might modify these effects. One study showed that healthy middle-aged adults with lots of friendly relationships had lower cholesterol and better immune function than others. The study's authors concluded that "social support systems may intervene between the stressful event and the physiological response to it."

GLEE AND SYMPATHY

What exactly is it about friendship that protects you against stress? "For one thing, friends provide emotional nurturance," says Dr. Sapadin. "They do things for you—concrete things such as bringing food over when you're sick and helping you through tough times by cheering you on, saying things like, 'You can do it!'" Friends also:

Make the world less threatening. Friendship offers vital reassurance that you are not alone, no matter what challenges life may send your way. "Intimacy, the feeling of closeness that comes from not being judged, is a vital component of friendship," says Dr. Sapadin.

Encourage self-expression. You get to share your worries and air what's on your mind. Not only is this soothing but it offers a practical benefit as well. By talking to others, you frequently discover new angles on your problems and additional information that you wouldn't have been able to come up with yourself. As the saying goes, two heads are better than one.

Provide perspective. When you're totally immersed in the crisis of the moment—a parent has been hospitalized or a child is having problems in school for example—friends can help you see the whole picture. "They can see, when you can't, that 'this too shall pass'—that life is a process and you won't always be stuck where you are," says Dr. Sapadin.

Facilitate fun. If walking outdoors, going shopping, listening to music, or eating out can lift your mood and keep stress at bay, doing it with a friend makes it feel even better. "Friends provide distraction," says Dr. Sapadin. "They get you outside yourself. When you're alone and thinking about your problems, you're basically chasing your tail. It's easy to get your stress-response system going in high gear, making you miserable and ultimately causing a great deal of damage to your body. Friends get you out of that mode."

How to Cultivate Companionship

You can't write yourself a stress-fighting prescription for friendship as you can for, say, exercise or meditation. But there are things to keep in mind as you build this type of relationship with someone.

Join the optimist's club. If support is what you're after, then spend time around supportive people. "It's important to have friends who are positive, nurturing, and optimistic about life," says Dr. Sapadin. "Some people are just the opposite. Whatever the situation, they make it sound worse. And just when you need them most, they isolate themselves from you." With friends like that, you don't need enemies. Gradually shift your allegiances to people who are good medicine.

Tune out the psychic network. Many of us expect our friends to be mind readers. Speak your mind and be specific about what you need. For example, say, "I want to talk about something that's on my mind," "I'd just like you to listen and not tell me what to do," or "I'd love for you to hear about this and offer whatever advice you have."

Lift your veil. The key to intimacy is mutual self-disclosure. That's *mutual*, as in you opening up, too, and telling the other person how you really feel. What makes a close friendship close is talking about things that you wouldn't share with just anyone.

Close your mouth and say "hmmmm." Another key is being able to listen—really listen—when a friend opens up. One of the biggest obstacles to intimacy is jumping in with your analysis and your suggestions too quickly, without waiting to digest the information and finding out if your friend even wants your input.

This brings us to another important point: What most people want when they're blue is empathy, not advice. "It has to come first," says Dr. Sapadin. "When a little kid falls on the playground and his knee is bleeding, the first thing he wants is for you to kiss the boo-boo. Only then is he really receptive to being told that he should walk instead of run." Adults are no different.

Be sensitive to the nuances of conversation, whether the problem at hand is yours or your friend's. When you react to another's problem, "make sure it's an empathetic 'I know what it's like' response," Dr. Sapadin says. If it's clear that you're really listening, all should go well.

The recipe for friendship comes down to a simple variation on the golden rule: Treat your friends as you would a precious commodity, and you'll be a lot richer for it.

See also Communication, Intimacy

G

GARDENING

SOW THE SEEDS OF SERENITY

When real life seems to be spinning out of control, you may sometimes wish that you could escape to another world. Well, you can—and it could be as close as your own backyard.

The garden is a world all its own. One that you create with your own hands. One that's filled with living things that grow and flower at a slow, unhurried pace. One where you can see, smell, and even taste the fruits of your labor.

Since ancient times, the garden has been a place of rest and restoration. "Living vegetation expresses a life force that's all over the planet, and we're part of it," says Charles Lewis, retired research fellow at Morton Arboretum in Lisle, Illinois, and author of *Green Nature-Human Nature*. "Through gardening we experience an intimate relationship with plants over time."

PLANT POWER

A growing body of research supports Lewis's viewpoint, documenting the revitalizing power of gardening and of nature in general. Not surprisingly, this research suggests that we need to be around green things to heal. In fact, it may be programmed into our genes.

The therapeutic benefits of working with plants are the foundation of horticultural therapy, "one of the oldest healing arts," according to Diane Relf, Ph.D., extension specialist for environmental horticulture at Virginia Polytechnic Institute and State University in Blackburg. Gardening has become an increasingly integral part of rehabilitation and psychological treatment in a wide variety of settings. It's now encouraged in hospitals, nursing homes, prisons, and schools for the developmentally challenged.

Tending plants helps people with serious psychiatric illness re-enter the world, doctors say. It also encourages elderly people to remain active. "The basic premise is that working with and around plants brings about positive psychological and physical changes that improve the quality of life for the individual," says Dr. Relf.

Lewis witnessed such changes in abundance during the decades that he helped set up community gardens in poor neighborhoods of New York City. "When people grew gardens, a kind of happiness came into their lives," he says. "It increased their self-esteem. They came to believe that they could make changes in their world."

These kinds of feelings very likely account for much of gardening's power over stress. The ability to take charge of a situation has time and again proved to be a key factor in stress reduction. In a survey conducted by the American Horticultural Society, respondents cited "a sense of control over my environment" as a significant, perhaps predominant, reason why they find gardening so satisfying.

A GREEN THUMBS-UP TO STRESS RELIEF

If you've ever tried your hand at gardening, you know how good it feels to dig into the dirt, to nestle a seedling into a shallow depression and gently pat the earth around it, to watch that seedling flourish and thrive. You can get even more from your gardening experience by keeping these strategies in mind.

Just dig in. If you're new to gardening, you might want to read up on the subject by checking out a book or two from your local library. Then head for a nearby nursery and make your plant picks. In general, "novice gardeners tend to grow vegetables, more experienced gardeners gravitate toward flowers, and the most experienced get involved in rock gardens," says Stephen Kaplan, Ph.D., professor of psychology at the University of Michigan in Ann Arbor. But don't take these as absolutes: Choose whatever tickles your fancy.

Bloom where you're planted. Gardening does not necessarily

ROOM TO GROW

You don't need a big backyard to experience the joys of growing tomatoes or roses. Throughout the country, gardeners sow, sweat, and reap side by side in community gardens. There are an estimated 15,000 such enterprises, ranging from a couple of people dividing up a common area to 11-acre fields with 20- by 20-foot plots for a whole neighborhood, according to Sally McCabe, board member of the American Community Gardening Association. The greatest number of community gardens is in Philadelphia, which has between 1,000 and 1,500 plots shared by local residents. The next biggest center of community gardening is New York City.

When you garden the community way, "you get to know neighbors you might not otherwise meet," says McCabe. In Philadelphia a yearly City Gardens Contest brings together people from all walks of life. "You'll see a hairdresser next to a cop, both helping out a 100-year-old lady," McCabe observes.

And since community gardeners love to share their experience and expertise, they'll give you lots of advice and encouragement if you're a novice.

Is there a community garden in your neighborhood? The American Community Gardening Association will let you know. You can write to the organization at 325 Walnut Street, Philadelphia, PA 19106.

mean tending a 20- by 20-foot plot that's overflowing with tomatoes and zucchini and bordered with nasturtiums. If you're looking for stress relief, you can get it just by growing African violets on your windowsill.

Ask the pros. Every state has branches of the U.S. Department of Agriculture Cooperative Extension Service that can support your back-to-earth efforts with pamphlets, information, and even seeds.

You may even want to sign up for the service's eight-week Master Gardener courses, which teach the ins and outs of gardening in your particular area.

In addition, many communities have botanic gardens and arboretums that offer courses and programs for every level of expertise, from beginner on up. Or you may want to just ask fellow gardeners for their advice: They're usually more than happy to share their tricks of the trade with others.

Accept the pace. Once you've planted your garden, it's time to let nature take its course, so to speak. "In our society, there's too much instant gratification," Lewis says. Gardening forces you to slow down and get back in sync with nature. It's a perfect antidote to the "hurry sickness" that's especially common among folks with hard-driving type A personalities.

"Growing plants isn't like turning on a switch," Lewis notes. "You sow the seeds, then you wait for the plant to come up. Over time, as you nurture the plant, you become more deeply involved in its well-being." You derive pleasure and pride from milestones such as the appearance of leaves, the first buds, and the setting of fruit.

Put your garden's needs first. When you tend garden, you learn to subordinate your desires to the needs of other living things. "When the weather is dry and the tomatoes are drooping, you simply have to water them," says Dr. Kaplan.

Focus on the flora. When you garden, you tend to become completely immersed in your work. Your attention is riveted to your plants—but not in a way that fatigues and depletes. And like all pleasing distractions, gardening takes your mind off everyday worries and concerns that lead to stress.

See also Hobbies, Nature

H

HERBS

STRESS RELIEF THAT'S STEEPED IN TRADITION

Forget powerful prescription pills. These days folks are reaching for a different kind of stress remedy—one that's as mild and soothing as a cup of herbal tea.

Herbal therapy, of course, is nothing new. The use of herbs to heal dates back to primitive times, and many modern-day medicines—aspirin, for one—are actually synthetic versions of these plants. But herbs are gentler to the body and produce fewer side effects than their man-made counterparts.

What's more, while prescription medicines perform highly specific functions within the body, herbal remedies offer multiple therapeutic benefits. Herbalists refer to this as a tonic effect. In other words, since herbs contain a mixture of active ingredients, the body can draw on those that it needs to get back into balance and reduce stress.

For example, an aromatic tea such as peppermint, catnip, or chamomile can be either stimulating or relaxing, depending on the state of the nervous system of the person who drinks it, says Daniel B. Mowrey, Ph.D., director of the American Phytotherapy Research Lab in Braper, Utah. "Herbs not only can calm you down, they can invigorate you, too," he says. "If you want to relax and shut out the world, they allow you to do that. But at the same time, they can sharpen and increase your attention span."

THE PLANT PHARMACY

Patients of Alan Gaby, M.D., a Baltimore physician and former president of the American Holistic Medical Association, routinely receive herbal prescriptions for their stress-related symptoms: valerian root for anxiety and insomnia, peppermint oil for tummy troubles, feverfew for migraines. "While I don't recommend long-term treatment of stress symptoms without analyzing the underlying causes, I still have confidence in these herbs because they've been well-researched," he says.

Which healing herbs should you choose? While there are enough varieties to fill a book, Dr. Mowrey says that just a handful are suited to stress relief. He recommends the following, which you can find in various forms at your local health food store. Follow package directions and heed the cautions at the end of this chapter for safe use.

Valerian. Popular in Europe and elsewhere as a sleeping aid and a balm for jangled nerves, valerian works much like a tranquilizer, but without the toxicity and side effects. In marked contrast to drugs such as Valium, which can leave you drowsy and forgetful and may be dangerous in combination with alcohol, valerian increases your concentration and energy levels.

The active ingredients of valerian appear to work both on the autonomic nervous system (which regulates the body's stress response) and the central nervous system (which is involved in thinking and feeling). Valerian has been shown to increase the brain waves associated with sleep and relaxation.

Passionflower. After valerian, passionflower is the most popular herbal sedative in Great Britain, according to Dr. Mowrey. Its therapeutic roots extend back to the sixteenth century, when Spanish explorers discovered it being used for medicinal purposes among the mountain tribes of Peru and Brazil. Today it's used to relieve anxiety, nervous tension, and high blood pressure, and it's often combined with valerian as a sleeping aid.

Some of passionflower's power comes from its ability to increase the supply of the chemical messenger serotonin in the brain. In this sense, it may parallel the activity of antidepressants such as Prozac and Zoloft.

Saint-John's-wort. The active ingredient in this herb, hypericin, works like the antidepressant drugs Parnate and Nardil: It inhibits enzymes called monoamine oxidases from breaking down natural feel-good brain chemicals. Control monoamine oxidases, and you'll keep your mood positive.

Ginseng. This well-known oriental root helps your body keep functioning normally in the face of stress, so you stay calm, cool, and collected. It works by maintaining the health of the adrenal glands and buffering the body's fight-or-flight response.

Studies have shown that ginseng can also improve circulation (which means greater mental clarity), blood sugar regulation (a boon to people with diabetes and borderline diabetes), and resistance to disease. For decades, it has been administered to Russian athletes to help them withstand the physical rigors of strenuous exertion.

Licorice root extract. No, this isn't the stuff that you find in the candy aisle at the supermarket. In fact, most American-made licorice candy contains no real licorice root extract. This herb appears to mimic the effect of the hormones that keep the body in balance. It can help restore these hormones during times of physical stress.

Note: While whole licorice root will balance body processes, a person with high blood pressure or heart or kidney problems should avoid licorice root extract because of its effects on these systems.

Chamomile. A tea made from this herb can induce relaxation without impairing the performance of tasks that require coordination. It can also quiet an upset stomach, a frequent consequence of stress. It works by relaxing the smooth muscle that lines the digestive system.

USING HERBS SAFELY

Because herbs can have significant effects on the body, it's critical that they be used with care. Those described here are not dangerous if you take them as directed, but they could be toxic if used inappropriately, warns Dr. Mowrey. So before you try any herbal remedy, heed this advice.

Do some research. It's best to consult an herbalist for advice before using a remedy. But if you decide to try any herbal product on your own, read up on it first to see if it poses any risk of toxicity, Dr. Gaby advises.

Always follow package directions. If a little is good, don't assume that more is better. More can give you a stomachache—or worse. Herbs deserve the same place in a healthy, low-stress lifestyle that they have in wholesome, flavorful cooking: Just a pinch of the right stuff can make all the difference.

Don't consider herbs a panacea. It's a mistake to try to cover up stressors that could be controlled or eliminated. "I don't recommend herbs for long-term use," Dr. Gaby says. "I urge people to exercise more, to eat better, to avoid caffeine and alcohol, and to deal with the emotional factors that are increasing their levels of stress."

HOBBIES

PURSUE YOUR PASSION

Chances are you know at least one person who's an avid hobbyist. Perhaps it's a co-worker who spends her lunch hour bird-watching in a nearby park. Or a neighbor who devotes his free time to restoring antique furniture. Or a nephew who trades baseball cards as though he were buying and selling shares on Wall Street.

You may wonder how that person can devote so much time and energy to such a seemingly inconsequential activity. Before you pooh-pooh his pastime, consider this: A hobby can help you escape the daily grind and all of its inherent hassles and heartaches—and delivers healthy doses of joy and satisfaction to boot. In other words, whether your tastes run to painting a landscape or flying an airplane, a hobby is a great way to short-circuit stress.

FOR THE LOVE OF LEISURE

Hobbyists are amateurs in the best sense of the word. "*Amateur* comes from the Latin for 'to love,' " points out Geoffrey Godbey, Ph.D., professor of leisure studies at Pennsylvania State University

THREE STRIKES AGAINST TELEVISION

For many people, leisure means spending time glued to the boob tube. The average American adult watches three hours of television a day, says Seppo Iso-Ahola, Ph.D., professor of social psychology in the College of Health and Human Performance at the University of Maryland, College Park.

Television is far from an ideal leisure pursuit. Here's why.

It's totally passive. Dr. Iso-Ahola points out that when you're watching television, your sense of control—one of the essentials of stress reduction—is limited to switching channels.

It cuts down on human contact. Think about it: How much do you talk to your family members or friends when you watch television together?

It's inactive. The tube may seem especially tempting after a trying day at work, but it's not truly restorative in the way that a brisk walk or an engrossing hour of gardening might be. "The research evidence is clear," says Roger Mannell, Ph.D., professor and chair of recreation and leisure studies at the University of Waterloo in Ontario. "People feel worse, not better, after an episode of television viewing."

None of this is to say that you should never turn on your television. Rather, you should avoid doing so automatically. People who get the most out of television are those who plan when and what to watch.

"What I do is impose restrictions on myself," Dr. Mannell says. "I scan the program guide when I get it and choose a few upcoming shows that I really want to see. Then I set aside that time."

in University Park. These folks do what they do for the sheer pleasure they derive from it.

They may not realize it, but they're getting some serious stress-busting benefits to boot. Here's how hobbies can help derail stress.

Forging stronger social bonds. Serious leisure—Dr. Godbey's term for hobbies—very often provides opportunities for lots of social interaction, which is a stress reliever par excellence. "There's a whole social world that goes with these activities," says Robert Stebbins, Ph.D., professor of sociology at the University of Calgary in Alberta. You have a chance to meet and mingle with other folks who share your interests.

There's a special sense of community in those activities that lead to group accomplishment—staging a play, for example. Each person has something unique to contribute to the production, and everyone from the stars to the stagehands is rewarded by the applause on opening night.

Instilling self-confidence. The sustained attention that you give to a hobby pays off with growing competence: As you hone your woodworking or knitting skills, for example, you derive a sense of mastery that dabblers will never know. "In serious leisure, the fun often comes from the expression of ability," says Dr. Stebbins. "If you're an accomplished figure skater, the joy you get from just whirling around the ice is all the greater because of your skill."

Fostering self-esteem. Your sense of self-worth gets a substantial boost from a leisure pursuit. You'd take great pride in telling others that you're a violinist in the civic symphony, for example. "A lot of people would prefer to identify themselves with their leisure activities instead of their work. They'd rather be known as amateur bicycle racers than office workers," Dr. Stebbins notes.

Keeping you occupied. Plain and simple, hobbyists don't have time to sit around and dwell on how life has done them wrong. This may be especially important for older folks, as demonstrated in a survey of retirees conducted by Roger Mannell, Ph.D., professor and chair of recreation and leisure studies at the University of Waterloo in Ontario. He concluded from his survey that "those who were happiest had become involved in challenging activities that allowed them to develop a sense of competency—and they spent at least 40 percent of their time in these pursuits."

PICKING YOUR PASTIME

Taking up a hobby is a little like embarking on a career. You have to choose something that's of genuine interest to you—something that you find relaxing and rewarding, so you'll stick with it. The following tips may help you decide.

Grow a passing fancy into a passion. If you're already engaged in something with serious leisure potential, consider making it a stronger focus of your free time, says Dr. Stebbins. Why watch television for another hour when you can devote that time to your garden and transform it into a masterpiece?

Remember: The sky's the limit. If you're having trouble deciding which hobby would suit you best, you might start by simply listing all of the activities that you can think of. Ask friends about their pursuits. Read up on other options. Then see if anything interests you and investigate further.

Also, adult education classes can introduce you to a lot of activities. Any one of them might turn into a real love affair.

Get lost in your leisure. One of the most crucial questions to ask is: Does this activity absorb all of your attention? "Sitting around and watching television isn't that absorbing," Dr. Stebbins notes. "On the other hand, a man can become completely immersed in practicing music. Or a woman can arrive home from a theater rehearsal and realize that she hasn't thought about her problems at work all evening."

Develop existing talents. "For serious leisure to be rewarding, you need a certain amount of talent for it," says Dr. Stebbins. "Someone who is all thumbs won't do well at fiddle playing or sewing. If you keep on trying hard at something yet it never goes quite right, it ceases to be leisure."

Welcome a challenge. A hobby isn't a hobby unless it involves some struggle. Becoming an amateur actor requires getting through the stage fright of opening night, for example. "When you get better, there's a huge sense of accomplishment," Dr. Stebbins says.

Find the right level for you. If what you're doing is a group activity, find the group that suits your skills best. "Many activities have stratified groups. There are local church choruses and symphony choruses and a lot in between," says Dr. Stebbins.

Be happy. The most important thing about your hobby is to love what you're doing. Unlike work, you can shape the activity any way you like. And that's what makes it so fulfilling. "Freedom is the quintessential nature of leisure," says Dr. Stebbins. "Having the biggest stamp collection in the state isn't the bottom line. Feeling good about it is."

See also Dancing, Gardening, Reading

HUMOR

A LAUGH A DAY KEEPS STRESS AT BAY

"I don't know what's wrong with me, Doc," the man sighed. "Some days I feel like I'm a circus big top, other days I feel like I'm a tepee."

"That's your problem," the doctor replied. "You're two tents."

Okay, so it's a bad joke. But if you're too tense, even a groaner like this one can change your attitude and outlook faster than you can say "Three Stooges."

How does humor deflate stress? With its amazing ability to transform how you look at the world around you. "Stress isn't an actual event," explains Joel Goodman, Ed.D., director of the Humor Project in Saratoga Springs, New York. "It's your perception of an event. How you see and react to reality determines whether or not stress will take its toll.

"Humor is also the ability to take yourself lightly," continues Dr. Goodman. "You have to take your work in life seriously, but taking yourself seriously is self-destructive. Humor bridges the gap between the perfection you may be seeking and the imperfection we all live with."

"Humor enables us to face stressful events squarely, without needing to evade or distort them," adds Christian Hageseth III, M.D., a psychiatrist in Fort Collins, Colorado, who writes and lectures on humor. He believes that humor is one of the healthiest ways of responding to the stress in our lives.

YUK-Y MEDICINE

Indeed, humor does a whole lot more than simply help us look on the brighter side of a difficult situation. Studies have shown that it produces positive changes within the body that offset the effects of stress. Here are some examples of what humor can do.

Enhance immunity. The act of laughing actually inhibits the body's production of stress-related hormones such as cortisol while beefing up the supply of disease-fighting white blood cells. The subjects of one study also experienced a signficant increase in interferon, a key chemical in the body's immune response, after watching an hour-long funny video—and the higher level was still present the next day.

Improve blood pressure and heart rate. When you laugh, both your blood pressure and your heart rate rise briefly, then fall below their original levels. The same thing happens when you exercise.

Reduce tension. Of course, not every stressful event lends itself to chortles and guffaws. Still, you may find it easier to get through especially painful or difficult times by seeing things from a more lighthearted point of view.

In one study researchers showed a violent video, then asked audience members to describe it two ways—seriously and humorously. Heart rate and other measures of stress rose when the people described the video seriously but dropped when they described it humorously.

FLEXING YOUR FUNNY BONE

Honing your ability to laugh in the face of stress doesn't mean you have to be another Rodney Dangerfield, able to come up with a side-splitting one-liner every time life throws you a curveball. "I've asked more than 750,000 people, in workshops and lectures that I've given, if they think they can tell jokes well," says Dr. Goodman. "Consistently, only about 1 percent say that they can. But 85 to 90 percent perceive that they have a good sense of humor."

Even if you're convinced that your skeleton didn't come equipped with a funny bone, you can learn to lighten up when the going gets rough. Here are some suggestions.

See no misery, feel no misery. One common trait among folks who can laugh at life's foibles is their ability to reframe stressful situations in a humorous way. A good way to begin, says Dr. Goodman, is to look to your favorite "humor mentors."

Say you've been in a fender bender. Simply ask yourself, "How would Groucho Marx respond?" Or maybe your boss is giving you a hard time. Stop and think, "What would Seinfeld have to say about this?"

Kid like a kid. The television show *Art Linkletter's House Party*, which aired in the 1950s and 1960s, featured a segment in which the host interviewed schoolchildren on a variety of topics. While the youngsters' words gave the mostly adult audience some real belly laughs, they also revealed how the grown-up world looks through a child's eyes.

Kids see things differently than adults, and that's what makes them natural role models for humor. "We need to recapture the fresh, spontaneous perspective of a child," says Dr. Goodman.

When you're sinking, grab a line. Find sayings that you can trot out for yourself in times of need. One of Dr. Goodman's favorites is from the poet Robert Frost: "The brain is a wonderful organ. It starts the moment you get up in the morning and doesn't stop until you get to work." Keep your laugh lines handy on self-stick notes or taped to your bathroom mirror.

Prop up your humor. Use visual props to give yourself a chuckle. A clown nose may lack sophistication, but it can transform stress into silliness. Or keep a bubble pipe in your glove compartment to pull out when you're stuck in traffic. "Blow some bubbles out the window. You'll get smiles instead of horn blasts," Dr. Goodman says.

Fight for your right to chuckle. Dr. Goodman favors a form of stress combat that he calls aikido humor. In the martial art aikido, instead of struggling against your opponent's strength, you turn it around to work for you. "Aikido humor is like a magic trick that reframes negative situations as positive ones," Dr. Goodman says.

A striking example: Visiting Minnesota on a lecture tour, Dr. Goodman saw the terrible devastation left behind by tornadoes that had battered the area the day before. "It was the worst destruction I had ever seen," he says. "Houses were demolished, cars destroyed." One car was literally crushed flat by a huge tree trunk. But standing next to it, the owner was waving at passersby, holding a hand-lettered sign that read "Compact Car."

"That man found a way to manufacture humor out of a terrible situation," Dr. Goodman says. "Mother Nature had thrown a punch, but he rolled with it, danced with it, turned it to his advantage. He was able to help others lighten their loads."

A LIFT THAT LASTS

Like any other kind of learned behavior, laughter gets stronger with practice, as do the upbeat feelings that go with it. "People have to loosen up to allow humor to express itself," says Dr. Hageseth. "A lot of folks have trouble with that. They feel that to laugh freely is immature. But if you practice that response, your brain will learn to interpret reality more lightly, and you'll feel the world is a brighter place."

The laughter response escalates in stages, Dr. Hageseth says. It starts with the stiff smile, then advances to twinkling eyes, giggling, and ultimately the out-and-out belly laugh. "So when you feel like laughing, take it to the next step," he suggests. Instead of smiling a little, smile a lot. Instead of chuckling sedately, let your laughter flow. "I advise patients to practice with a video that most people agree is funny," Dr. Hageseth adds. "Watch it, preferably with another person, and amplify your reaction to it."

In the final analysis, humor works as a kind of emotional insulation. If you can laugh at yourself, stress can't touch you, says Dr. Goodman. Considering that fact, it pays to start looking for things to laugh at right now.

"Have you ever been in the midst of a crisis and thinking, 'Twenty years from now, we'll laugh about this'?" Dr. Goodman asks. "My question is, why wait?"

See also Smiling

HYDROTHERAPY
WASH AWAY YOUR WORRIES

Now you know why they call it the daily grind: It sure has made mincemeat out of you. You're tense, you're tired, you're tied in knots. And you just can't wait to get home to relax and unwind.

What better way to give stress the slip than with a soothing soak in a warm bath? If it seems like an indulgence, consider this: Water—that pure, natural substance so essential to human life—has proven medicinal benefits, too.

In fact, water therapy—also known as hydrotherapy—has been around for centuries. The ancient Greeks took therapeutic baths, as did the Babylonians and Egyptians before them. And both the Chinese and Native Americans make the most of water in their traditional medical systems.

Good ol' H_2O does seem to have special powers against the world's enervating forces. "The use of water is rivaled only by physical exercise as a reliever of the intolerable, physically unpleasant symptoms of stress," says Richard Hansen, M.D., medical director of the Poland Spring Health Institute in Maine.

THE WONDERS OF WATER

At Poland Spring, guests can bathe in natural spring water. For stress relief, though, any water will do—even the stuff that flows out of your tap at home.

How does water work its medicinal magic? "It primarily affects the skin and muscles," explains Dr. Hansen. "And it calms the lungs, heart, stomach, and endocrine system by stimulating nerve reflexes in the spinal cord."

When you submerge yourself in a bath, a pool, or a whirlpool, you experience a kind of weightlessness. To your skin and muscles, this buoyancy is a welcome release from the constant pull of gravity. "It's extremely relaxing," Dr. Hansen says. "It's like having hun-

SCINTILLATING SOAKING

You don't have to go to a pricey spa to enjoy hydrotherapy. Here's how to make your own bath extra-special.

- Create a soothing environment: no slamming doors, barking dogs, or screeching car alarms. Turn off overhead lights if they're too bright and arrange subdued, indirect lighting.
- Showering? Adjust the shower head to deliver a fine spray. "It should simulate a gentle rain," says Richard Hansen, M.D., medical director of the Poland Spring Health Institute in Maine. The round, flat shower heads are ideal for this purpose.
- Add oil or aromatic plant extracts. Mint essence, pine essence, and lavender are all particularly good choices for increasing your bath's stress-quelling potential. But don't put bubble bath in the water: Soaking in soap dries out your skin and makes you itchy.

dreds of hands supporting you. And it's one reason that baths have never been completely replaced by showers, even in this country."

Flotation tanks take the buoyancy principle one step further. Salt is dissolved in the tank's water to create extra buoyancy. The prolonged weightlessness, in combination with the complete absence of light and sound, is said to quell many of the body's physical stress symptoms.

Water also has a hydrostatic effect, which refers to the massage-like feeling that water produces as it gently kneads your body. Water in motion stimulates touch receptors on the skin, boosting blood circulation and releasing tight muscles.

In fact, the more that water is in motion, the greater its stress-relieving benefits. In a study of 40 healthy men and women at the University of Minnesota Hospital and Medical School in Minneapolis, 85 percent of the participants preferred a whirlpool bath to a still bath. Although 10 minutes of either kind of immersion produced similar reductions in anxiety, only the whirlpool lowered the participants' re-activity to stress—that is, their susceptibility to anxiety-producing events. "For some people," the researchers concluded, "prudent use of whirlpools may serve as a healthy alternative to activities like the use of alcohol or drugs as a means of reducing tension."

THE BASICS OF BATHING

You might not think that modern science would have much to say about the pure and simple pleasure of soaking in a tub. But there's a surprising wealth of information to immerse yourself in. These tips should help fine-tune your bath experience.

Select a sedating temperature. For overall tension reduction, Dr. Hansen recommends a neutral bath, where the water is close to skin temperature (92° to 94°F). "In hydrotherapy texts, this is called a seda-tive bath," he observes. If your sensation is normal, you don't need a thermometer to check the temperature: The water is just right when you don't feel it at all—it seems neither warm nor cool to the touch.

To relieve soreness, turn up the heat. A hot bath (or shower) is more effective for loosening tight, tense muscles and reducing the pain of stress-linked conditions such as backache. As a bonus, it steps up your body's production of white blood cells, which fight infection and improve your resistance to disease.

How hot is hot? Not very, advises Dr. Hansen: 102° to 106°F is best. Because your body is unable to discharge heat in a bath, no matter how much you sweat, water much hotter than that can raise your core temperature in a matter of minutes, inducing an artificial fever. As a guide to the correct temperature, "don't make the water so hot that it's hard for you to step into the bath," Dr. Hansen says.

Chill out. Don't just step out of the tub and dry off when you're done. Dr. Hansen suggests following up with a brief cold shower. "In Finland and Germany, folks roll in the snow after a sauna," he says. "We've had patients who do that, too. It brings an immediate rush of blood through your system, as well as a rush of energy. You feel like you just won the lottery."

120

If you're showering, alternate between 3 minutes of hot water and 30 seconds of cold water for an invigorating contrast, recommends Dr. Hansen. "It leaves you feeling refreshed, awake, and energetic," he says. "It's better than a morning cup of coffee."

Keep it short. A good time frame for a hot or neutral bath is 15 to 20 minutes. But if you have high blood pressure or cardiovascular problems, don't stay in long enough to raise your body temperature.

Do it late. Evening is a great time to enjoy the calming effect of a warm bath. An English study found that people who soaked shortly before going to bed slept more readily and deeply. Be sure to dry yourself gently, not briskly, to avoid overstimulating yourself.

See also Flotation Tanks

I

IMAGERY
A VISION OF INNER PEACE

Think back to the last time you felt completely, blissfully re-laxed. Maybe you spent the day lounging on a secluded beach or walking along a wooded trail. Maybe you treated yourself to a weekend getaway with your spouse or returned to your childhood home for a holiday celebration. Whatever the occasion, just reflect-ing on it fills you with a sense of calm and contentment.

Wouldn't it be wonderful if you could return to that place when-ever life's hassles and heartaches become a little too much to bear? You can, with the help of a relaxation technique known as imagery.

As you might guess from its name, imagery simply means that you re-create an experience by conjuring the scene in your mind. But it's not just visuals: You can actually smell the ocean saltwater, hear the wind rustling through the pines, taste your mom's home cookin'.

Using brain wave monitors, researchers have determined that the parts of the brain that become active during a real event also turn on when the event is merely imagined. Messages from the brain then move downward to stimulate emotions and arouse ap-propriate responses throughout the body.

It's the pictures in our minds that can stoke the fires of stress—or lull our bodies into healing calm. "Imagery, in one form or an-other, initiates everything we do," says Patricia Norris, Ph.D., clinical director at the Life Sciences Institute of Mind-Body Health in Topeka, Kansas.

THE PICTURE OF HEALTH

While not everyone agrees on the effectiveness of imagery, some of its practitioners believe that it can just about work miracles. They suggest, for example, that visualizing your immune system successfully fighting off cancer cells can help win the battle against a deadly malignancy.

Imagery can also help minimize the daily wear and tear of stress. "I teach my patients to use images that will quiet the stress response, wherever in the body it's taking place, and help them work with the source of turmoil," Dr. Norris says.

One of Dr. Norris's patients suffered from the severe stomach cramps and diarrhea that characterize irritable bowel syndrome. It appeared that her digestive troubles were directly related to conflicts with her husband.

As part of her therapy, the woman was asked to take an imaginary trip inside her own intestines and to describe what she saw. "There were wrenching, accordion-like spasms," Dr. Norris recalls. And the spasms kicked in whenever the woman had trouble with her spouse. Eventually, she learned to smooth out the contractions and maintain that relaxed state while visualizing a confrontation with her husband.

Similar exercises can ease stress even when it runs very deep, Dr. Norris says. People have used imagery to cope with the death of a loved one and to treat post-traumatic stress disorder, which is characterized by profoundly disturbing flashbacks to a devastating life event such as a violent crime, combat experience, or a natural disaster.

CLOSE YOUR EYES AND SAY AHHH

Researchers have documented the healing effects of imagery for stress-related conditions as diverse as sexual dysfunction, asthma, and insomnia.

It can reduce tension, relax muscles, open up circulation, and undo much of the physical damage of stress.

Imagery works remarkably well in quelling the devastating anxiety that can accompany stage fright. Most of us get a little uncomfortable at the prospect of having to speak before others. But when stage fright is severe, it can derail career advancement and personal success.

In a study at Washington State University in Pullman, 109 of 669 students taking a public speaking class scored very high on a test that measured anxiety about communication. Half of the high-anxiety students then learned a visualization exercise that helped them maintain a relaxed state of mind and body as they prepared and delivered speeches.

In the exercise, the students envisioned themselves going through the whole day prior to the speech. They saw themselves getting up in the morning full of energy and optimism and, later on, arriving for class feeling clear-headed and confident. They visualized themselves moving eagerly to the front of the classroom to give their speeches. And they imagined the actual presentation, feeling their own sense of confidence and mastery and seeing the approving audience—people nodding their heads and smiling. When it was all over, they felt themselves filled with energy, purpose, and a general sense of well-being.

Six weeks later the students were tested again. Those who practiced the visualization exercise had significantly less anxiety than those who practiced either a standard relaxation technique or nothing at all.

Another study, conducted at Schneider Children's Hospital in New Hyde Park, New York, used imagery to bring about substantial relief for youngsters with fibromyalgia, a chronic disease of aching muscles, disrupted sleep, and emotional suffering. Seven female patients between the ages of 8 and 18 were taught to relax their muscles and to see themselves in a scene from the past, at a time when they were free of pain.

The patients then chose an image for their pain and practiced changing the image in a way that would ease their pain. One girl who described the pain in her leg as pressing, for example, was coached to envision a vise mercilessly gripping her leg, then to feel the vise gradually loosen. Another imagined the pain as a bright color, then watched the color slowly fade.

Of the five girls who finished the treatment and were contacted 4 to 24 months later, four reported having no pain at all. One had occasional mild pain that was easily controlled.

See Where You Want to Be

Imagery is quite easy to learn. In fact, you've probably conjured images on occasion without really being aware that you were practicing a relaxation technique. These tips from Dr. Norris will turn you into an imagery pro and have you reaping its stress-busting benefits in no time.

Breathe in relief. Imagery begins with your nose. Take several slow, deep, even breaths. Each time you exhale, silently say the word *relax* to yourself and breathe out as completely as possible without straining.

Concentrate on comfort. "Think of a favorite place where you feel very, very comfortable," Dr. Norris suggests. "If you have several such places, you can combine them." For example, you might focus on a room that makes you feel safe and reassured, with a window that looks out to a beautiful landscape.

Set the stage. Envision the scene clearly and vividly, adding in as much detail as you can. If you're visualizing the woods, for instance, hear birds singing and the wind softly rustling through the trees. Smell the scent of pine. Feel the cool air on your face.

Box up bad vibes. If you find it hard to leave your day-to-day concerns and responsibilities behind, imagine a big box with a strong lock sitting right in the middle of your mental refuge. Deposit your worries in it one by one, no matter what's on your mind: what to make for dinner, an upcoming dental appointment, a forgotten birthday. Make a deal with yourself to forget about those things while you're "visiting" your favorite place, then take them out again when you leave.

Imagine anytime. You can practice imagery for 15 minutes or so to start or end your day, or you can use it for on-the-spot escapes whenever you feel the need. "Once you've created the place in your mind, you can visualize it whenever you're feeling tense," Dr. Norris says. "In the middle of a big meeting, for instance, you can go there for a moment and then bring the good feelings back with you."

See also Daydreaming

INTIMACY
YOUR STRESS-DEFYING SAFETY NET

"We all need somebody to lean on," as the song goes. And at no time is that more true than when stress complicates our lives.

Those closest to us—those who know us best—share a unique ability to mellow our moods, reinforce our resolve, and help us keep things in perspective. In fact, studies have shown that people with strong social networks are more likely to live longer and stay healthier than those who are socially isolated.

But these studies also indicate that when it comes to good health, intimacy is more of a deciding factor than the number of social contacts. "What's really important is quality, not quantity," says Thomas Campbell, M.D., associate professor of family medicine and psychiatry at the University of Rochester School of Medicine and Dentistry in New York.

CLOSING IN ON CALM

"Intimacy is a feeling of closeness, a feeling that you're not alone in the world," says Linda Sapadin, Ph.D., director of the Biofeedback and Stress Reduction Center in Valley Stream, New York. In a truly intimate relationship, both people can open up to and confide in each other without fear of being judged.

What fosters intimacy is sharing those parts of yourself that you normally keep private from the rest of the world. "Intimacy in friendship grows out of mutual self-disclosure," Dr. Sapadin observes.

Keeping secrets, on the other hand, can create unnecessary physical and mental stress, according to Dale Larson, Ph.D., associate professor of counseling psychology at Santa Clara University in California. "When we keep parts of ourselves hidden from everyone, it's a stressful, demanding process," Dr. Larson notes. "We have to work at it constantly." And when you're trying so hard to

126

conceal your thoughts, feelings, or impulses, your health may suffer, he observes.

SHARING AND CARING

So how can we develop the type of intimacy that combats stress? Here are some of Dr. Larson's suggestions.

Fess up. You're more likely to get support if people know what you're going through. "When other people don't know what you're experiencing, you feel alone," says Dr. Larson. Not sharing your doubts and uncertainties fosters the highly stressful fallacy that your problem, guilt, or flaw is unique.

Reveal yourself—warts and all. We all enjoy the occasional pat on the back. But if you believe that you've received it under false pretenses because you haven't been completely open about your thoughts and feelings, that can actually create stress.

The solution is to be more open about what's going on in your head and heart. If you share the good, the bad, and the ugly and still get kudos, you can feel confident that they're genuine.

Dig deeper to stop the symptoms. Quite simply, keeping secrets can have profoundly negative effects on your health. Dr. Larson surveyed 300 adults about the extent to which they revealed themselves to—and concealed themselves from—others. He found that those who bottled things up the most were much more likely to suffer stress-related symptoms such as headaches, fatigue, depression, and anxiety.

Twenty percent of the people questioned had some deep, dark secret that they had never shared with anyone. The secrets ran the gamut from affairs or drug use to "I'm not in love with my wife anymore" or "I feel that life has no meaning." These folks had the most stress symptoms of all.

Don't give up. When you open up for the first time about something you've been concealing, you may end up wondering whether you've done the right thing. Indeed, about half of the participants in Dr. Larson's survey reported that they initially had mixed feelings when they revealed their secrets. Some worried that what they said would become public knowledge. Others wondered whether the self-exposure would damage the relationship between themselves and the other person.

But by a wide margin, the participants said that sharing their secrets ultimately had positive effects on their bond with the person they told. "Ninety percent said it strengthened and deepened their relationship with the confidant," Dr. Larson says.

Choose someone. "Don't tell your secrets to everyone," advises Dr. Larson. "But you should have one person to whom you can really reveal yourself." Your confidant could be a best friend, a family member, a clergyperson, a counselor, or a therapist. The important thing, says Dr. Larson, is having the opportunity to let someone know you intimately, accept you, and love you for the person you really are.

See also Communication, Counseling, Family, Friendship

L

LIGHT AND SOUND MACHINES
STIMULATE YOUR SENSES

You don a set of goggles and earphones. Lights flash and sounds pulsate in a precisely timed way. And before you know it, you feel relaxed . . . deeply, utterly relaxed.

This may seem like the ultimate in cutting-edge, twenty-first–century technology. But the fact is, the ideas behind these devices—known as light and sound machines, or brain wave machines—have been around a very long time.

"That a flickering light can cause mysterious alterations in consciousness is something humans must have known since the discovery of fire," says Michael Hutchison, publisher of *MegaBrain Report: A Journal of Mind Technology*. And the ancient Greeks noted that sunlight filtered through a spinning wheel could induce euphoria.

As for sound, pounding percussion has always been central to trance-inducing religious rituals. And in the early 1960s, Hutchison says, researchers observed that drumming could alter brain wave activity.

If light and sound can influence your frame of mind by themselves, just imagine what a powerful antistress tool they make when combined.

CATCH A WAVE

To understand how light and sound machines work, you first need to know a little bit about brain waves. What we call waves are

129

actually tiny bursts of electrical energy produced by brain cells. Fast waves are called beta, slow waves are called alpha, and very slow waves are called theta.

Everyone has a little bit of all three types of brain wave activity going at any given time, according to George Fritz, Ph.D., a psychologist in private practice in Bethlehem, Pennsylvania. But if you want to feel relaxed, you need to boost the proportion of alpha waves. "Increase alpha, and you get a calmer state of mind," says Dr. Fritz.

In fact, an increase in alpha waves is one of the physical changes characteristic of the so-called relaxation response, which is a kinder, gentler way for your body to react to stress. The relaxation response can also be induced by techniques such as meditation, progressive muscle relaxation, and yoga.

But just how do light and sound machines affect your brain waves? The key is what scientists call entrainment. When the brain is stimulated at a steady, rhythmic pace, it tends to adapt that pace. So if you see light flashing at 10 beats per second and hear sound throbbing at 10 beats per second—which, incidentally, is the frequency of alpha waves—"the brain itself will follow those signals," says Dr. Fritz.

IT'S ALL IN YOUR HEAD

A number of pilot studies are pointing at the effectiveness of light and sound machines, says psychologist Julian Isaacs, Ph.D., professor in the Graduate School of Holistic Studies at John F. Kennedy University in Orinda, California and president of Marin Biofeedback Associates in San Rafael, California. Thus far, these devices have been used successfully to reduce tension, relieve depression, and treat other stress-related ailments. And according to the latest research, they may also:

Slow heart rate. Officers of the Metro-Dade Police Department in Miami received 10 sessions of light and sound therapy along with nutritional counseling and massage. At the end of the sessions, their resting heart rates were lower than the heart rates of other police officers who did not take part in the program.

Alleviate anxiety. College students who received six sessions of light and sound therapy showed significant reductions in anxiety and were better able to cope with stressful events, compared with a group of students who did not receive the therapy.

Relieve chronic pain. A study of men suffering from severe chronic pain found that light and sound machines reduced their pain levels, minimized their need for medication, improved their sleep, and enhanced their ability to handle stress over a period of 9 to 17 months. "The patients reported that learning how to use light and sound gave them greater control over their lives," Dr. Isaacs says.

A HIGH-TECH TUNE-UP

If light and sound therapy seems intriguing to you, the following tips will help you make the most of the experience.

Get equipped. Light and sound machines come in all sizes and in all levels of complexity. Acceptable ones usually range in price from $60 to $600. A basic device that has a few preset programs is adequate, says Dr. Isaacs. (One source is Tools for Exploration. You can call 1-888-748-6657 to request a catalog.)

Be like clockwork. "You need to practice light and sound therapy consistently to keep the benefits of the relaxation response going," says Dr. Isaacs. Daily 30-minute sessions are typical.

Enhance the effects. Dr. Fritz advises practicing meditation or some other relaxation technique while using a light and sound device. "You have to be doing something with your mind anyway," he says. "Most people will feel more deeply into the experience by meditating at the same time."

Expect some bumps. The road to deep relaxation via light and sound therapy doesn't always run smoothly. "The release of built-up tension in the body and mind may produce some shooting pains or some feelings of anxiety," notes Dr. Fritz. His point: Along the way to achieving the effects you want—peaceful, calm, at-ease feelings—you could experience some temporary unpleasantness.

Get the sensation. Your first experience with a light and sound machine will most likely be very relaxing—but you'll realize even more valuable benefits over time. Ultimately, you should learn to achieve a relaxed state voluntarily, without the machine's assistance, says Dr. Fritz. "The machine is like a tour guide; it shows you how to get there, so you can find your way back on your own."

Heed the warnings. Light and sound machines are not for every-one. You should not use one if you have a history of epilepsy or if there's a history of seizure disorders in your family, Dr. Isaacs cautions. The reason is that because these devices directly affect brain function, they can trigger seizures in people who are vulnerable to them.

Likewise, people who have severe liver disease or who are un-dergoing drug or alcohol detoxification are vulnerable to seizures and should avoid using light and sound machines. These devices are also not suitable for people with severe psychiatric disease or for pregnant women, Dr. Isaacs adds.

See also Relaxation Response

MASSAGE

GET RUBBED THE RIGHT WAY

Sometimes stress socks you right between the eyes, crowning you with a throbbing tension headache. Other times it seizes you by the neck and squeezes mercilessly, tying your muscles in knots.

When it does, you instinctively reach for the tender spot and gently knead it with the tips of your fingers. The pain begins to dissipate in minutes.

Just goes to show what a little massage can do for you.

Massage works wonders in alleviating the physical and mental strain that usually accompany stress. It makes the most of the proven power of human touch to calm, to soothe, and to heal. And it just plain feels good. Maybe that's why massage ranks as the third most popular form of alternative therapy in this country according to a study at Beth Israel Hospital and Harvard Medical School in Boston. (Relaxation techniques and chiropractic hold the top two spots.)

HANDS-ON RELIEF

Scientists believe that the stroking, rubbing, and pressing motions used in massage trigger a natural relaxation response in the human body. "Massage has been shown to increase the activity of the vagus nerve, which slows down the whole nervous system," says Tiffany Field, Ph.D., professor of pediatrics, psychology, and psychiatry and founder and director of the Touch Research Institute, both at the University of Miami School of Medicine.

133

Other studies suggest that massage defuses stress by:

Increasing circulation. Often we carry tension and anxiety in our neck and shoulder muscles. Massage alleviates this tightness and tenderness by moving oxygen- and nutrient-rich blood into the muscle tissues. It also hastens the removal of lactic acid, a pain-producing by-product of muscular exertion, says Robert Edwards, president of the Somerset School of Massage in New Jersey.

Enhancing mental skills. In a study at the Touch Research Institute, people completed math problems twice as quickly—and made half as many mistakes—after receiving a massage. Tests showed that the rubdowns increased both beta and theta brain waves, which are associated with alertness, while lowering anxiety.

Cutting down on stress hormones. For reasons not yet clear to scientists, massage produces a significant reduction in the amount of cortisol and other stress hormones floating around the bloodstream. It also increases levels of serotonin, a brain chemical that brings about relaxation and feelings of well-being.

Easing breathing. People with chronic sinus problems suffer even more when they're under stress, says Edwards. "Tense facial muscles can prevent the cavities in the skull from venting properly," he explains. "Fluids build up and create pressure on the nervous system, eventually leading to sinusitis, headaches, and jaw problems." Massaging the facial muscles releases tension and allows the sinuses to drain freely, he says.

SOOTHING STROKES

Self-massage is perfect for on-the-spot stress relief—when you're marooned in a traffic jam, for example, or waiting in a long line. But for all-over relaxation, you might want to enlist the help of a partner. In fact, massage is a great way to reconnect with your spouse after a trying day. "First and foremost, massage is communication between two people," says Emily Weinstein, an occupational therapist and massage therapist in Brooklyn, New York. "You're sharing a mutual space of calm and connectedness."

What's more, exchanging massages with a partner appears to

benefit both the giver and the receiver, according to Dr. Field. In a study that she conducted, volunteers who gave massages to infants reported feeling less anxious themselves. They also experienced fewer depressive symptoms and improved mood. In fact, they benefited more from giving a massage than from receiving one.

These findings are backed up by anecdotal reports, Dr. Field adds. "Massage therapists, for example, say that they themselves are in good health because they're always doing hands-on work."

You don't have to be a professional massage therapist to give a massage. The one thing you do need is confidence. "What communicates best through the hands is caring confidence," Weinstein says. "If you're tentative, massage is not relaxing."

These pointers should help ensure a good massage experience for both you and your partner.

Get in position. If you're giving the massage, have your partner lie on the floor or on a bed on his stomach. Then kneel at the person's side.

Engage in effleurage. Begin by using the long, smooth strokes known in Swedish massage as effleurage. (See "Relaxation That's Oh-So-Swede" on page 136 for descriptions of the hand movements used in Swedish massage.) "Use your whole hand and palm to stroke upward along the person's back, leaning into the body," says Weinstein. "Use just your fingertips when you move your hands downward, so you apply less pressure."

Rub in rings. Using just your thumbs, make small circles right alongside the spine. Be careful not to press on the spine itself.

Treat the feet. "The feet have a lot of nerve endings. Just squeezing them feels terrific," Weinstein says. Using your knuckles and thumbs, apply pressure to various points all over the sole of each foot. Then very gently—no yanking—stretch each toe.

Play taps. Finish up with light taps along the spine, which improve circulation and stimulate nerve receptors. "Be sure to keep your wrists loose," Weinstein says. Have your partner inhale deeply. Then as he exhales, press a little more on any tense areas.

RELAXATION THAT'S OH-SO-SWEDE

Swedish massage—probably the most familiar and most widely practiced of all massage styles—uses five basic hand strokes, explains Robert Edwards, president of the Somerset School of Massage in New Jersey. You may hear your massage therapist using the following terms.

Effleurage. The long, gliding hand motions of this stroke relieve tension and increase blood flow to the muscles.

Petrissage. This involves lightly grabbing and lifting the muscle away from the bone, then rolling and squeezing it. Practitioners say that petrissage helps clear away lactic acid, a by-product created by the muscles when they work extra hard.

Friction. For this stroke, the therapist uses his thumbs and fingertips to make deep circles near the spine and joints. Like effleurage, friction increases circulation, but in a more localized way.

Tapotement. You might recognize this stroke for its light blows that resemble karate chops. It is said to stimulate the muscles, though it's rarely used in a relaxation massage.

Vibration. The therapist presses his fingers or flattened hands on a muscle, then rapidly shakes it for a few seconds. It's believed that this stroke helps stimulate the nervous system.

Pay attention. For a truly relaxing and pleasurable massage, keep communication lines open. "Ask your partner what feels good—how much pressure to apply, how fast or slow to move your hands—and make sure he tells you if anything is uncomfortable," Weinstein stresses.

Don't even go there. Be careful where you move your hands. "It's not a good idea to put a lot of pressure along the backbone—

there are all kinds of nerves there," Dr. Field says. "I'd also stay away from varicose veins." Massaging these could dislodge a blood clot.

GOING PRO

If you prefer, you could enlist the services of a professional massage therapist. Since the majority of states don't require therapists to be licensed, you'll need to do some checking around to find someone reputable. A good place to start is the American Massage Therapy Association, which will provide you with a list of qualified therapists in your area. You can write the organization at 820 Davis Street, Suite 100, Evanston, Illinois 60201-4444.

When selecting a therapist, you'll want to consider the massage style that he practices. Not all styles are the same, and one might make you feel better—or worse—than another. Here's a sampling of what's available.

Swedish massage. Mention massage, and this is the style that usually comes to mind. Typically, you disrobe and lie on a hard table with a sheet covering the genitals and, for women, the breasts—the parts of your body that a massage therapist should never touch. The therapist will tell you to focus on your breathing and on the part of your body that is being worked. A full-body Swedish massage lasts about an hour. Relax and enjoy it.

Oriental massage. This style is becoming more popular in the United States. Oriental massage emphasizes the application of pressure either all over the body or at specific points. It follows a different healing tradition than Swedish massage: Its objective is to balance the body's flow of energy.

Rolfing. This actually consists of a series of very deep massages that aim to break up unhealthy patterns of muscular tension that develop as a result of emotional trauma, Edwards says. These patterns may persist long enough to distort the body's natural alignment. Rolfing has a reputation for being painful, but new techniques for working the body have made it much more tolerable.

See also Touch

MEDICATION
AN RX FOR THE HIGHLY STRESSED

When stress gets the best of us, we can usually shake it off fairly easily. A long walk, a warm bath, some soothing music, and everything is all better.

But once in a while life batters us relentlessly or knocks us to our knees with one devastating blow. We can't seem to do anything to overcome the onslaught and ease the resulting tension, anxiety, and pain.

It's times like these when your doctor may suggest medication for relief. Not everyone feels comfortable with the prospect of taking drugs for this purpose. Certainly, you should carefully consider your options in consultation with your doctor before deciding if this is the route you should go.

Those who treat stress tend to view medication as a last resort and agree that it should never be handed out indiscriminately. But most acknowledge that drugs can be of value when symptoms such as nervousness or sleeplessness are riding roughshod over our lives.

"If stress reaches a point where a person is not able to carry out his role as a parent or an employee—especially if the symptoms are very physical, such as disturbed eating and sleeping patterns and agitation—then some help is in order," says Jerilyn Ross, director of the Ross Center for Anxiety and Related Disorders in Washington, D.C.

DIFFERENT PILLS FOR DIFFERENT ILLS

Medication treats the symptoms of stress, not stress itself. And while powerful barbiturates were once routinely prescribed for almost any kind of mental or emotional distress, doctors today usually opt for the weakest medicine that's still effective.

For stress-related insomnia, for example, doctors often recommend a drug from the benzodiazepine family. Benzodiazepines

THE DEPRESSION CONNECTION

Clinically speaking, stress and depression are two very different conditions that require two very different courses of treatment. "I'd ordinarily be reluctant to prescribe antidepressants for stress," says Eliot Gelwan, M.D., a psychiatrist and associate medical director of Community Counseling of Bristol County in Taunton, Massachusetts.

But there are times when one condition precipitates the other. For example, a major stressor such as bereavement or unemployment can trigger the symptoms of depression: loss of appetite, poor sleep, sadness or numbness, fatigue, loss of self-confidence or sex drive, or the inability to derive pleasure from life. Or a stressor can bring underlying depression to the surface.

"Many people just clock along for decades with depression," Dr. Gelwan says. "They're not even aware that they're depressed until they lose their jobs or have relationship difficulties"—the proverbial straw that breaks the camel's back.

Among antidepressants, newer drugs such as Prozac, Zoloft, and Paxil are the most widely prescribed. Their one-pill-a-day dosing makes them easy to take, and people seem to find them more physically tolerable. Two older classes of drugs, tricyclics (such as Tofranil) and monoamine oxidase inhibitors (such as Parnate), can be especially effective in treating chronic depression, Dr. Gelwan says.

Research shows that antidepressants work best when used in conjunction with talk therapy. Some people find that they can stop taking the pills after just a few months and do just fine. Others discover that they've been living with the burden of depression for years and want to stay on medication indefinitely.

differ in how quickly they act and how long their effects last. Which one your doctor prescribes will depend on the type of insomnia you have.

"If you have trouble falling asleep, then you want something that acts right away," says Eliot Gelwan, M.D., a psychiatrist and associate medical director of Community Counseling of Bristol County in Taunton, Massachusetts. "On the other hand, if you fall asleep easily but your sleep is broken and you wake up frequently, then you need something that keeps on working for hours."

Depending on the severity of your insomnia, you may not even need a prescription, Dr. Gelwan adds. Over-the-counter sleep products contain an antihistamine-like ingredient called diphenhydramine, which produces drowsiness as a side effect. This may be perfectly adequate for a mild case of stress-related insomnia, he says.

Benzodiazepines may also be prescribed to help people regain control of runaway fear and anxiety. As with insomnia, the characteristics of your anxiety will determine which particular benzodiazepine you should take. "If you can anticipate extremely stressful moments and want something that will work rapidly and then wear off, a drug such as Ativan or Serax may be best," says Dr. Gelwan. "But if your anxiety symptoms persist throughout the day, you may need a drug that acts more steadily and gradually."

When anxiety becomes incapacitating—especially in the wake of a catastrophic event such as a death in the family or a divorce—you may require more than a pill to get better. It's important that you see your doctor in such circumstances. He may advise longer-term treatment with counseling, medication, or a combination of the two.

BENEFITS IN A BOTTLE

Taking medication won't eliminate the source of your stress or teach you appropriate coping mechanisms. What it can do is make nondrug stress-relieving strategies work more effectively.

Jump-start your engine. Stress may be robbing you of the energy to exercise, or the concentration to meditate, or the capacity to enjoy the activities that you usually find soothing. "Medication can restore your level of functioning so that you can use other resources to spur healing to take place," says Dr. Gelwan. "After starting medication, patients have told me, 'I found myself able to go out and run for the first time in weeks.' "

Rev up motivation. While medication is for the most part a short-term measure, it can catalyze the changes you need to make for long-term stress reduction. "When people take medication, they may feel more confident, less tired," Ross says. "Their self-esteem is better, and they're more hopeful about the future."

Restore sound sleep. Since restless nights can sabotage your waking hours, your doctor might recommend medication to re-establish a normal sleeping pattern. "I most readily resort to medication to relieve sleep loss and fatigue," says Dr. Gelwan. "If disturbed sleep isn't treated, it becomes self-perpetuating. Fears and worries about insomnia can themselves cause insomnia."

But Dr. Gelwan notes that you may get maximum benefit by reserving a sleep aid for occasions when you need it most. "A bereaved person, for example, may be getting along most the time," he says. "But suddenly there's a big assignment at work, and that person is afraid he won't be able to sleep. A few days of medication can really help."

BEFORE YOU DECIDE

Clearly, medication has a lot to offer. But it also has its downside—cost and side effects, to name just two. To help you choose wisely, experts offer these suggestions.

Give nondrug options a shot. Since doctors usually prescribe medication for stress-related symptoms only as a last resort, why not try self-care first? You may find that after a few weeks of deep breathing exercises, meditation, or yoga, you no longer have a need for a medicinal cure.

Consider the severity of your stress. Medication is more effective—and safer—in helping someone who has been overwhelmed by an event such as divorce or bereavement than someone who is ground down by chronic, low-level hassles, says Allen Elkin, Ph.D., program director of the Stress Management and Counseling Center in New York City.

Do your part. Medication can relieve the symptoms of stress, but it's up to you to learn how to manage stress better. Seize the opportunity to make lifestyle changes in diet, exercise, and use of leisure time, says Ross.

Don't expect miracles. Keep in mind what medications can and can't do. "They can't change the situation. They can't make you happy," says Emily Stein, Ph.D., director of Human Resources at Mount Sinai Medical Center in New York City. "They're like a splint when you break your arm—an aid to healing."

TAKING DRUGS SAFELY

Should you and your doctor decide that medication is an appropriate treatment for you, you'll want to make sure that you understand exactly what your prescription is for and how to use it safely and effectively. Doctors advise the following strategies to minimize potential problems.

Start on a weekend. That way, you can find out if the drug makes you drowsy. And if it does, you'll be able to rest instead of going about your weekday chores or following your work schedule.

Watch for signs of dependency. If you've been prescribed a drug for stress-related sleep problems, you're better off taking it for a limited time only—no more than two to four weeks, Dr. Gelwan says. After about a month, benzodiazepines start to lose their punch and require larger doses to work.

If you find yourself needing more pills or higher doses to get the same effect—whether to reduce anxiety or improve your sleep cycle—you may be developing a physical dependency on your medication. Speak to your doctor about this problem immediately. You'll need to slowly taper your dosage with your doctor's supervision.

Be aware of side effects. All drugs used to treat stress-related symptoms produce some side effects, ranging from decreased appetite and diminished interest in sex to grogginess and memory loss. Know what to look out for before you start taking your medication, and if side effects become severe or intolerable, report them to your doctor.

In the end, stress and your reaction to it are highly individual matters. Any time that you feel overwhelmed by tension, anxiety, or despair, don't hesitate to seek help from a psychiatrist, a psychotherapist, or another qualified counselor. Together, you can explore the sources of your stress and figure out what kind of assistance you need, whether it be counseling, medication, or simply better self-care.

MEDITATION
THERE'S NO PLACE LIKE OM

Have you ever tried meditation?

Before you answer, think of an occasion when you got so wrapped up in what you were doing that you became completely oblivious to the world around you. It could have been anything: digging in your garden, watching your pet play with a favorite toy, putting a puzzle together. It made you lose track of time and place and focus wholly on the moment.

Probably most of us can recall experiences like this. In fact, some experts say that we have them several times a day. They're what meditation is all about.

Meditation has long had a reputation as the domain of turbaned gurus who contorted themselves into pretzel-like positions and stayed that way for hours on end. But that began to change when Herbert Benson, M.D., founder and director of the Mind/Body Medical Institute at Deaconess Hospital in Boston, introduced the idea that meditation could actually override the human body's normal reaction to stress.

CLEAR THE MIND, CALM THE BODY

In the late 1960s Dr. Benson studied a group of experienced meditators and found that the practice produced all of the physical changes characteristic of deep relaxation: slowed breathing, slowed pulse, a reduction in lactate (a chemical associated with anxiety), and an increase in the brain wave activity that indicates profound rest. He later found that meditation could reduce blood pressure as well.

Dr. Benson dubbed this phenomenon the relaxation response— an intentional allusion to the so-called fight-or-flight response that puts our bodies on red alert when stress comes calling. He reasoned that stress puts us at the mercy of our anxious thoughts, while meditation allows us to regain the upper hand.

"Meditation means learning to take control of your attention," says Roderick Borrie, Ph.D., a psychologist at South Oaks Hospital in Amityville, New York. Take control of your attention—and the thoughts and feelings that dominate it—and you can keep stress at bay.

MENTAL MEDICINE

As Dr. Benson points out, there are scores of techniques besides meditation that can evoke the relaxation response, including yoga, progressive muscle relaxation, autogenic training, and rhythmic physical exercise such as jogging or swimming. But meditation appears to offer other therapeutic benefits as well. Researchers have documented its ability to:

Reduce work-related stress. In a study of 46 nurses at three large Chinese hospitals, those who participated in a relaxation program that combined meditation and imagery reported significantly less work-related stress than those in a control group. Stress-related symptoms, including physical aches and pains, anxiety, and depression, declined substantially within a week after the nurses began practicing the relaxation techniques.

Overcome anxiety. In another study 20 of 22 patients who suffered from anxiety severe enough to interfere with normal life showed significant improvement after eight weeks of meditation training. What's more, the positive effects lasted through the patients' three-month follow-up.

Guard the heart. One of the most impressive demonstrations of the power of meditation occurred in a pioneering study conducted by Dean Ornish, M.D., president and director of the Preventive

Medicine Research Institute in Sausalito, California. He had 48 people with severe heart disease—a condition in which stress is believed to be a contributing factor—follow a program that combined daily meditation with yoga, a very low fat vegetarian diet, and moderate physical exercise.

After a year, the cholesterol deposits blocking the patients' coronary arteries had become smaller—meaning that their heart disease had actually reversed. And their chest pain was reduced by more than 90 percent, an improvement that began within the first few weeks of the study.

Provide perspective. Meditation enables us to step back from life and observe it in a more detached way. From this vantage point, we can objectively view the demands that others place on us and the expectations that we place on ourselves.

This can help us avoid the stress that comes from simply trying to do too much. "We have to be able to let go of things," says Stephen Nezezon, M.D., a physician who specializes in natural therapies and a yoga teacher at the Himalayan International Institute of Yoga Science and Philosophy in Honesdale, Pennsylvania.

TUNING OUT, TURNING IN

Should you decide to give meditation a try, you'll discover that there are many different forms to choose from. Generally, they fall into one of two main categories: concentrative meditation or mindfulness meditation.

Concentrative meditation uses a word (or mantra), an object, an image, or a sensation to focus the mind. Probably the best-known concentrative form is transcendental meditation.

Mindfulness meditation is a little more abstract. You simply allow thoughts, feelings, and images to float through your mind.

Most forms of meditation emphasize proper breathing. "The breath is the link between mind and body," explains Dr. Nezezon. "Breath awareness is easy to understand and accept."

To try a simple meditation, follow these four steps recommended by Dr. Nezezon.

1. Sit quietly and comfortably. You should be upright but not rigid.
2. As you inhale, be aware of your breath as it travels from the bridge between your nostrils up to the point between your eyebrows.
3. Focus your attention on the in-and-out motion of your breathing.
4. When thoughts float into your mind, briefly acknowledge them but don't get absorbed by them. Let them go and return your attention to your breath.

Start by practicing this exercise for 5 to 10 minutes, gradually increasing to 20 to 30 minutes. A few minutes of meditation every day is better than a occasional lengthy session, Dr. Nezezon says.

"Meditation is a way of becoming your own therapist," Dr. Borrie adds. "You'll be surprised how much better you'll get to know your thoughts in a deeply relaxed state."

See also Mindfulness, Relaxation Response

MINDFULNESS
LIVE IN THE HERE AND NOW

You know the tale of Ebenezer Scrooge: miserly grouch meets three prophetic (not to mention creepy) ghosts, decides to mend his ways, and turns into Mr. Yuletide. He learned a valuable lesson from his spectral sidekicks—one that we can benefit from even in this day and age. What matters most is how we live in the present.

Experts call this here-and-now focus mindfulness. It has proven itself as a highly effective stress-reduction technique.

"Mindfulness is a moment-to-moment awareness of everything that's passing through your mind," explains Roderick Borrie, Ph.D., a psychologist at South Oaks Hospital in Amityville, New York. By staying tuned to the moment, you turn off troubling thoughts about events that have already come to pass or that will happen sometime down the road. "Think about it: Most stress isn't derived from the present," Dr. Borrie says. "It comes from thinking about the project that's due next week or the comment that you wish you hadn't made last week."

When you dwell on what's over and done with or what's to come, your body responds as if the event were happening right now. "If you worry about missing a deadline, for example, your body reacts as if you already have," says Dr. Borrie. By keeping your mind in the present, he adds, you stop the event from flicking the internal switch that launches the body's stress response.

THERE'S NO TIME LIKE THE PRESENT

You're probably already familiar with the mindful state and the physical calm and mental clarity that it induces. "Many people experience mindfulness on a random basis—when they go fishing, for example, or when they listen to music," says David Harp, author of *The New Three-Minute Meditator*. "They know that a comforting mental space exists, but they can't readily access it. It's like coming across a wonderful station on the radio from time to time: If you never learn the call numbers, you can't find it again, except at random."

Tuning in to mindfulness at will works against stress in several ways, according to research. Among its therapeutic benefits, this technique has been found to:

Inhibit stress-related illness. At the stress reduction clinic of the University of Massachusetts Medical Center in Worcester, more than 6,000 patients with medical problems as diverse as high blood pressure and cancer have participated in an eight-week program in which they learn mindfulness. Overall, patients report a substantial decline in both physical and psychological symptoms during and after their training, according to Jon Kabat-Zinn, Ph.D., program director at the clinic. And the benefits persist through years of follow-up.

Minimize mental distress. Mindfulness training made a big difference for one group of people with serious psychiatric problems, including anxiety, panic, and depression. After going through the University of Massachusetts Medical Center program, 20 of the 22

MAKING MINDFULNESS A HABIT

You can set aside time each day to practice mindfulness. But to get the full benefit of this stress-deflating technique, you might want to incorporate it into your everyday activities. For example:

- When you're eating, be conscious of how the food looks on your plate before you take the first bite. Then focus on the texture of a single mouthful and the way the taste changes as you chew and swallow. "When I want to eat mindfully, I switch the hand I hold my fork in," says David Harp, author of *The New Three-Minute Meditator.* "Since my left hand is so uncoordinated, I have to pay more attention to what I'm doing."

- When you're walking, "make a conscious effort to move slowly," suggests Roderick Borrie, Ph.D., a psychologist at South Oaks Hospital in Amityville, New York. "Think to yourself: 'I'm not going anywhere.' Feel yourself being in your body as you move. Be aware of your breathing, and feel how your weight shifts from one leg to another as you proceed." Counting steps is helpful, too, suggests Harp.

- "If you work in an office and need to go to the copier six to eight times a day, turn your path into a place for medi-

---

participants showed marked improvement: less anxiety, fewer and milder panic attacks, and relief from depression.

Pacify pain. In one study nearly three-fourths of patients with chronic pain reported that their discomfort declined by at least one-third when they began practicing mindfulness. Even more impressive: 61 percent said that their pain was at least half as intense as before. Patients also experienced significant improvements in their ability to go about their daily lives and in their moods.

tation," says Harp. "Instead of obsessing about what you should have said last night or what's waiting for you on your desk, be mindful of your walking."

- When your phone rings, consider it a mindfulness cue. "I never answer the phone before the third ring," says Harp. "From the moment I become aware of the first ring, I focus my attention on my breathing: how it feels as it hits the back of my throat, how it comes out on my tongue and the back of my front teeth."
- Even when you're washing dishes, don't do it on automatic pilot, according to Thich Nhat Hanh, a Vietnamese author whose books have introduced many Americans to the Buddhist tradition of mindfulness called *vipassana*. "I enjoy taking my time with each dish, being fully aware of the dish, the water, and each movement of my hands," writes Hanh in *Peace Is Every Step*. "If I am incapable of washing dishes joyfully, if I want to finish them quickly so I can go and have dessert, I will be equally incapable of enjoying my dessert. . . . I will always be dragged into the future, never able to live in the present moment."

THOUGHT CONTROL

Entering a mindful state on the spot is simple to do. It comes down to being in touch with your bodily sensations, Dr. Borrie says. "The mind is a time traveler, but the body is always in the present," he explains. "Be aware of where your body is . . . what sights, sounds, and smells are registering."

And when an unpleasant or disturbing thought crosses your mind, address it head-on. "Identify it—'This is impatience,' 'This is worry'—and recognize it as something you've experienced many times before," Dr. Borrie says. This robs the thought of its power and lets it drift away. Then return your attention to your here-and-now bodily sensations.

To help you evoke mindfulness, Dr. Borrie suggests this simple exercise.

Scan your body. Lying quietly and comfortably, focus your attention on each part of your body in turn. "You're not trying to relax or do anything," says Dr. Borrie. "You're just accepting your body the way it is." Start at the top: Become aware of the sensations in your face and head . . . in your neck . . . in each arm, from shoulder to fingertips . . . in your chest . . . in your abdomen . . . all the way down to the tips of your toes.

Meditate mindfully. Now sit quietly in a peaceful, comfortable place. As you sit, pay attention to your breathing. Be aware of the sensations in your body as the air enters your nose and travels down deep into your lungs, then leaves again. When your mind drifts, be aware of the thought or feeling. Label it—"thinking" or "judging" or "worry," for example—then refocus on your breathing. Continue for 20 minutes.

See also Meditation

MUSIC

CHANGE YOUR TUNE WITH A SONG

So maybe Snow White was on to something when she lyrically advised her animal companions to "whistle while you work." Lots of us turn to tunes to usher us through tedious, tense, or turbulent times. Indeed, in a Gallop poll of more than 1,000 people, 77 percent chose music as their favorite way to beat the blues—twice the number who chose exercise.

What is it about music that can transform our moods from mad to mellow, from melancholy to motivated? While the melody may be what catches our ears, some experts say it's really the cadence that calms and comforts. "We feel the rhythm in our bones," explains music therapist Helen Lindquist Bonny, Ph.D., director of the Bonny Foundation in Salina, Kansas. "It makes us want to move and dance."

Our affinity for music is completely natural, even innate, Dr. Bonny adds. "Research has shown that our first hearing of sounds come from the womb," she says. And of course, what better way to soothe an infant than with gentle rocking and a lullaby?

POWER CHORDS

Perhaps this primal connection explains why music produces such profound physical effects when we listen to it. Among the first stress-fighting changes to take place when we hear a tune is an increase in deep breathing, says Trudy Shulman-Fagan, a music therapist in Newton Highlands, Massachusetts, who treats people with anxiety disorders, chronic pain, or high levels of stress. The body's production of serotonin—a brain chemical that brings about relaxation and feelings of well-being—also accelerates, studies have shown.

But this just scratches the surface of what music can do for us. Among its other benefits:

Music de-stresses dental appointments. In one study dental patients who listened to music reported less pain, less discomfort, and a greater sense of control than those who just grin and bear it.

Tones make toiling tolerable. Music can work its magic even if your mind is on something else. Just playing it in the background while you work can relieve stress. One study, from the State University of New York at Buffalo, had cardiovascular surgeons who routinely listened to music while performing surgery complete difficult arithmetic problems. The doctors showed significantly lower levels of stress when their favorite selections played in the background than when all was silent.

Music helps the heart to heal. Among 80 patients recovering from heart attacks in coronary care units, those who learned to relax while listening to their choice of music had lower heart rates and higher body temperatures (an indicator of relaxation) after each session than those in a control group. A lower heart rate reduces the strain on a damaged heart and eases the healing process.

What's more, combining music with a relaxation technique had greater therapeutic benefits than practicing a relaxation technique by itself.

RELAXING REFRAINS

While using music to de-stress can be as simple as popping in a favorite tape and slipping on some headphones, you can take steps to maximize the positive effects of the experience. First and foremost, you have to choose the right tune to listen to.

"There's no one piece of music that will relax everyone," says Shulman-Fagen. "And what you need to relax may be very different from one day—even one moment—to the next." Still, the following general principles apply.

Go slow for soothing. Researchers have found that music with a beat slower than the natural heart rate—about 72 beats per minute—has a calming effect. Select a piece with a cyclical quality, Shulman-Fagen suggests. Classical music or mellow jazz that repeats the same theme and pattern but varies it in an interesting way creates a safe and secure feeling, she explains.

Pick up the pace for a pick-me-up. If you've been sitting all day, your body and mind are likely to hunger for renewal by stimulation. "You may need to let loose with rock and roll or a rousing rendition of the *New World Symphony*," Shulman-Fagen says.

Go for the oldies but goodies. With music, personal taste is everything. Favorite selections that you've found stress-reducing in the past have the added benefit of familiarity. A piece that you've loved since childhood can be that much more comforting when the going gets rough.

Explore the options. If you're feeling adventurous, you might want to lend an ear to some less mainstream strains. Among the styles you can choose from:

- Minimalist: This modern classical music uses a lot of repetition and evolves very subtly and gradually, explains music therapist Frank Bosco, director of the Sound Health Studio in New York City. He recommends works by composers such as Philip Glass, John Adams, and Steve Reich as well as tapes from the Kronos Quartet.

MOVE TO THE MUSIC

When stress turns your day topsy-turvy, it's nice to know that you can go home, slip on some sweats, and curl up on the couch with Tony Bennett, Beethoven, or the Beach Boys. But time and place don't always permit such an indulgence.

To work off stress in a flash, just tune in to your favorite music meister and hit the pavement, says Trudy Shulman-Fagen, a music therapist in Newton Highlands, Massachusetts, who treats people with anxiety disorders, chronic pain, or high levels of stress. "Be sure to choose music that makes you feel good—something with a rhythm that's easy to breathe to." As you walk, inhale and exhale in time with the music. "Let the music take you," Shulman-Fagen says. "Feel your body and whatever sensations come your way."

If worries, demands, and other troubling thoughts intrude on your walk, don't try to stop them. "Let the laundry list of problems run through your head," Shulman-Fagen says. "Even if you have a hundred things to do, the list will run dry fairly quickly." You'll arrive back at your home or workplace feeling calm and in control.

- New Age: This style is specifically designed for relaxation, with light sounds and slow, flowing rhythms. "The sense of space in the music is supposed to create space in the mind," says Bosco. Some people find it extremely soothing.
- Chants: The slow, serious, spiritual sounds of Gregorian chants have a unique power to induce a peaceful, trance-like state.

See also Relaxation Tapes

N

NATURE

ANSWER THE CALL OF THE OUTDOORS

The next time you find yourself tested by stress, why not take a walk on the wild side? That's right: Trade in your briefcase for a backpack, your housework for hiking boots, and head for the great outdoors.

Actually, you don't even need to get all that extravagant to make your great escape. Just strolling through a nearby park on your lunch break or stopping to watch the sun set as you make dinner can buoy your spirits and put problems—and life—in perspective.

We humans seem to have an inborn affinity for all things natural. Scientists even have a name for it: *biophilia*, which literally means "love of nature." Their work has suggested that we're drawn to the natural world because we know instinctively that it can undo the ravages of stress and make us feel better.

Some experts theorize that our tendency to seek solace and strength in nature is genetically programmed. Thousands of years before biofeedback machines and relaxation tapes, our ancestors had to resort to other means of defusing the body's fight-or-flight response to a stressful situation. "During the long period of human evolution, it would have been useful not only to quickly react in the face of a threat but also to quickly return to a calm state once the threat had passed," says Roger Ulrich, Ph.D., an environmental psychologist at Texas A & M University in College Station.

Humans who developed this ability, explains Dr. Ulrich, had better odds of survival than those who didn't, because they could bounce back faster from traumatic events and generally function better. He believes that for our ancestors, nature became a refuge—a source of much-needed relaxation and renewal.

CALMING COMMUNION

These days, it's not saber-toothed tigers and woolly mammoths but surly spouses and workplace hassles that fill us with tension and anxiety. Although the stressors have changed, the human body's response to them remains the same. And our natural surroundings still make for a soothing, stabilizing antidote.

Specifically, nature neutralizes stress by:

Stifling the stress response. In a study led by Dr. Ulrich, 120 people watched a stressful movie, then a videotape of either natural settings or urban scenes. The people who watched the nature video showed almost immediate improvements in heart rate, muscle tension, blood pressure, and other physical indicators of stress. "After only four to six minutes of exposure . . . significantly greater recovery was evident in all physiological measures," Dr. Ulrich says.

Moderating mood. In another study Dr. Ulrich showed color slides of either green vegetation or urban scenes to college students facing the pressure of final exams. The students who viewed the greenery demonstrated significant reductions in fear, anger, and aggression and corresponding increases in positive emotions.

Allaying anxiety. Nature appears to have especially therapeutic effects for folks undergoing or recovering from medical procedures. Patients who gazed up at serene naturescapes while awaiting surgery had significantly lower blood pressure than patients who looked at an unadorned ceiling. Likewise, people facing dental surgery showed fewer anxious feelings when they were instructed to watch an aquarium. And patients recuperating from gallbladder surgery experienced fewer complications, needed fewer painkillers, and were out of the hospital faster if their beds overlooked stands of trees rather than brick walls.

Toppling tension. Nature can stave off stress in the workplace, too. Employees who had views of trees and flowers found their jobs less stressful and reported fewer physical ailments than their co-workers who could see only buildings and pavement, according to research by Rachel Kaplan, Ph.D., professor of environmental psychology, and Stephen Kaplan, Ph.D., professor of psychology, both at the University of Michigan in Ann Arbor.

Fending off fuzziness. Dr. Stephen Kaplan believes that nature also helps ease what he calls mental fatigue: the inability to concentrate and resist distraction that comes upon us as the result of stress. "Of everything we've studied, the natural environment has turned out to be the most powerful setting for reducing mental fatigue," he notes.

GETTING A FIX FROM FLORA AND FAUNA

What makes nature such a super stress reducer is its accessibility: It can be as close as a glance out the window or a step out the door. To get the most benefit from your moment in the sun, try these tips.

Go for the real thing. If you absolutely can't break free of whatever it is you're doing, you can still take advantage of nature's calming effects with the help of the nearest available window (one with a good view, of course). But if you can spare the time, getting real outdoor exposure is more beneficial. Actually being in a park, the woods, or a garden reduces mental fatigue and stress in a matter of minutes, Dr. Stephen Kaplan says.

Step out for a break. Instead of juicing up on caffeine and a candy bar, use your coffee break to squeeze in a short walk, advises Dr. Stephen Kaplan. Here are some other ideas for integrating brief nature breaks into your daily routine.

- Have lunch in a nearby park—or a well-planted mall.
- Go for stroll rather than watching the six o'clock news.
- Commute to work by foot. If you live farther than walking distance, park your car a half-mile or more from your workplace and hoof it the rest of the way.

Keep a journal. Not everyone reacts to nature in the same way, points out Charles Lewis, retired research fellow at Morton Arboretum in Lisle, Illinois, and author of *Green Nature-Human Nature.* "Try to discover the part of you that responds to green," he urges.

One way of doing that, says Dr. Stephen Kaplan, is to document your exposures to nature and how you feel on each occasion: your

SHAKING THAT SHUT-IN FEELING

Snow and cold weather can drain your desire to spend time outdoors. But just when you want to do it the least, that may be when you need it the most. "There really is such a thing as cabin fever," says Stephen Kaplan, Ph.D., professor of psychology at the University of Michigan in Ann Arbor.

When winter threatens to drive you to distraction, keep these tips in mind.

Flex your green thumb. Fill your home or workplace with greenery. You can do something simple, like plant a philodendron. Or you can learn the Japanese art of bonsai or ikebana, which involves arranging flowers to capture a sense of life. Or make a miniature landscape of your own with mosses, small plants, and rocks in a terrarium.

Hang a picture. You can also bring nature indoors with the help of a landscape painting or photograph. Opt for an image with elements that are known to be especially calming: an open area that's shaded but not crowded with trees, a winding trail into the woods, or a lakeside scene.

Take time out for nature. Try this two-minute exercise for a quick nature boost, recommended by Mel Bucholtz, a psychotherapist in Lincoln Center, Massachusetts, who organizes outdoor adventures for stressed-out professionals through his Returning to Earth Institute. Find a place in a room that is bathed in sunlight. Close your eyes and just feel the light on your face and on your hands. Or sit quietly next to a rock or a plant, then breathe slowly and become aware of how you feel in the presence of an object from nature.

mood, your anxiety level, your ability to focus and perform. "People aren't always aware of the restorative effect of nature unless they look for it," he explains.

Write your own nature Rx. The notes you take should give you a clearer understanding of how nature influences you, says Dr. Stephen Kaplan. Many of his students discover that they need certain regular doses of "green therapy" to be at their best—perhaps a half-hour a day or three to four hours a week.

Do something wild. Why not spend your next vacation trekking into the Grand Canyon or hiking the Appalachian Trail? Such intense exposure to nature will recharge your batteries in a way that a short stroll in the park cannot.

"Deep immersion in a natural setting restores a sense of proportion and of living in the present," says Mel Bucholtz, a psychotherapist in Lincoln Center, Massachusetts, who organizes outdoor adventures for stressed-out professionals through his Returning to Earth Institute. These overdriven folks sign up to spend as many as 14 days in primitive wilderness areas. They walk away with a feeling of connectedness, Bucholtz explains.

"The experience accentuates the fact that people are part of something larger," he says. "It's a psychological passport back to self."

See also Gardening

NUTRITION

FUEL YOUR BODY RIGHT

Your mechanic just called with the news you've been dreading: Your car's engine has unceremoniously expired, and getting it fixed is going to cost you a pretty penny. You heave a sigh, head for the fridge, and grab (A) a pint of your favorite ice cream or (B) some spinach and brown rice left over from last night's dinner.

Okay, so you can probably guess which is the "right" choice. But be honest: Which would you really go for? Most of us would opt for A. There's no denying that this sweet treat can melt away tension with each soothing spoonful. The downside is that the lift is only temporary and can actually drain the body's energy supply, leaving us feeling physically and mentally fatigued.

A nutrient-packed snack would do a much better job of keeping our energy levels steady. That's important to the body's efforts to cope with stressful situations. "The stress response often consumes great amounts of energy, and as our energy is depleted, we are less able to handle stress," says Derrick Lonsdale, M.D., a preventive medicine physician in private practice in Westlake, Ohio.

CRAVING COMFORT

If we know what's good for us, why do we so often forsake healthful foods when we're feeling frazzled? Eating self-indulgently rather than sensibly is a habit that starts at an early age, says Larry Richardson, M.D., author of *Diets and Weight Loss*. As we're growing up, he notes, many of us learn to associate foods such as ice cream, cake, and candy with feelings of well-being.

"When you were a child and you would fall and scrape your chin, your mother probably didn't say, 'Let's get you a nice dish of broccoli,' " Dr. Richardson says. "Now Mom's not around to help you through the crisis, but your friend the ice cream cone is. The foods that people eat when they're anxious, depressed, or upset tend to be smooth, sweet, creamy things."

These so-called comfort foods may provide more than just a psychological lift. Research suggests that the fat and sugar in them causes the brain to step up its production of opioids and serotonin. These two feel-good chemicals deliver a biological boost that people find calming and soothing.

Trouble is, these effects last only a short time—and they're likely to make you feel worse in the long run. That jolt you get from drinking a cola or eating a candy bar floods your bloodstream with sugar. Your body responds by releasing more insulin, the hormone that's responsible for mopping up blood sugar. The surge in insulin causes your blood sugar to quickly drop to a normal or below-normal level.

This little roller-coaster ride can leave anyone feeling drained. But in people who are already prone to low blood sugar, or hypoglycemia, the reaction can be especially severe. "Those with a tendency toward hypoglycemia may experience it more in times of stress," says Richard Podell, M.D., clinical professor of family med-

THE RIGHT FOOD FOR YOUR MOOD

When you must munch, you want to be sure to select a nutritious snack that's low in both fat and sugar. You should also keep in mind that what you eat can intensify or change your mood, says Cheryl Hartsough, R.D., head nutritionist at the PGA National Resort and Spa in Palm Beach Gardens, Florida.

The chart below can help you choose the food to best counterbalance your mood.

WHEN YOU FEEL...	AVOID...	EAT...
Tense, anxious, stressed	Chocolate, alcohol, cake, ice cream, coffee	Fresh fruit, dried fruit, or pasta, whole-grain bread, baked potatoes, rice, vegetables
Sleepy and lethargic	Sweets, wine or beer, pizza, high-fat food	Low-fat, high-protein foods, such as broiled or baked fish, veal and poultry, low-fat cheese, egg-white omelet, fruit
Depressed	Cake, ice cream, bread, pastries	Whole-grain entrées, such as pasta primavera, rice and beans

icine at the University of Medicine and Dentistry of New Jersey Robert Wood Johnson Medical School in New Brunswick.

A TASTE OF TRANQUILLITY

Scientists are busy looking for nutrients that will bolster the body's ability to withstand stress, but without the negative aftereffects common among the comfort foods. Some of the most intriguing research involves a group that is subject to extremely high stress: soldiers in combat.

A report from the Military Nutrition Research Committee of the National Academy of Sciences suggests that tyrosine, an amino acid, and choline, a B vitamin, have potential stress-fighting properties. The body uses both nutrients to manufacture neurotransmitters, nervous system messengers that may be depleted by stress.

In one study tyrosine supplements increased the physical endurance and mental alertness of soldiers exposed to cold weather and high altitude. In another study soldiers who took choline supplements were able to run a grueling 20-mile course about five minutes faster than they had before.

As fascinating as these findings are, experts caution that loading up on tyrosine and choline supplements would be premature. Researchers need to establish the safety of such supplements and to determine proper doses, says Robert Nesheim, Ph.D., who chaired the committee that issued the report. Taking too much tyrosine, for example, could disrupt the normal balance among amino acids in the body, with unknown results.

Scientists are also examining the stress-defying effects of the B vitamins and vitamin C. In one study at Georgia State University College of Education in Atlanta, patients at health centers and counseling centers completed questionnaires about their dietary habits and stress levels. Those who consumed the most B vitamins and vitamin C showed significantly less anxiety than those who consumed the least. "High intakes of stress vitamins may serve as a coping resource under high-stress conditions," concluded Dottie Dixon Brock, Ph.D., the author of the study.

FOOD FOR THOUGHT

While nutrition therapy shows a lot of promise in helping us manage stress effectively, much work remains to be done. For now, your best bet is to make sure that you eat lots of healthful foods that give your body the raw materials it needs to function properly. A balanced, nutrient-rich diet also helps keep your blood sugar as steady as possible. Dr. Podell recommends meals and snacks that emphasize carbohydrates and protein and minimize fat. Here are some other dietary do's and don'ts for tough times.

161

FIGHTING THE URGE TO SPLURGE

Eating is a common way of coping with stress. But when we reach for rich, sugary treats, we're putting ourselves at risk for overeating, according to Larry Richardson, M.D., author of *Diets and Weight Loss*.

"Many Americans are overweight as a result of eating in response to emotions," Dr. Richardson says. He cites one national survey that found Americans to be 8 percent heavier today than 10 years ago. "There's so much more stress these days—I think that has a lot to do with it," he adds.

Stress eating is a lifelong habit that's hard to break. These tips from Dr. Richardson should help.

Get it in writing. Become aware of the relationship between your eating habits and stress by keeping a food-mood diary. Write down what you eat, when you eat it, and how you feel. Are you truly hungry? Or are you anxious, tired, or blue?

Stall before snacking. When you get the urge to munch, don't head for the fridge right away. "If you can delay eating for 20 to 30 minutes, often hunger will pass," Dr. Richardson says.

Think of substitutes. Make a list of your 10 favorite things to do. Then when stress strikes, choose one of those activities instead of eating.

Be prepared. Make healthy snacks accessible—for example, have vegetables cut and ready in the front of your refrigerator. If you must have sweet treats in your house, put them in a place that's hard for you to get to. "Most of us take the path of least resistance," Dr. Richardson says.

Stick to your list. It's also a good idea to plan ahead for your grocery shopping. When you stock up on snacks, make a list of the foods you like that are low in sugar and fat, then stick to it.

Stay on schedule. Stress can mess with your mealtimes, and that can wreak havoc on your blood sugar level. "Many people say that they feel much worse when they delay or skip meals," says Dr. Podell.

To keep your blood sugar on an even keel, you need to set an eating schedule and stick with it. Even if you don't have time for a substantial sit-down lunch, make a point of grabbing a nutritious snack—a banana and a serving of low-fat yogurt, for example—as close to your regular mealtime as possible.

Multi-ply your defenses. The B vitamins and vitamin C aren't the only nutrients that take it on the chin when your body battles stress. A multivitamin can make up for any shortfall and ensure that your body has a sufficient supply of all of the essential vitamins and minerals, says Dr. Podell.

Get all wet. Remember to drink plenty of liquids. For one thing, you tend to perspire more when you're under stress, which means that your body is losing fluids that need to be replaced. What's more, if your body is low on fluids, certain stress symptoms such as dry mouth and heart palpitations may get worse.

Most experts recommend drinking at least eight eight-ounce glasses of water daily. While this is especially important when you're stressed, it's a good practice anytime.

Don't forget fiber. The digestive system is perhaps the most common—and the most sensitive—target of stress. Among the usual consequences: cramps and constipation. An adequate intake of fiber—from fruits, vegetables, and whole grains—can offer some protection against these symptoms.

A word of warning: Don't abruptly dump a lot of extra fiber into your diet. Too much too soon can actually contribute to digestive upsets.

Be careful with caffeine. When we're under pressure, many of us find comfort in a hot cup of coffee or tea. The caffeine in these beverages increases energy, heightens alertness, and gives a welcome lift to mood.

But all of this comes at a cost. The boost we enjoy is borrowed, not created. Sooner or later it wears off, and we get dragged down by fatigue.

Also, too much caffeine can cause jitters and anxiety. Researchers at Duke University Medical Center in Durham, North Carolina, found that 300 milligrams of caffeine—the equivalent of two to three cups of coffee—more than doubled production of the stress hormones cortisol and adrenaline and raised blood pressure in people facing stressful situations.

Caffeine is a stimulant that apparently revs up the sympathetic nervous system, which is responsible for the body's stress response. Many people who kick the caffeine habit report reduced anxiety and the elimination of problems such as hand tremors.

O

OPTIMISM

LOOK ON THE BRIGHT SIDE

Is the glass half full or half empty?

Is it a doughnut or a hole?

We often use these simple images to convey the fundamental difference between optimism and pessimism. In reality, the contrast between the two is much more profound. Optimists and pessimists live in two very distinct worlds—and the optimist's is a good deal more relaxed. "Research suggests that an optimistic nature helps people cope with stress much more effectively," says Lisa G. Aspinwall, Ph.D., assistant professor of psychology at the University of Maryland at College Park.

If we think positively, the daily setbacks that we all experience don't seem to hurt us as easily. "There's good evidence that optimists appraise the threat of a negative event as less severe," says Dr. Aspinwall. At the same time, they have a more favorable view of their own abilities to deal with life's challenges and to handle stressful situations.

HOPE SPRINGS ETERNAL

Just to set things straight: Optimism is not an absolute conviction that nothing bad can possibly happen, nor is it an unwavering adherence to some pie-in-the-sky belief system that's steeped in blind faith and wishful thinking. It's more accurately described as a kind of upbeat realism. In other words, optimists see themselves and the world in such a way that the problems and pitfalls are manageable.

When a crisis does arise, optimists weather the storm with the help of two essential survival skills. First, they always look for the proverbial silver lining and then use it to their advantage. They believe that they're better off for having the experience, Dr. Aspinwall says, because in it they've found new faith, or discovered something really important, or become stronger. In effect, they manage to make some kind of spiritual lemonade out of the most unlikely lemons.

Second, optimists have confidence that "this, too, shall pass." Unlike pessimists, who tend to view a setback as a permanent state of affairs with far-reaching consequences, optimists are more likely to believe that the situation is transient, limited, and the result of circumstance. This attitude makes them feel that they're in control of things.

Both of these traits enable optimists to cope with stress in a more positive way. These folks don't need crutches such as drinking, smoking, and overeating to make them feel better. And they don't try to evade the stressor by sleeping more, staying away from people, hoping for a miracle, or engaging in another avoidance activity.

THE PERKS OF POSITIVE THINKING

Adopting an optimistic outlook does more than help us change the self-defeating behaviors often brought on by stress. These are among the benefits that researchers have recorded thus far.

Optimism facilitates change. For people moving from one life situation into another—because of a divorce or a new job, for example—a positive outlook can ease the transition. In a study conducted by Dr. Aspinwall, 672 college freshmen completed a personality assessment during the second week of their first semester. Then three months later, they answered another questionnaire that measured their adaptation to college life—how happy they were, whether they felt able to deal with pressure. "Only one personality predisposition—optimism—had a direct, positive effect on adjustment to college," Dr. Aspinwall reports.

In a separate study researchers found that optimistic students were, in general, much less stressed, less depressed, and less lonely than their pessimistic counterparts at the end of their first semester of college.

Optimism speeds postoperative recovery. In a study of coronary bypass patients, those who kept their spirits up fared much better than those who were down in the dumps. The optimists were much less likely to suffer heart attacks during surgery. Afterward, they sat up in bed and walked around their rooms sooner. Six months later, they were much more likely to be exercising vigorously.

Optimism fosters acceptance. Researchers found that among women with breast cancer, pessimists had a much harder time coming to terms with their condition as long as one year after surgery. "Optimistic women appear to more readily accept the reality of the challenge they face, whereas pessimistic women try to push this reality away," the researchers concluded.

Optimism nurtures good health. Ninety-nine male Harvard University graduates underwent physical examinations at age 25, then every five years through age 60. When researchers reviewed the men's medical records, they found that over the years the pessimists in the group experienced significantly poorer health than the optimists.

ATTITUDE ADJUSTMENT

Clearly, looking on the bright side in bad times can pay off big. If you consider yourself a dyed-in-the-wool naysayer, keep this in mind: Optimists are not born, they're made.

"Many of us were trained to look at the negative side of things," says Susan Jeffers, Ph.D., author of *End the Struggle and Dance with Life*. "But what's learned can also be unlearned." The following tips should help you see life from a rosier perspective.

Speak a new language. One way to enhance your optimism is to make slight alterations in the messages you send yourself—the so-called self-talk that's constantly going on in your head. Do you catastrophize? ("I burned the roast. The whole dinner is ruined!") Do you overgeneralize? ("Nothing ever works out for me!") Do you habitually judge yourself harshly? ("I'm a complete failure!") Learn to recognize such negative thoughts and then replace them with positive ones.

Stay in the present. "If you're treating yourself in a critical, judgmental, punitive way, rehashing the past and worrying about the future, you're cutting off access to your own natural optimism," says Richard Sackett, Ph.D., director of Integrative Psychotherapy Services in New York City. "By connecting with the here and now, you'll experience a realistic sense of optimism."

Learn a lesson. "In any situation focus on what there is to be learned, what can enrich your life," urges Dr. Jeffers. She recalls her own experience with breast cancer a dozen years ago: "I knew I had a choice. I could say no and be a victim, or I could say yes and find something positive." She chose the latter and believes that it helped her overcome the disease.

Take notes. Dr. Jeffers suggests looking at the abundance in your life rather than the shortcomings. "We look at the world so superficially," she says. "We can't see the many things that make life pleasant."

One way to correct this, Dr. Jeffers says, is to make a list. "Every night before bed, write down 50 things to be grateful for: The car started, you had a delicious salad at lunch, you saw a flower," she explains. "If you know that you're going to write them down at night, you'll get into the habit of looking for them during the day."

Take charge. Instead of adopting a victim mentality—"Why did this happen to me?"—get into the habit of asking yourself how you can change what you don't like. "The three most important words that you can say to yourself are, 'I'll handle it,'" Dr. Jeffers says. "'I'll handle whatever comes into my life and make something worthwhile and beautiful out of it.' You can train yourself to feel this way."

Pal around with positive people. "Your friends are a reflection of your outlook," Dr. Jeffers says. "You need to create a circle of upbeat friends to go with your more optimistic attitude."

See also Self-Talk

ORGANIZATION
GET YOUR LIFE IN ORDER

When it comes to stressors, most of us probably wouldn't rank messy closets with something like losing a job or ending a relationship. True, a disorganized lifestyle may not make your heart race, or your muscles tense, or fill you with anxiety. But it does create a persistent, low-level friction that builds up over time and ultimately leaves you feeling overwhelmed and out of control.

"Being disorganized can create enormous stress," says Ronni Eisenberg, time-management consultant and co-author of *Organize Yourself*. "You spend minutes or even hours looking for a sweater, a photo, a piece of paper. You never get to appointments on time. You don't get things done."

Eventually, she adds, the sense that you're still in the starting block while everyone else heads toward the finish line takes its toll. You feel inadequate. Your self-esteem erodes.

The good news is that unlike many other stressors in our lives, disorder is one that's correctable—even preventable. All you need is a little fine-tuning of your organizational skills. And that's easy to do, according to Eisenberg. The key, she says, is "learning to think like an organized person."

A Place for Everything and Everything in Its Place

Getting organized does not require you to do any soul-searching or make profound personal changes. It does call for a slightly different outlook and a little discipline. What's more, it need not take place overnight—but to be effective, it must extend to the smallest details of your life.

In your bedroom, for example, you need to designate specific drawers for socks, for underwear, for T-shirts. In your study, you must set aside a place to store your bills and receipts. In your kitchen, you need to plan which utensils you want handy and which ones you can tuck away for special occasions.

All this means setting up a system—and yes, that might require some up-front effort. But the time and energy you put into it is quickly rewarded.

"People avoid getting organized because they think it takes time," Eisenberg says. But as she points out, it's less time-consuming to figure out where to put the mail than to spend time searching for misplaced bills and letters.

HOME NEAT HOME

You can start your personal reorganization on the home front. The following guidelines can bring some order to your day-to-day routine and reduce stress in the process.

Put things back. Be scrupulous about returning everything to its storage space when you're finished with it. "I've taught this to my 10-year-old daughter and 3-year-old twins," says Eisenberg. "If they take a toy from the playroom to the bedroom, they know it goes right back to the playroom when they're done playing."

Categorize closets. Keep like clothes together: coats next to coats, slacks next to slacks. Arrange clothing by color, from dark to light. (Tie a ribbon around the hanger or use some other marker to help distinguish navy from black.) In the hall closet, group together the coats for each family member.

"Also, if you need to get at something often, keep it accessible," Eisenberg suggests. "Make sure it's visible, not hidden behind a box." Ask yourself, "What do I need to find most often? How can I most easily find it?"

Redesign dresser drawers. Organize your chest of drawers according to the order in which you get dressed: Put the article of clothing you put on first—say, underwear—in the top drawer, then work your way to the bottom drawer. Get as many dividers as you need to create separate spaces for different articles of clothing. As in your closets, group items within each clothing group by color, and keep the most frequently used items at the front of the drawers.

Systematize your kitchen. The only visible appliances should be the ones that get used every day, like the toaster or microwave. Stash the rarely used blender or mixer in nearby cabinets, where you can still get at them.

Cluster companions. Group the cookware and utensils that are used together—such as the spaghetti pot and the colander—on one shelf, where you can find them easily. Any item that you need only occasionally, like a picnic thermos or a fondue dish, should be stored outside the kitchen, where space is at less of a premium.

Coordinate your calendar. Get a big wall calendar with enough space to write down all date-related family information:

appointments, birthdays, meetings, social events. It might help to use a different color ink for each family member.

If you have school-age children, transfer all of the information about activities, holidays, and the like to the wall calendar at the start of the school year. It may take a couple of hours, but then you can throw out the separate schedules that your kids bring home.

Use it or lose it. If you never use an item—any item—get rid of it. Period. Garage sale, anyone?

RETOOL YOUR WORKSPACE

While you're at it, you may want to take some steps to streamline your work environment, too. It can certainly enhance your productivity and whittle away at job-related stress. And even if you're not a desk jockey, you can use the following tips to keep the business of home and family running like clockwork.

De-clutter your desk. Whether it's the executive type handmade from solid mahogany or a makeshift structure fashioned from milk crates and plywood, the desk is the greatest test of organizational skills. "The most basic rule is to keep it clear, not stacked with a lot of unused piles," says Eisenberg.

If you work in an office, "at the end of the day—every day—take a few minutes to file everything that needs to be filed, to pass on everything that needs to be passed on, and to plan for the next day," Eisenberg suggests. "It makes an enormous difference when you arrive the next morning and your desk is all clear."

Reserve your space. The work surface of your desk should be restricted to those things you use constantly, such as your appointment book. Personal items, such as family photos, should be allowed only if there's room—and even then you should be sparing. Every time you add a new memento, take one away.

Store tools neatly. Keep pencils, paper clips, stationery, and other things that you use frequently in desk drawers, using separators liberally to spare yourself the need for constant rummaging.

Be a better mail manager. Desks are notorious depositories for incoming mail. Leave a couple of unopened letters in your in-box, and they seem to multiply into forbidding stacks of correspondence in a matter of days. Here's what Eisenberg suggests to prevent this sort of paper pandemonium.

- Set aside 10 to 15 minutes of each day to go through your mail pile. Immediately identify the things you have no interest in—circulars, catalogs you're not going to buy from, solicitations from groups you don't donate to—and toss them.
- Sort mail by family member and always leave it in a designated place—say, on a hall table.
- Act promptly on the mail you're keeping. If it's notification of an address change, update your address book and then throw the card away. Time for your dental checkup? Make the appointment and toss the card. Reply to any invitation, note the necessary information on your calendar, then file or toss the invitations themselves. Read letters, note your reply on the top, then answer them right away or file them for response the next day. If it's a personal letter you want to answer at your leisure, set it aside until you have more time.
- When bills come in, circle the due dates and put them in their own file in chronological order. Then set aside time once or twice a month for bill paying. To make this process even easier, pick up an accordion file with separate compartments in a stationery store or office-supply store. Put unpaid bills in one compartment and paid bills and receipts in another. You'll breathe easy at tax time.

Control magazine buildup. Read weekly magazines within a week, monthly magazines within a month. When the new issue arrives, throw out the old one, whether you've read it or not.

If you can't bear to discard a magazine that you haven't read, scan the contents page as soon as the magazine arrives and clip out the stories that look promising. Create a file folder for the articles and take it with you to read while you're waiting in the doctor's office or riding the bus to work.

Become a fan of files. If you don't already have a file cabinet in your home, you should get one—a two- or four-drawer model will do. They're indispensible when it comes to managing paperwork. You can create an efficient filing system with these tips from Eisenberg.

- Divide the file cabinet into sections according to your needs: automobile expenses, credit cards, medical records, mortgage, taxes, and warranties, to name a few. Give some thought to other areas of your life that may require their own files.
- Use color coding. For example, mark everything related to taxes with a green tab, everything related to medical records with a blue tab, and so on, so you can spot what you need at a glance. Within each color, place the file folders in alphabetical order.
- Regularly purge your files of materials that are out of date. Every time you take a piece of paper out of a folder, check to see if there's anything else that no longer belongs in there.
- Create a set of 12 "tickler files," one for each month of the year. When something comes in that will need action three months from now, put it in the appropriate file. Include notes to remind you of important future obligations. Once your tickler file system is operating smoothly, you might want to add a "this week" file for everything you'll need to take care of in the coming week.

See also Time Management

P

PETS

CALMING COMPANIONSHIP—
AND MUCH MORE

Sometimes we joke about how we prefer the company of animals to that of our own species. After all, dogs, cats, and other members of the pet set don't nag us about doing our share of the housework, or steal our ideas and present them to the boss as their own, or blare their stereos until 4:18 in the morning.

In exchange for the few things they do ask for—food, shelter, an occasional warm lap—pets give us a lifetime supply of joy, comfort, and unconditional affection. It's no wonder, then, that they can protect us against the ill effects of stress.

In fact, we humans have known about the healing powers of pets for quite a long time. They were "prescribed" as a cure for the mentally ill in late-eighteenth-century England. And in 1919 dogs were assigned as companions for patients at St. Elizabeth's Hospital in Washington, D.C.

These days, pets encourage nursing-home residents to perk up, interact, and take an interest in their surroundings. They've also been found to reduce depression and hostility among prison inmates. In one program that allowed inmates to care for small animals, the number of fights dropped, as did the incidence of suicide.

CREATURE COMFORTS

What is it about pets that enables them to tame our tension so effortlessly? At the most basic level, animals are a distraction, says Alan Beck, D.Sc., director of the center for applied ethology and human-animal interaction at Purdue University in West Lafayette, Indiana. "Anything that holds your attention without challenging you will produce a kind of relaxation response," he explains. This, in turn, can help switch off your body's usual reaction to stress—and the elevated blood pressure, accelerated pulse, and rapid, shallow breathing that go with it.

Interacting with animals can also:

Help you perform under pressure. In a study at the State University of New York at Buffalo, female college students performed a stressful mental task either alone or in the presence of their closest female friends or their dogs. Interestingly, the students exhibited a greater stress response—that is, their blood pressure and heart rates rose more—when they had human company than when they were alone. With their dogs by their sides, the students stayed calm, and they naturally performed the task more slowly and accurately.

The researchers speculate that even a close friend made the women feel that their performances were being critically evaluated. But a dog was a nonevaluative companion who provided support without judgment.

Get your mind off your worries. "When an animal comes over and licks you and wants to play, it's hard to stay totally self-absorbed," says Joel Gavriele-Gold, Ph.D., a psychologist in private practice in New York City. "I try to get some of my very depressed and stressed-out patients interested in pet ownership."

Give you a sense of security. This may seem obvious when Rover is a fanatically loyal 150-pound Rottweiler. But even birds, fish, hamsters, and other small pets have the same effect. "Animals, we believe, are sensitive to their environment," says Dr. Beck. "We learn to associate normal animal behavior with feelings of safety."

Some scientists suggest that our tendency to look on our pets as an early warning system for danger is encoded in our genes. Throughout the animal kingdom, one creature keeps its eyes on another for signs that trouble is brewing. When antelope scatter from the watering hole, for example, giraffes and zebras take note—and take off. So when you come home and find Penelope the Persian napping in her favorite chair, you get a gut-level message that all is well.

Put a leash on loneliness. Loneliness and isolation are proven sources of stress that can increase your risk of disease and shorten your life span. A pet is there for you through thick and thin, 24 hours a day. People—especially older folks—invariably cite companionship as the major dividend of pet ownership.

In a study presented at a conference sponsored by the National Institutes of Health, children between ages 7 and 10 described their relationships with their pets the same way they talked about family members. For these children, animals offered both the companionship of a sibling and the warmth and affection of a grandparent.

Widen your social circle. Human contact helps fend off stress, too. And while you're out walking Fido, it's only natural to meet and chat with others who are similarly engaged.

Studies have shown that people tend to look at you in a friendlier way if you're with an animal, Dr. Beck says. Folks in wheelchairs, for example, receive smiles rather than uncomfortable stares when accompanied by their pets.

Release inhibitions. People who find it hard to express warmth and emotion to family and friends get downright demonstrative with their pets. The same restrained fellow who believes that real men don't express their feelings has no difficulty hugging, playing with, and talking doggy to the family beagle.

Letting go in this manner is critical if you are to find inner peace, say the experts. "Stress is not so much being overcome by feelings as denying them," says Dr. Gavriele-Gold. "If a pet can help you reconnect emotionally, it will relieve some of that stress."

Strengthen relationships. Your family is a vital bulwark against stress—except when it's the center of nerve-jangling conflict. A pet can be the glue that fixes family bonds.

In many marriages a pet provides common ground, says Alan Entin, Ph.D., a psychologist in private practice in Richmond, Virginia. "A couple may experience difficulties in other areas of their relationship. But they can talk about and relate to their pet together," he explains.

ANIMAL PHARM

Spending time around your pet—whether he's furry, feathered, or finned—can help short-circuit the physical effects of stress, too. Research so far has shown that pet ownership can:

Reduce stress-induced symptoms. In one widely cited study people about to undergo oral surgery spent a few minutes watching tropical fish in an aquarium. Measurements of blood pressure, muscle tension, and behavior revealed that these folks were significantly more relaxed both before and during the procedure than folks who did not watch the fish. What's more, the fish watchers were just as calm going into surgery as another group of patients who had been hypnotized to relieve stress.

Keep the doctor away. For most people, a stressful event such as divorce, retirement, or job loss leads to an increase in the number of visits they make to the doctor. But in a study of older patients, Judith M. Siegel, Ph.D., associate dean of the School of Public Health of the University of California, Los Angeles, found that dog owners required much less medical care for stress-related aches and pains than non–dog owners.

Add years to your life. In a classic study conducted by Erika Friedmann, Ph.D., chairperson of Health and Nutrition Sciences at Brooklyn College of the City University in New York, heart patients who owned pets were significantly more likely to be alive a year after they were discharged from the hospital than those who didn't own pets. The presence of a pet gave a bigger boost to the survival rate than having a spouse or friends.

PICKING THE PERFECT PET FOR YOU

Whether you own a German shepherd or a goldfish, a parakeet or a Persian, the therapeutic benefits are surprisingly similar. "We haven't seen any significant difference in blood pressure among dog people, cat people, and bird people," Dr. Beck says. "If the animal is of interest to you, it probably doesn't matter what it looks like."

Needs and tastes vary enormously, however. A pet that doesn't fit your temperament, lifestyle, or living space can contribute to stress rather than relieve it. If you're in the market for an animal companion, keep these guidelines in mind.

Size 'em up. "There are some obvious logistic questions that need to be addressed," Dr. Beck says. "If you live in a studio apartment and are never home, you don't want a St. Bernard."

Test temperament. Cats are a lot more self-reliant than dogs. They don't require walking, and you can leave them alone for a day or two—with adequate food and water, of course. "But you have to be prepared to live with feline independence," Dr. Entin points out. For some people, an aloof Siamese that cuddles only when the mood strikes is a source of frustration.

Look at your lifestyle. A cat that prefers to curl up for a nap in a human lap would be great for a confirmed couch potato—but not for a hiking enthusiast who craves companionship on the trail.

Know your expectations. "Some people demand a closer relationship with a pet than others," Dr. Entin says. If you find it soothing to stroke a warm, furry body, don't buy a parakeet.

Meet your match. Once you've decided on the type of pet that best suits you, you can proceed with the actual selection process a bit more scientifically. Purebred dogs, for example, are predictable in temperament as well as in size and shape. Great Danes are laid-back, gentle giants, while Yorkies are little bundles of energy. A Maltese will follow you from room to room. Labrador retrievers are patient with kids and eager to please but need a lot of exercise.

In the final analysis, though, there's no substitute for instinct and chemistry. "It's like choosing a human partner," says Dr. Beck. "You meet the right one, and you redefine what you're looking for."

See also Relaxation Response

PLAY
FEEL LIKE A KID AGAIN

When was the last time you indulged in some good old-fashioned, unadulterated fun? No, playing hide-and-seek with your shoes every morning doesn't count. Nor does driving ring-around-a-rosy until you find a parking space at the shopping center.

The fact is, most of us packed up our games and playthings sometime in our teens, when we decided that we were too mature for that sort of kid stuff. And it's a shame, really, because the pastimes we now view as child's play are actually a perfect antidote to the hassles and headaches of the grown-up world.

Oh, we may take time out for leisure once in a while. But the activities we choose have little playfulness about them. Think about it: What is your game of choice? Bridge? Tennis? Scrabble? Especially if you're the kind of person who strives for perfection in your pastime, you have to ask yourself: Are you really having fun?

We may say that we're playing, but the true spirit of play is all too often absent. And when an activity involves do-or-die competition, "it becomes useless for stress reduction," says Roger Mannell, Ph.D., professor and chair of recreation and leisure studies at the University of Waterloo in Ontario.

ARE WE HAVING FUN YET?

In real, honest-to-goodness play, the outcome—who wins and who loses—doesn't make much difference. The idea is to have a good time and to genuinely enjoy what you're doing.

Now lots of us might feel a twinge of guilt when we do something just for the fun of it. One word of advice: Don't. We need play for diversion, for relaxation, for release.

And we shouldn't treat pleasurable pastimes as an afterthought, to be squeezed in when we have a few minutes to spare. Regular play sessions are among the best defenses we have against the negative effects of stress.

No Contest?

Competition in games and sports is a good thing—up to a point. "It can boost the pleasure of moving around, of honing your skills, of companionship. But it shouldn't be the primary reason for play," says Roger Mannell, Ph.D., professor and chair of recreation and leisure studies at the University of Waterloo in Ontario. "That's a tough line to walk."

Here are some suggestions to help you get the most from your matchup but still keep things friendly.

Know your motivation. Why are you involved in this activity? If winning is the first thing to come to mind, then you're not playing in a way that has anything to do with stress reduction. You should be participating for enjoyment and recreation.

Choose playmates carefully. The competitive virus is very contagious. If you habitually play with someone for whom winning is the only thing that matters, you're sure to get caught up in the frenzy.

Don't be perfect. It's up to you whether you pursue your activity with rigid perfectionism or in the true spirit of play. Choose the latter, and it won't matter who wins and who loses.

Dr. Mannell points out that play:

Offers escape. "To the extent that you get caught up in an activity, you're distracted from your everyday problems," says Dr. Mannell. "Play creates its own little world."

Tightens ties. When you choose an activity that involves your family and friends, it can strengthen the bonds between you—provided the level of competition isn't too high.

Sharpens skills. Play gives your imagination and creativity a workout. Not only does this divert your attention from your problems, it might also help you come up with some innovative solutions.

FILLING YOUR FUN QUOTA

Most of us are probably a little rusty in the recreation department. Not to worry, says Betsy Smith Higgins, a kindergarten teacher at Abington Friends School in Jenkintown, Pennsylvania: "Adults don't lose their knack for play. They can recapture it." We all have the ability to transform stressful circumstances into belly laughs and whimsical smiles by having a little fun.

A good place to start, Higgins says, is to revive favorite games and hobbies from your childhood. You can also give these strategies a try.

Figure out what's missing. Take an inventory of the sorts of things that your daily activities do and don't provide. Then look for a pastime that can supply the elements that are important to you but that are missing from your daily routine, whether it's physical work, privacy, challenge, communication, or leadership.

Find out what's available. Once you know what you're looking for in an activity, you can get some ideas by checking out course listings at a nearby community college or by watching your newspaper for announcements of club meetings. Or go to your local library and browse through the *Encyclopedia of Associations*, which offers brief descriptions and contact information for hundreds of organizations.

Go back to school. Higgins leads a workshop called Kindergarten for Adults that's a veritable laboratory of grown-up playfulness. Participants bring a favorite pillow or blanket for nap time—as well as something for show-and-tell. They get to choose among a number of activities, including building with blocks, working with clay, gluing and cutting papers, and weaving ribbons.

All of this is open-ended: There's no project to complete or objective to achieve. Whatever happens, happens. The best part: You get to make a mess with fingerpaints.

Remember the reason. The whole point of play is to give your imagination free rein. While the toys and trinkets are fun, they're by no means essential. "Play means being able to stretch what you have," Higgins says. "All you really need is yourself and your thoughts."

In other words, play is a coping mechanism that you can evoke anytime you wish. Suppose you're stuck in traffic. Don't waste

181

FUN STUFF FOR BIG KIDS

You don't need to recruit your grandchildren or the grade-schoolers next door to have an excuse to play. Make your own fun with the following activities, suggested by Betsy Smith Higgins, a kindergarten teacher at Abington Friends School in Jenkintown, Pennsylvania.

- If you want to do something really "kindergarten," there's nothing better than fingerpaints or clay. Just put on old clothes, spread newspaper over the floor, and dig in.
- Pour milk into a dish or large saucer and add food coloring—about three drops each of red, blue, and yellow. Then add a few drops of mild dish detergent. "Something wonderful will happen, and it will keep going for quite a while," Higgins promises. For extra fun, try 2 percent, 1 percent, or skim milk or half-and-half.
- Fill a tall drinking glass with seltzer water, ginger ale, or 7-Up. (Alka-Seltzer will work, as well.) Drop in 5 to 10 raisins and watch what happens.

---

your energy fretting and fuming. Instead, pass the time by creating stories about the other drivers or inventing fanciful limericks about your situation.

See also Hobbies

PROBLEM SOLVING
IF IT'S BROKEN, FIX IT

The easiest way to deal with stress is to simply pretend it doesn't exist. If we go about our business, paying our troubles no mind, they just might go away on their own. Ignorance is bliss, as the saying goes.

There is only one catch: Our minds may push our problems aside, but our bodies don't. They know something is amiss, and they rev up to react with rapid, shallow breathing, quickened pulse, and elevated blood pressure. When we allow our bodies to constantly simmer in this red-alert mode, it can set the stage for some serious health problems.

A much better way to tackle our troubles is to face them head-on. We can do this by practicing what psychologists call problem-solving coping. The name may sound intimidating, but the technique is quite simple: First you identify what needs to be done to resolve a stressful situation in your life, then you take practical steps to make a change, says Timothy R. Elliott, Ph.D., associate professor in the Department of Rehabilitation Medicine at the University of Alabama at Birmingham.

HONESTY IS THE BEST POLICY

Of course, to practice problem solving, you must first admit that you do indeed have a problem. This isn't always easy. But until you accept that something needs changing, you won't make much progress.

Suppose, for example, you feel stuck in a hopelessly stagnant relationship. You need to admit that all is not well, even if only to yourself. We're all tempted to say, "It's okay," "It doesn't really matter," or "Nothing is going to help." But when we do that, we allow the problem to fester. Why not work to bring about a solution instead?

Simply acknowledging that something is amiss can give you relief. Using problem-solving skills to deal with your dilemma will make you feel even better because it:

Puts you in control. "Problem solvers have a sense of mastery of the situation," says Dr. Elliott. "They feel in charge of their emotional lives and have faith in themselves."

Banishes blame. When things don't go according to plan, we too often dwell on finding out why—and who's responsible. Problem solvers don't feel compelled to point fingers. Research has shown that this helps them sail through high-stress situations with less psychological distress, Dr. Elliott says.

183

Defeats depression. Dr. Elliott has observed that people who become paralyzed as the result of injury are able to cope better if their problem-solving skills are strong. "They're less prone to depression because they have greater acceptance of their disability," he explains. "They make plans for themselves and manage to deal with life's problems as they come their way."

Similarly, Dr. Elliot has also found that women who are effective problem solvers are less likely to experience postpartum depression.

RESOLVE TO RELAX

To become a skilled problem solver, all you need is the right frame of mind. These tips will help shape your attitude for calm, objective reasoning.

Keep things in perspective. Recognize a problem for what it is: a situation that needs to be worked through and resolved. It's not a catastrophe, an assault, or a conspiracy against you. "If you see things as extremely difficult and you have a negative view of yourself and your competence, you'll never get to the point of solving problems. You'll just tell yourself, 'Why bother?' " says Dr. Elliott.

Think positive. Stuff happens. That doesn't make you a failure; that makes you human. Welcome problems as challenges, as opportunities for growth and gain, rather than as threats to your well-being. Expect to find a solution, and you will.

Talk to yourself—nicely. What is that little voice inside you saying? If it has a tendency to be critical of you, practice replacing those negative messages with positive ones.

Learn good timing. Don't try to solve a problem when you're stressed out. You'll be far more motivated to simply avoid dealing with it than to work out a truly effective solution. "If you're preoccupied with bad feelings, if you're overaroused and anxious, you can't think clearly," says Dr. Elliott. "A positive mood, on the other hand, facilitates good problem solving."

Calm down. If stress has you in its grip, you can defuse it by practicing any one of a number of relaxation techniques, such as deep breathing, imagery, and meditation. Wait until you've regained your composure, then use your problem-solving skills to address the situation at hand.

LOOK FOR THE ANSWER

Okay. You've settled into problem-solving mode. You're now ready to run your problem through the following four-step process, recommended by Dr. Elliot.

1. Gather information. Define and clarify the problem. You can do this by asking yourself these questions: "What is it that's troubling me? What would I like to see happen? What results am I hoping for?"

2. Consider the alternatives. Generate as many solutions as you can. Think broadly and creatively, and don't worry about what's realistic and what's silly. The idea is to bring to the surface all of the ideas that might be buried in your subconscious.

Give yourself plenty of time to imagine the possibilities. It's also helpful to think about your problem in a variety of settings: at home, at work, on your daily walk. "An important idea for a paper I was writing came into my head while I was jogging," recalls Dr. Elliott.

3. Weigh your options. Here's where you evaluate and judge the solutions you've come up with. Compare one with another. Try to envision the consequences of each alternative—for yourself and for others. Ask yourself, "What is my most important goal?" Then find the alternative that might get you there.

Notice that coming up with solutions and assessing them are two distinct steps. This encourages you to maximize your creativity and prevents you from mentally scuttling an option before you give it full consideration.

4. Follow through. Once you have settled on the solution that you think will work best, implement it and then monitor the results. You can always modify your plan of action if it doesn't seem to be working or if new information becomes available. If you've made a mistake, learn from it. Allow yourself to make changes for the better.

See also Decision Making, Deep Breathing, Imagery, Meditation

PROGRESSIVE MUSCLE RELAXATION
PUT THE SQUEEZE ON STRESS

Your neck and shoulders are so taut with tension that it feels like some Boy Scout was practicing knot tying with your muscles. Naturally, you want relief. But tightening up even more, on purpose, probably isn't what you had in mind to ease your discomfort.

Yet that's exactly what you do when you use a technique called progressive muscle relaxation, or PMR. Developed in the 1920s by Edmund Jacobson, M.D., a Chicago physician, PMR involves tensing and then releasing groups of muscles in succession until your entire body has loosened up.

Since muscle tension is such a common symptom of stress, affecting as many as 90 percent of us, you'd think that deliberately creating more tension would just compound the pain. But PMR works, proponents say, because it actually increases blood flow to the muscles, helping them relax.

FIGHT FIRE WITH FIRE

Muscle tension is a central part of the stress experience, explains Gary Grody, Ph.D., a clinical psychologist in private practice in Lawrence, New York. "It's not a cause but a by-product of stress," he notes. But it might be the first physical reaction we have to anxious thoughts or a pressure situation.

When we become aware that our muscles are stiff and tight, we perceive that we're under stress. This, in turn, escalates the stress response: The muscles contract even more, and the heartbeat increases. Muscle tension also contributes to a host of other stress-related symptoms, including headache, backache, fatigue, and even high blood pressure, Dr. Grody says.

The methodical muscle contraction and relaxation of PMR breaks the stress cycle before it can get the better of you. Once you learn the technique, you can induce a calmer, more tranquil state in minutes. That means you can protect yourself against the other physical problems associated with stress. "If you learn to recognize the early warning signs of stress, before the headache or backache develops, you can go right into PMR and thwart the pain," Dr. Grody points out.

RELIEF FROM HEAD TO TOE

The deep relaxation produced by PMR does indeed appear to bolster our bodies' defenses against stress. Research so far has zeroed in on PMR's ability to:

Deflate high blood pressure. Back in 1938, Dr. Jacobson conducted a study in which he found that people with and without high blood pressure could lower their readings by using PMR. More than 50 years later, Korean researchers got similar results when they had people with high blood pressure practice a combination of PMR and biofeedback: The participants' blood pressure readings declined significantly.

Head off headaches. In a study at the State University of New York at Albany and Albany Medical College, people with chronic headaches learned PMR and then were instructed to practice the technique for 20 to 25 minutes every day. They were also told to use PMR as needed to help them deal with stressful situations. After eight weeks their headaches had become less frequent and less severe, and their use of painkillers had dropped significantly.

Alleviate anxiety. Forty children and adolescents with depression or other psychiatric problems severe enough to require hospitalization participated in a relaxation program that combined PMR, yoga, and massage. The therapy reduced the youngsters' anxiety and anxious behaviors and also lowered their blood levels of cortisol, a hormone that our bodies secrete when we're stressed.

Fortify feelings of well-being. In a study at Florida State University in Tallahassee, runners who practiced PMR daily for eight weeks had greater optimism and less perceived stress than runners who served as controls. Members of the PMR group also reported that the hassles in their lives seemed less frequent and less intense.

WHO SHOULD USE PROGRESSIVE MUSCLE RELAXATION?

With all of the relaxation techniques available, you want to make sure you choose the one that suits you best. According to a Yale University study, the deciding factor should be your comfort level. The more you enjoy a particular technique, the study showed, the more likely it is to work for you. Researchers theorize that you're more apt to faithfully practice an activity if it's something that brings you pleasure.

That said, progressive muscle relaxation (PMR) seems to work especially well for the following populations.

People with type A personalities. PMR caters to these time-oriented, high-pressure folks by offering them quick release. There's no element of introspection or contemplation. You just do it.

"And with PMR, you notice an immediate contrast between tense and relaxed muscles," says Gary Grody, Ph.D., a clinical psychologist in private practice in Lawrence, New York. "It can be very gratifying."

People with physical symptoms of stress. "PMR is a great exercise for folks with problems such as chronic stomach pain and muscle aches," Dr. Grody says. "It means that they always have something they can do to feel better."

People prone to spiraling anxiety. You can use PMR on your own, whenever you need it. That means you can take action at the first sign of discomfort and short-circuit symptoms that can blossom into a full-fledged panic attack. "Sometimes just knowing you're good at PMR will inhibit the stress response," says Dr. Grody.

FLEX SOME MUSCLE

PMR is quite simple to learn. You just sit or lie quietly, then tense and relax each muscle group in turn. You learn to focus on the process and to let other thoughts drift out of your mind.

The sequence outlined below, recommended by Dr. Grody, will take about a half-hour for a beginner to complete. Once you're accustomed to it, you'll be able to move through it much more quickly and easily. Then you can use PMR whenever you like for on-the-spot stress relief.

1. Sit in a comfortable chair or lie down. Close your eyes and think of a pleasant, relaxing image. (If you find it hard to do this, just let your mind fill with something neutral, such as the color white or black.)
2. Breathe deeply, in through your nose and out through your mouth. As you inhale, tighten your muscles. Then exhale with a "whoosh" and let your muscles completely relax. Keep thinking of your relaxing image.
3. Contract and then relax each group of muscles, starting with the muscles in your hands and arms. Feel the tension as you make really tight fists, as if you were showing off your biceps. Hold for several seconds, then release the tension. Let your hands and arms become limp.
4. Press your upper arms hard against your sides. Relax.
5. Lift your shoulders in an exaggerated shrug, tensing your neck and shoulder muscles. Let your shoulders drop.
6. Tighten your forehead muscles by wrinkling your brow. Let it go smooth.
7. Shut your eyes tight. Relax.
8. Open your mouth wide. Relax.
9. Clench your teeth together. Relax.
10. Take a deep, deep breath and tighten your chest. Let it out.
11. Suck in your stomach as hard as you can. Let it out.
12. Continue the sequence as you tense and relax your hips and legs. When you get to your feet, curl your toes down, then up.
13. Sit or lie quietly for a time, feeling the deep relaxation that has spread through all of the muscles of your body.

Q

QUIET

TURN DOWN THE VOLUME OF LIFE

It starts first thing in the morning, with the jarring jingle of the alarm clock. From that moment on, the day just gets louder: Everything from humming hair dryers to honking horns, from beeping computers to blaring stereos assaults our eardrums and sets our nerves on edge.

Noise is a stressor, and like any other stressor, it triggers the body's fight-or-flight response, explains Evelyn Talbott, Ph.D., associate professor of epidemiology at the University of Pittsburgh.

Perhaps the obvious solution is to just eliminate the repulsive racket. But that may be easier said than done. "There's no real silence anymore," says Bruce Davis, Ph.D., adjunct professor of consciousness studies in the Graduate School of Holistic Studies at John F. Kennedy University in Orinda, California, and a psychologist in San Anselmo, California. "Even the national parks are noisy. A lot of people have never experienced true silence."

AUDITORY AGITATION

Sounds don't have to be ear-splitting to set the body's stress response in motion, especially if they're constant, according to Dr. Talbott. As a general guideline, daytime noise levels shouldn't exceed 75 decibels, or about the loudness of a dishwasher or washing machine. The desired nighttime limit is even lower: 55 decibels, or about the equivalent of a quiet conversation in the next room.

Certain types of sounds seem to aggravate us regardless of their

THE ESTROGEN CONNECTION

Studies have shown that people have varying degrees of sensitivity to noise. In particular, women seem less able to tolerate noise than men, especially when it comes to high-frequency sounds. While the gender difference isn't fully understood, it appears to be related to the female hormone estrogen, says Carolyn Dow, Ph.D., associate professor of communications at the University of Evansville in Indiana. Women who are noise-sensitive tend to be more irritated by sounds at times of the menstrual cycle when their estrogen levels are high.

If you are noise-sensitive, it's a good idea to carry earplugs with you wherever you go. Look for the kind that blocks out high-frequency tones but allows you to hear sounds in normal conversational range.

volume. Just the thought of fingernails scraping on a blackboard can send shivers down our spines. And so-called Chinese water torture used sound—the steady dripping of water on a bell—to drive people out of their minds.

But most troublesome are those sounds that we simply can't control. "If you're trying to concentrate and someone is revving a motorbike outside your door, whether it's your kid or the neighbor's kid who's responsible makes a big difference," says Jerome Singer, Ph.D., professor and chair of medical and clinical psychology at the Uniformed Armed Services University of Health Sciences in Bethesda, Maryland. "It's the same noise. But if it's coming from your kid, your belief that you can control it makes it less disturbing, even if you don't actually take steps to do so."

The importance of feeling in control was demonstrated in a study that subjected two groups of people to the exact same noise. Members of one of the groups had buttons that they could press to stop the noise. Even when these folks didn't use their buttons, they performed test tasks significantly better than those who had no way of controlling the noise. "Higher-decibel noise with the button was less bothersome than lower-decibel noise without the button," Dr. Singer says.

Unexpected sounds can also send our stress levels skyward, according to Dr. Singer. "If noise occurs at a regular level, people adapt to it," he notes. "Those who live next to highways don't even hear it after a while."

HEAR NO EVIL

Even if you manage to mentally tune out the sounds around you, the racket of everyday raucousness can still take a tremendous toll. Persistent, excessive, unnerving noise has been linked to a host of health problems ranging from hearing damage to heart disease. Here are some examples.

High blood pressure. Dr. Talbott examined the blood pressure readings of 240 retired men who had labored for 30 years or more in noisy factories that stamped out car bumpers and machine parts. More than half of the men between the ages of 64 and 68 who suffered hearing loss also had high blood pressure. In comparison, less than one-third of the men who didn't have enough noise exposure to damage their hearing had high blood pressure.

Increased anxiety. At the University of Evansville in Indiana, a mystifying situation developed when a class of older students moved to a new room that contained computers for them to work with. "Some of the women started showing severe stress reactions," recalls Carolyn Dow, Ph.D., associate professor of communications at the university. "They had high levels of anxiety or went aggressive on us."

The problem: The computers were making noise. It was not a loud noise but a very high-pitched, unwavering tone with a unique ability to torment.

Poor concentration. Dr. Dow and her colleague Douglas C. Covert, Ph.D., associate professor of mass communication at the University of Evansville, had groups of women take a standard examination in two separate rooms. The women in the room where noise was piped in scored significantly worse than the women who completed the exam in relative quiet.

THE SOUND OF SILENCE

While you can't eliminate noise from your life completely, you can take steps to ensure that you're getting regular doses of peace and quiet. Dr. Davis organizes excursions to European monasteries, where participants learn meditation and revel in the relative silence. But he points out that you needn't do anything so extravagant to find a serene spot in your life.

Your personal retreat could be something as simple as sitting for a half hour in the most remote corner of your local public library. Or taking a walk through snow-muffled woods. Or waking up an hour early, before the rest of the world is stirring, to experience your surroundings while they're fresh and undisturbed.

You can also try these simple strategies for securing more silence in your life.

Take a noise inventory. In order to lower the volume of your life, you first have to figure out where the sounds are coming from. "Most people have no idea how much noise they're living with and how much of it they have control over," says Dr. Davis. Do you turn on the radio or television as soon as you enter a room? Is your refrigerator humming? Is your air conditioner whirring?

Stand up for silence. Speak out to your neighbors if their noise bothers you. Then contact local authorities should your words fall on deaf ears. "Sometimes it doesn't take much more than a few complaints to make things happen," says Dr. Davis. "But if people don't take some control over noise, it will keep getting worse and worse."

Seal out the sound. When you find yourself in a situation where the noise level is out of your hands, you can keep the peace—and protect your hearing—with a pair of foam rubber earplugs. Wearing them will also give you a sense of control over the situation, which is key to stifling the stress response.

Go for an upgrade. Older computers tend to generate a lot of noise, subjecting you to constant whirring and humming while you work. State-of-the-art models are much quieter, making hardly any sound at all.

Insulate. Rubber and cork make great sound barriers. "Putting up a corkboard on a wall that abuts a loud neighbor can make a tremendous difference," Dr. Talbott says.

Seek quieter accommodations. If you find noise virtually intolerable, take it seriously enough to influence your choice of home and job, says Dr. Talbot. If you're considering a change in residence, for example, check out airline flight patterns in the neighborhood where you plan to move. Also find out whether any major construction projects are planned for the immediate area.

READING

MASTERMIND THE GREAT ESCAPE

Peace at last: You have the house all to yourself. It's the perfect time to slip into something comfortable, grab a pillow, and curl up on the couch with a good book.

What will it be? Mystery, romance, sci-fi, or classic? Pick your favorite, and within a few pages you're so engrossed in the plot, so fascinated by the characters that you become oblivious to everything around you.

That's what makes reading such a powerful weapon against stress: It captivates and distracts you, drawing your attention away from the problems and concerns of everyday life. "Reading takes you into another world," explains Edna Bauer, a psychotherapist in private practice in Binghamton, New York. "Why do we read to children at bedtime? To spiral them down, to calm them down. Books can serve the same function for adults as they do for children."

WORDS TO THE WISE

Unlike watching television and other purely passive pursuits, reading sets your mind in motion. It doesn't give you the same blah feeling that you may have experienced after being glued to the tube for an extended period of time. "Our data suggest that reading is much better at reducing stress than watching television," says Roger Mannell, Ph.D., professor and chair of recreation and leisure studies at the University of Waterloo in Ontario.

Here's how reading works its tension-taming magic.

FROM PASTIME TO PASSION

Many of us consider reading a retreat—a way of stepping outside the daily routine to relax and unwind. But some folks are truly passionate about perusal, so much so that it has become what Robert Stebbins, Ph.D., professor of sociology at the University of Calgary in Alberta, calls a serious leisure pursuit.

These bibliophiles invest a lot of time and energy in mastering the works of a good contemporary writer, for example, or exploring the literary world of Shakespeare. Dr. Stebbins says this intense immersion in the written word has a special ability to restore mood, regenerate spirits, and repair the toll of a stress-filled life. It offers the following unique benefits.

Greater self-esteem. Pursuing reading as a hobby gives you a sense of accomplishment. "You're developing your capacity to do something substantial and worthwhile," notes Dr. Stebbins.

Personal enrichment. Developing expertise in a particular area has its own rewards. Just ask the Civil War buff who can tell you what happened in each hour of the Battle of Bull Run, or the armchair meteorologist who has learned to predict the weather by the shape of the clouds. Knowledge makes you feel that you have control over something in your life. That's vital to stress relief.

Connection to others. Joining a book club will introduce you to people who share your interests, giving you a sense of community, says Dr. Stebbins. You can link up with these groups at work, at your place of worship, or by watching your local newspaper for meeting announcements.

Immediate relaxation. Reading is portable, which means you can break out a book whenever and wherever the urge strikes. "The hobbyist can read in a tranquil place in a city park, on a front porch, or at a public library," Dr. Stebbins points out.

Stimulating your brain. "When you read, you do a lot of think-ing," Dr. Mannell notes. "You have to imagine. You have to see things in your mind's eye."

Putting you in charge. Reading gives you the feeling of control that experts say is essential to effective stress reduction. Unlike tele-vision programs, which are usually interrupted by commercials and continue on without you when you have to answer the phone, a book is in your command. You decide how fast or how slow to turn pages. You can even skip whole chapters, if you wish.

Securing your slumber. Stress is responsible for countless sleep-less nights. Some people develop the mind-set that when they can't get their shut-eye, they're just frittering away valuable minutes, says Bauer. These folks lie awake at night, obsessing not only about their problems but also about their inability to snooze. This can set the stage for insomnia.

"These folks see reading as productive behavior," explains Bauer. "They sense that they are not wasting time as they would be if they were tossing and turning." They can stop dwelling on the fact that they can't sleep and instead get wrapped up in their stories. And they just might find themselves lulled into peaceful slumber.

GET YOUR RELIEF IN WRITING

Whether reading can subdue stress and mend your mood has a lot to do with the material you choose to peruse. When browsing your local bookstore or library, you might want to keep these guidelines in mind.

Consider complexity. Some literary works require a lot more concentration and contemplation than others. If you don't have the frame of mind for that kind of intensity, you're not going to get much relaxation from the experience.

"I have every possible kind of reading matter in my house," says Bauer. If you don't, she adds, go out and stock up. Choose material from each of the following categories.

- No-demand reading. Sometimes you may be so preoccu-pied that you're unable to shift your focus or grasp even the simplest plot line. "When I'm exhausted, the only thing I can look at are catalogs," Bauer says. "That's the bottom level."

- Low- to medium-demand reading. Let's say you are feeling a little beat at the end of the day, but you still have some mental energy to spare. Your best bet: brief, entertaining magazine articles.
- Medium- to high-demand reading. In a word, books—fiction and nonfiction, lightweight and heavyweight. Choose whatever tickles your fancy.

Know what to expect. Some books, both fiction and nonfiction, can stimulate your emotions in an unpleasant way. You may find the subject matter upsetting or offensive, particularly if it hits close to home. Or you may become so involved in the lives of well-crafted characters that you experience powerful, pervasive feelings about them and their actions.

The Greek philosopher Aristotle praised tragedy for its ability to arouse pity and terror and to relieve the specter of these powerful emotions. But it may not work for you. You have to decide for yourself whether the subject matter is going to subdue your stress or exacerbate it.

Select for the situation. When and where you're doing your reading should influence your choice of material. "A lot depends on your circumstances," says Bauer. "If you're on vacation, for example, it might feel great to give your emotions a workout. But if a story gets you agitated in the middle of the night, that's not so good."

Don't feel obligated. Forcing yourself to read just because it's supposed to be good for you is no way to relax. "And if you're a compulsive type who has to finish any book you start, no matter how boring you find it, that's hardly calming," says Bauer.

See also Hobbies

RELAXATION RESPONSE
STOP STRESS IN ITS TRACKS

You know the feeling. You're snuggled up on your sofa, completely engrossed in the pages of a murder mystery, when . . . yikes! You feel a tap on your shoulder from behind.

Your spouse's stealthiness triggers a flood of changes in your body. Your blood pressure and heart rate soar. Your breathing becomes rapid and shallow. Your muscles tense. Adrenaline pours into your bloodstream.

These changes make up what is known as the fight-or-flight response. Essentially, it's a chemical reaction that fuels your body so that you can either defend yourself against the "attacker" or run like the wind to flee.

The fight-or-flight response can be a good thing—say, when you're crossing the street and you suddenly find yourself in the path of an oncoming car. It's not so good when it's switched on by more everyday matters that don't require you to fight or flee: family problems, traffic tie-ups, and job pressure, to name a few. Because you're not releasing all that pent-up energy, the stress chemicals just simmer. That means your blood pressure goes up and stays up, and your heart, lungs, and adrenal glands work overtime day in and day out.

What we need is a way to shut down this stress response, so our bodies aren't constantly functioning in crisis mode. That's where the relaxation response can help.

NATURAL R AND R

We know about the relaxation response thanks to the pioneering work of Herbert Benson, M.D., founder and director of the Mind/Body Medical Institute at Deaconess Hospital in Boston. Through his extensive research, he proved that just as the body turns itself on in the face of stress, it can also turn itself off and restore itself to a calm, tranquil state.

199

EXERCISE YOUR RIGHT TO RELAXATION

Physical activities such as running, swimming, walking, and biking may not seem to have much in common with more traditional relaxation techniques. But believe it or not, they, too, can evoke the relaxation response.

Repetitive muscle movements account for the stress-reducing effects of exercise, says Herbert Benson, M.D., founder and director of the Mind/Body Medical Institute at Deaconess Hospital in Boston. He believes that they're also responsible for the so-called runner's high that active people sometimes experience.

It seems that the secret of relaxing exercise is maintaining mental focus while you're going through the paces. In a study conducted by the University of Massachusetts Medical School in Worcester and the Marsh: A Center for Balance in Minnetonka, Minnesota, participants were instructed to walk regularly at either a brisk or a slow pace. The slow walkers who learned to evoke the relaxation response by focusing on their footsteps and disregarding distracting thoughts experienced substantial reductions in anxiety as well as improvements in self-image. Their stress levels dropped as much as those of people who exercised at a faster pace.

To try this for yourself, just add an extra dimension to your regular exercise routine: Pay attention to your steps as you walk or jog or your strokes as you swim. (You can count "one-two" if you wish.) When distracting thoughts enter your mind, let them go. See what happens.

When you elicit the relaxation response, your blood pressure drops, your heart rate slows, your breathing stabilizes, and your muscles loosen up. In other words, you experience physical changes that are the exact opposite of what occurs during the fight-or-flight response.

Dr. Benson and his staff have found that the relaxation response produces more than just deep, soothing relaxation. Over the long term, it may reverse health problems as diverse as insomnia and cancer. "Physically, it can help in any situation that has been caused or made worse by stress," Dr. Benson says.

Thus far, research has shown that regular practice at evoking the relaxation response can:

Pacify pain. People who have chronic pain can cut the number of visits they make to the doctor by more than one-third when they learn to turn on the relaxation response, Dr. Benson says. "The pain may still be there, but they can get on with their lives," he explains. "They're less angry and depressed and more active."

Support sleep. A study of 10 people with chronic insomnia found that the relaxation response—combined with a program designed to make bedtime behavior more sleep-friendly—helped these folks effectively eliminate their problem. Over the course of the study, the average time it took the participants to fall asleep dropped from 1¼ hours to less than 20 minutes. That's a 77 percent improvement.

Lower blood pressure. Research into the effects of the relaxation response on high blood pressure has so far produced mixed results. But a recent meta-analysis (a study that combines data from a number of smaller trials) led to this striking conclusion: The relaxation response can lower blood pressure as effectively as many of the drugs that most doctors prescribe for that purpose.

Minimize menstrual discomfort. The relaxation response alleviates the physical and psychological distress associated with premenstrual syndrome, according to studies conducted at the Mind/Body Medical Institute and elsewhere. Improvement in symptoms averaged a solid 60 percent in women who practiced relaxation techniques for 15 to 20 minutes twice a day.

Ease serious illness. Though controversial, some studies suggest that the relaxation response can actually alter the course of diseases such as cancer and AIDS. Whether or not these findings are supported by further research, there's little question that the regular practice of relaxation techniques helps people cope with the stress of serious illness. It does this, Dr. Benson says, by reducing anxiety and depression, which are often just as intense as the physical symptoms.

201

CALLING FORTH CALM

Dr. Benson and his staff at the Mind/Body Medical Institute teach the relaxation response to more than 7,000 patients every year. It's interesting to note that not everyone evokes the response in exactly the same way. "There are many paths to stress. What's stressful for you may not be for me," Dr. Benson points out. "Likewise, the relaxation technique that works for one person may not work for another."

His research has focused on using meditation to trigger the relaxation response. "But there are scores of techniques that can bring about the same physical changes," he says.

As diverse as these techniques may be, they all seem to share two basic components. "One is the repetition of a word, sound, prayer, phrase, or muscular activity," says Dr. Benson. "The other is the passive disregard of thoughts that come to mind."

Working with these components, Dr. Benson has developed what he calls a generic relaxation program, which is outlined below. It's simple to learn, and it's perfect if yoga doesn't suit you or meditation isn't your thing. Most important, it works: It has helped thousands learn how to really relax.

1. Sit in a comfortable position and close your eyes.
2. Relax your muscles in turn, starting with your face and gradually working down to your feet.
3. Become aware of your breath as it enters and leaves your nose. Each time you exhale, silently say the word "one."
4. When distracting thoughts enter your mind (as they inevitably will), just disregard them and return to "one."
5. Consciously maintain a passive attitude—that is, don't worry whether you're "doing it right" or relaxing deeply enough. Let the process unroll at its own pace.

If you like, you can tailor the exercise to your individual belief system by replacing "one" with a word that's particularly meaningful to you—"peace" or "love," for example. A short prayer or religious phrase will also work perfectly.

That's all there is to it. Practice for 10 to 20 minutes twice a day. (Don't use an alarm, but check the time periodically.)

See also Autogenics, Deep Breathing, Exercise, Imagery, Meditation, Mindfulness, Progressive Muscle Relaxation, Walking, Yoga

RELAXATION TAPES
TUNE IN TO TRANQUILLITY

We all have days when we wish we could be "anywhere but here"—when we'd like to escape the world around us for even just a few minutes of complete, uninterrupted calm. So how about heading for some uncharted Caribbean isle? Or maybe a secluded mountain getaway? You can travel light: All you need are headphones, a recorder, and the relaxation tape of your choice.

Relaxation tapes allow you to get away from it all without ever leaving your home or workplace. They fight stress by separating you from the tension and challenges of day-to-day life, says Emmett Miller, M.D., stress-management consultant and president of Source Cassette Learning Systems in Menlo Park, California.

When you step outside of stressful circumstances, Dr. Miller explains, you stop catastrophizing with self-defeating thoughts of embarrassment and failure. You gain a whole new perspective on things, so you can respond in a more effective, productive way.

RECORDED RELAXATION

Relaxation tapes employ a variety of formats to guide you through these mental mini-vacations. You'll want to check them out and choose the one that best suits your personal preferences. You can purchase the tapes in most music stores and through mail-order sources. Here's a sampling of what's available.

Instructional tapes. If you want to learn a stress-relieving technique such as meditation, imagery, or progressive muscle relaxation, there's nothing like having an expert talk you through it.

TEACH YOURSELF ON TAPE

When you're trying to learn a new relaxation technique on your own, it can be difficult and distracting to follow written instructions. You might find it helpful to turn on your tape recorder and read the lesson into the microphone, suggests Phil Nuernberger, Ph.D., psychologist and president of Mind Resource Technologies and a faculty member at the Himalayan International Institute of Yoga Science and Philosophy in Honesdale, Pennsylvania. Then you'll be able to have a more passive attitude as you listen to your own voice leading you through an exercise.

Be sure to make the tape at a time when you're particularly relaxed, Dr. Nuernberger advises. That way, your voice will provide calm, clear guidance.

Instructional tapes "are quite helpful for learning specific skills," says Phil Nuernberger, Ph.D., psychologist and president of Mind Resource Technologies and a faculty member at the Himalayan International Institute of Yoga Science and Philosophy in Honesdale, Pennsylvania. "They make great adjunct tools."

Nature tapes. You might find it calming to listen to ocean waves washing up on the beach or pine trees rustling in the wind. If you can't actually get to your favorite spot, a tape might be the next best thing. Just tune in to the soothing sounds, breathing deeply and visualizing the scene as if it were real. "You'll eventually learn to relax the same way you learn anything else," says Dr. Miller.

Dual induction tapes. These are designed to overwhelm conscious resistance to an audio message by playing two versions of the message at the same time, one in each ear. The information that you hear is identical, but the presentation varies slightly. The voices are extremely slow and soothing, and they're backed by relaxing music. From time to time, the voices converge and deliver one powerful, clear message that summarizes the entire lesson.

When you listen to two voices at the same time, "it's too much information for the brain to process," says Lloyd Glauberman, Ph.D., a psychologist in New York City who has produced a series of these tapes. "Both the mind and the body shut off." With normal barriers down, the positive suggestions are free to enter your subconscious mind.

Dual induction is a fairly new technique, so more research needs to be done. So far, one study has found that dual induction produces a significant increase in theta waves, the kind of brain activity associated with deep sleep.

Subliminal tapes. You might think you're listening to your favorite classical music, but underneath the lilting melody are scores of hidden messages instructing you to relax. They're spoken so softly and quickly that you're not aware you've heard them. But by the time the tape is over, you notice a sense of calm that you didn't feel before.

Subliminal tapes are extremely controversial. At issue is whether the ear is capable of responding at all to a message that is pitched below the level of hearing. While some research supports the effectiveness of this technique, critics liken it to looking at an object in complete darkness. In fact, an analysis of several subliminal tapes by a researcher at the University of Waterloo in Ontario found that there was nothing on them that resembled a hidden message. "I believe these tapes are a waste of money," says Dr. Nuernberger.

HEARING IS RELIEVING

Once you've found a tape that you're comfortable with, these strategies can help you make the most of your relaxation session.

Go solo. Dr. Miller instructs his clients to listen to a relaxation tape once or twice a day to start. Then, once they internalize what the tape has to teach them, they can wean themselves off it, since they really don't need it anymore. "They may put the tape in a closet, keeping it handy the way you always have a bottle of aspirin on hand," says Dr. Miller. "Then they can reach for it in especially difficult situations."

Live the lesson. While a relaxation tape is great for on-the-spot stress relief, Dr. Miller says that their ultimate goal is to make you

205

see the world a little bit differently. That way, you can avoid becoming agitated in the first place.

"Relaxation is always inside you," Dr. Miller explains. "It's like the stars: They're always there, but in the daytime, the sun obliterates them. Likewise, the distractions of the outside world can make it hard to find relaxation within."

Know the limits. If you do choose to use an instructional tape for a physical relaxation technique such as tai chi or yoga, realize that it can't teach you all the nuances of the movements. Tapes are fine at the start, says Dr. Nuernberger, but past that point they're no substitute for a real live teacher. "A tape can't watch you and give you feedback," he observes.

See also Music

RELIGION

A SUPPORT SYSTEM FOR THE SPIRIT

These days the news can seem like nothing but gloom and doom. But if you look beyond the headlines, you'll often find inspirational stories of courageous individuals who have managed to overcome tremendous personal tragedy. When these folks are asked how they beat the odds, they invariably reply that their faith gave them the strength they needed to survive.

Research has shown that belief in a higher power can indeed be sustaining in times of crisis. It creates a buffer against stress by helping you maintain balance in your life. "It's an anchor, a rock, a fortress, a shelter in a storm," says David Larson, M.D., president of the National Institute for Healthcare Research in Rockville, Maryland.

A solid spiritual foundation makes troubled times easier to bear by reminding you that you are not alone—that someone is watching over you. And it silences that internal "Why me?" refrain that only compounds stress. "It gets you to think about God, then your neighbor, then yourself," says Dr. Larson.

FORTIFIED BY FAITH

People express their religious beliefs in many different ways. Some enjoy fellowship as a member of an established congregation. Others prefer daily sessions of private meditation or prayer. The common thread is a conviction that one has a personal relationship with a higher power. This sense of spiritual connectedness has proven benefits, such as:

Enhanced coping skills. Researchers asked 720 adults how often they attended religious services. These folks were then revisited at two-year intervals and asked about any traumatic events that had occurred in the interim—things such as a death in the family, divorce, relocation, and job loss. They were also tested for signs of psychological distress, such as anxiety and depression.

The people who seldom or never attended religious services experienced significant emotional wear and tear, while the "regulars"— those who attended services once a week or more—remained largely unscathed. "This is a classic example of the stress-buffering effects of religion," notes Dr. Larson.

Improved physical health. Numerous studies have examined the link between religion and health. In one huge analysis of data from 27 separate studies, researchers found a significant correlation between the frequency of participation in religious services and good health. It was so strong, in fact, that the researchers suggested that an absence of such participation "should be regarded as a risk factor for morbidity and mortality."

A longer life span. Spirituality can actually add years to your life. In one study, researchers interviewed elderly men and women who had just been through cardiac surgery about their religious beliefs. Those who reported that they received strength and comfort from religion were three times more likely to be alive six months after their surgery.

A built-in support network. Places of worship are full of people who are willing and able to help fellow members in need, observes Dr. Larson. A congregation provides the same kind of acceptance and empathy that you'd find in a support group or among friends. So you know that should the going get rough, you have somewhere to turn for practical and emotional help.

THE ANSWER TO YOUR PRAYERS

If you are in search of the type of spiritual structure that a church can provide but aren't sure which one to choose, your best bet is to simply explore your options. Talk to clergy and to members of different congregations. Trust your instincts: If you feel comfortable in a particular house of worship, perhaps you've found the right place.

If you already have a religious affiliation, the following tips will help you get the most stress-relieving benefit from your spiritual experience.

Be a regular. Dr. Larson believes that merely espousing a particular religion or belonging to a particular house of worship has fewer positive effects than actually participating in religious services. Make the effort to attend services, and you'll be rewarded.

Give it a chance. "For someone who hasn't done it in a while, going to services can actually be stressful at first," says Dr. Larson. It may take months before you start feeling comfortable and supported.

Say a prayer. There's real comfort in communicating with a higher power. It doesn't matter where, how, or why you pray. In fact, those who are uncomfortable with traditional religious practice may want to try combining a repetitive prayer with a relaxation technique such as meditation.

Don't judge yourself. Be accepting of your motives for pursuing religion. There's nothing hypocritical about seeking divine intervention when your life has been turned upside down. "People often turn to God in their own self-interest," says Dr. Larson. "The spiritual part doesn't need to be there at first. It comes with time."

See also Meditation

S

SELF-TALK
WORDS THAT SPEAK VOLUMES

It's a crisp, sunny autumn afternoon, and you've decided to take your daily constitutional through a nearby park. As you're striding along a wooded trail, you spy a long, skinny something lying directly in your path.

Now one of two things can happen. You can shrug and say, "That's a stick," in which case you'll just brush it aside and continue on your way. Or you can freeze and shriek, "That's a snake!"—in which case adrenaline will flood your body, your heart will race, your muscles will tense, and your blood pressure will skyrocket. In other words, you'll find yourself in the midst of a major stress attack, and all because you convinced yourself of something that isn't necessarily true.

This illustrates a very important point: While we naturally attribute stress to specific situations and events in our lives, what actually makes them stressful is how we perceive them. "Most stress is produced by the way we look at the world, by our attitudes and belief systems," explains Allen Elkin, Ph.D., program director of the Stress Management and Counseling Center in New York City. When our minds turn life's sticks into snakes, our bodies react by preparing to fight or flee those slithery stressors.

But just as negative thoughts can fire up the stress response, positive thoughts can dampen those flames. "If we can change how we think about life and its hassles, to a great extent we can eliminate stress," Dr. Elkin says.

DETECTING DEFEATIST ATTITUDES

Psychologists have identified several patterns of self-talk that can taint your perspective on life and raise your stress level unnecessarily. By recognizing these patterns in your own internal dialogue, you can take steps to change them and adapt a more positive point of view. Do any of the following seem familiar?

Catastrophizing and awfulizing. These terms describe a tendency to blow things way out of proportion—to make mountains out of molehills, so to speak. Let's say you're stuck in traffic. Your self-talk might go something like this: "Oh, no! I'll be stuck here for the next hour. I'm going to be late for that big meeting. The boss will be furious. I'm going to get fired. I'll wind up out on the street."

Can't-stand-it-itis. When you're in an unpleasant situation, you might think, "I just can't take this! This is unbearable!" You can bear it, of course. But your mind persuades your body otherwise, and you end up feeling as though you've been tied in knots.

What-iffing. You can worry about practically anything by stretching your imagination to ponder remote possibilities. An example: You're on an airplane. As your fellow passengers doze peacefully, you hear an odd little sound. "What if it's a loose bolt?" you think to yourself. If you allow your mind to continue along those lines . . . well, you're certainly not going to be getting any sleep.

Should-ing. Not everything in life can go your way. When something happens that's not to your liking, you have two choices: You can accept it and move on, or you can dwell on it and fume that things should be different. When you do the latter, you're turning a preference or a desire into a demand that you already know isn't going to be met. That only creates frustration and anger.

Ego-rating. Judging your self-worth based on your performance or the approval of others is a surefire formula for stress. You slip up, and your inner voice says, "I'm a failure. I'm no good." This kind of self-talk can leave you run-down, discouraged, and feeling worthless.

Black-and-white thinking. Statements that use words such as *always*, *never*, *all*, and *nothing* are overgeneralizations. They distort reality and create a fertile playing field for stress. If your spouse

210

WHAT TO DO WHEN THE SPOTLIGHT IS ON YOU

When you know about a potentially stressful situation in advance, you can plan ahead to shut down any negative self-talk that may try to sabotage your thoughts and actions. That's important if you're one of the millions of people who suffer from a common form of stage fright: the fear of public speaking.

If you want to bring that fear under control, some self-talk before your next presentation can be a big help. All you have to do is give yourself a series of instructions to stay calm and relaxed. "It's a lot like an air traffic controller talking a plane down onto the runway in fog," says Allen Elkin, Ph.D., program director of the Stress Management and Counseling Center in New York City.

Let's say you've been invited to address one of the service organizations in your community. Now the idea of speaking before an audience can give even the most confident, outgoing person the heebie-jeebies. It's the perfect situation for negative self-talk to run amok.

Don't wait until you're completely wired to try to regain your composure. The first sensation of physical tension that you notice is your cue to start positive self-talk.

You might try the following internal dialogue: "I can feel my heart pounding, but I know I'm in control of the situation. I've practiced this talk, and I know it well. I'll just take a deep breath and let it out slowly. I'll concentrate on how the breath feels as it goes all the way down to my belly, then back up and out my nose. I see lots of smiling faces out there. They like me!"

fails to take out the garbage, for example, it's hard to get too upset. But once you start an internal litany—"He never takes out the garbage. In fact, he never does anything around the house"— there's no limit to your righteous anger.

211

WHEN SELDOM IS HEARD A DISCOURAGING WORD

Simply acknowledging the distorted thought patterns that drive your self-talk is important. "But having the insight in itself won't change your feelings, because you don't really believe in it," Dr. Elkin says. You have to actually replace the negative statements with more positive ones. That's an ongoing process.

"You have to keep at it," Dr. Elkin notes. "You're internalizing a new belief system, and it's not going to take the first time out of the gate. You're not just uttering certain words. You're persuading yourself to look at life in a different, healthier way."

The following tips should help banish the internal bad-mouthing and give your self-talk a more supportive, upbeat tone.

Rate your reaction. You can create your own stress scale to ensure that you're in what Dr. Elkin calls stress balance. "Start by rating your emotional response to a given problem on a 10-point scale," he explains. "Then rate the problem itself compared with life's other disasters." As benchmarks, consider that a heart attack might earn a 10, while a broken shoelace might earn a 1.

"Now you have two numbers: one for the stressor and one for your response," Dr. Elkin continues. "How close are they?" Knowing that you're about to throw an 8-point fit for a 4-point problem can often help you cool down.

Argue the point. To change a belief system that supports negative self-talk, you have to learn how to challenge it. "Vigorously dispute thinking errors," Dr. Elkin says. "Ask yourself, 'Is this really true?' "

Rephrase your statement. When you find yourself thinking or saying, "I can't stand this. It's unbearable," give yourself a reality check. Is the situation truly intolerable? Or would it be more precise to say, "This is unpleasant. I wish it were different"?

Shake out the shoulds. The workplace, in particular, provides a lot of fodder for "should-ing": "I should have gotten that raise," "He should have taken responsibility for this," "She should treat me better." Statements like these won't change your situation. They'll only make the anger and disappointment run deeper.

Use the 3-3-3 technique. When you catch yourself catastrophizing, Dr. Elkin prescribes this corrective medicine: "Ask yourself, 'Is this something I'll remember in three months . . . three days . . . three hours?' " Often that simple question will put your problem in perspective.

See also Optimism

SEX

RELAX WITH A LITTLE ROMANCE

A warm embrace. A gentle caress. A tender kiss. Say . . . if this is what you do for relief, then maybe this stress business isn't so bad after all.

Make no mistake: You should try to keep the stress in your life to a minimum. But when the day's events take their toll, a romantic interlude may be just what you need for profound head-to-toe relaxation.

"Sex can be a great stress reliever," agrees Allen Elkin, Ph.D., program director of the Stress Management and Counseling Center in New York City. Maybe that's because making love gives you the opportunity to reconnect with your significant other. Or because it makes the most of the therapeutic power of human contact. Or because, quite simply, it feels good all over.

NOT TONIGHT, DEAR . . .

As wonderful as sex can be for the mind and body, we don't necessarily have an easy time reaping the benefits. It seems that when we're most stressed, we're also least likely to be in the mood. "Loss of desire is the most common sexual problem," says Dr. Elkin, who is a member of both the American Association for Sex Educators, Counselors, and Therapists and the American Academy of Clinical Sexologists. "When you're preoccupied in a worried way, sexual interest diminishes rapidly."

Researchers at the Uniformed Services University of the Health Sciences in Bethesda, Maryland, found that men who were unemployed—an especially high-stress situation—became less sexually aroused by an erotic videotape than men who had less stress in their lives.

Desire isn't the only thing to suffer. Anxiety can also interfere with the ability to function sexually—especially in men. Stress is known to reduce levels of testosterone, the primary male sex hormone. The bedroom damage can range from loss of desire to an inability to maintain an erection.

To complicate things further, a slide in sexual activity can lead to misunderstandings and hurt feelings. "We tend to be conclusion jumpers and mind readers," Dr. Elkin explains. "So when his desire starts to flag, she's thinking, 'He doesn't love me. He doesn't find me attractive anymore. It must be the six pounds I put on.' In reality, he's distracted and anxious about problems at work." This kind of a rift—and the distance and antagonism it creates—is the last thing you need during periods of stress.

TRANQUILLITY FOR TWO

What you need most when life gets a little crazy is to escape and unwind, to calm your body and quiet your mind. Sex offers all this and more. Research has shown that sex can:

Loosen up muscles. Dr. Elkin likens sex to a good sneeze: All of the muscles in your body tighten up and then release, much as they do with progressive muscle relaxation but in a spontaneous, natural way. You can also compare sex with a warm bath or a long walk in that the experience completely discharges physical tension.

Mend the mind. "Sex releases a lot of the pent-up emotions created by stress," says Dr. Elkin. It's also highly diverting. "If you're involved in a sexual fantasy or act, you're not thinking about balancing the family checkbook," says Dr. Elkin. "Sex allows your mind to let go of whatever problems you're facing." Many people have found that they feel less anxious and sleep better after having sex.

Soothe the spirit. Sex involves lots of touching, caressing, and hugging, which is vital to our emotional well-being. Human contact stimulates the body's touch receptors to release chemicals that stymie the stress response and restore calm.

Quell pain. Sex happens to be a good workout, too. And just like a game of tennis or a long walk, it triggers the release of brain chemicals known as endorphins, which are the body's natural pain relievers, says Dr. Elkin. People have reported that sexual activity lessens the pain of tension headaches, arthritis, and even menstrual cramps if these conditions are brought on or aggravated by stress. Scientists theorize that the endorphins are responsible.

Enhance intimacy. In a healthy relationship, sex promotes emotional intimacy. It brings couples closer together and fosters communication. It enables two people to share their deepest thoughts and concerns with each other and thus lighten the load of stress.

MAKING LOVE MAGICAL

Sex can work wonders in relieving stress. Just remember these few simple guidelines.

Speak freely. Many of us find it very difficult to talk openly about our sexual problems, even with those closest to us. But doing so is the key that unlocks the door to passion. Be honest with your partner: "I'm still in love with you. I'm just so worried about work right now that I'm finding it hard to get in the mood." Simple words like these can head off a lot of tension and grief.

Redefine sex. We often think of sex as "the act." In fact, it encompasses a lot more than just intercourse and orgasm. It's the whole experience: the anticipation, the fantasy, the cuddling, the touching.

Touching is especially important. "You can extend the benefits of sexual activity by exploring massage," says Dr. Elkin. "Like sex itself, massage reduces muscle tension and distracts you from your worries. It allows you to relieve stress in a more prolonged, gradual way."

Take it slow. While there's nothing wrong with the occasional quickie, the most relaxing sex takes time. And all too often the very people who have the most to gain from stress-relieving sex are simply too busy to avail themselves of this very natural resource.

"Busy couples sometimes need to make a date for sex," suggests Dr. Elkin. "Spontaneity is great, but it's overrated." You may not be able to schedule a romantic weekend at a country inn. But why not plan an evening for just the two of you, with candlelight and gourmet take-out, the phone off the hook, and the television unplugged?

Learn to love yourself. Sex in a warm, loving, trusting relationship is ideal, but for single people that may not be on the program. To be perfectly candid, that leaves masturbation—something nearly everyone does but most of us feel extremely guilty about. Scientists say we shouldn't: Self-stimulation is "a great idea," Dr. Elkin says.

And it's not just for single people needing stress release but also for partners with mismatched sex drives. Dr. Elkin points out that when the partner with a greater need for sex can find release in masturbation, it takes pressure off the relationship.

See also Intimacy, Massage, Touch

SMILING

PUT ON A HAPPY FACE

Come on, you can do it. Flex those facial muscles. Just slide the corners of your mouth back toward your ears. That's it. Now let's see those pearly whites. Beautiful.

Don't you feel better already?

Nothing works like a smile to foil bad feelings and brighten a blue mood. And you shouldn't wait for a good joke or a joyous occasion to break out a big grin. Just as smiling reflects your inner happiness, it can actually bring about a more positive, optimistic outlook. That's right: Wear a smile more often, and you'll find it a whole lot easier to look on the bright side of life.

"If you can get people to smile, they report feeling happier," says James Laird, Ph.D., professor and chairman of psychology at Clark University in Worcester, Massachusetts. And his research of the past three decades bears out this conclusion. Dr. Laird has shown that there's a powerful link between facial expression and emotion. In his studies, people who were instructed to look a certain way—say, happy, angry, or scared—reported increases in the corresponding emotion. Adopt a smile, and you're more likely to adopt a good mood.

To Temper Tension, Show Some Teeth

Funny thing about smiling, though: It seems we need it the most just when we feel like doing it the least. Just remember that mustering a grin can make managing stress a whole lot easier by:

Bolstering bonds. In the words of comedian Victor Borge, a smile is "the shortest distance between two people." It communicates affection and goodwill, which in turn help melt away the negative feelings associated with stress.

Summoning sunny thoughts. A smile evokes positive memories just as a scowl evokes negative ones. "You have an easier time recalling material that's consistent with your facial expression," says Dr. Laird.

In a study he conducted, students were asked to read either a short story by Woody Allen or an angry editorial about corruption in Congress. Those who read the funny story could remember it better later on if they were smiling. Likewise, wearing angry expressions enabled the students who read the editorial to recall it in more detail.

Pumping up positive thinking. Participants in another study were asked to share personal memories triggered by common words such as *car* and *tree.* They tended to relate pleasant experiences—a kiss at the drive-in, for example—while smiling. On the other hand, they were more likely to recall unpleasant car-related episodes—say, an epic traffic jam—while frowning.

Bring the Grin In

Everyone knows how to smile. Many of us simply don't do it often enough. To make the most of this most natural of de-stressors, you can give these tips a try.

Set it, then forget it. Smiling seems to produce its most positive effects when it's automatic. This may take some getting used to—it may even feel forced at first. After a while, though, it becomes completely natural. In fact, most people forget that they started out by deliberately planting smiles on their faces. "They experience smiling as true happiness," Dr. Laird says.

Make your grin a real eye-opener. "The most critical part of a smile is the look in your eyes," says Christian Hageseth III, M.D., a psychiatrist in Fort Collins, Colorado, who writes and lectures on

217

humor. "The mouth is a liar. If your mouth smiles but your eyes don't, you seem insincere."

If you're trying to communicate warmth, support, and empathy, Dr. Hageseth suggests, "smile with your eyes, and your mouth will follow." It's hard to pin down just what creates that special twinkle, but it seems to involve the wrinkling of the little muscles around the eyes.

Check your mirror image. To work on your "eye-smile," take a good look in a mirror the next time you're feeling genuinely merry. Note the way it feels around your eyes, then try to reproduce that sensation—as well as the good vibrations that go with it.

Monitor your mood. Not everyone reacts in precisely the same way to smiling, Dr. Laird says. Some people report that it has a strong influence over their emotions, while others don't seem affected at all. You'll have to test the waters to see whether it changes your mood. To do that, Dr. Laird suggests that you simply "smile as naturally as you normally do . . . then don't think about it."

See also Humor

STRETCHING
LIMBER UP TO UNDO TENSION

Few things make us feel as good as a nice, long stretch. It wakes us up in the morning and primes our bodies for the day ahead. It soothes the stiffness that accompanies long periods of sitting or standing. And it dusts off the mental cobwebs that are often produced by pressure, boredom, or the blues.

Perhaps most important, stretching offers a fast-working antidote to stress by ridding our bodies of pent-up tension. Our muscles naturally contract when we're distressed as part of the so-called fight-or-flight response. Being sedentary—because you're desk-bound, for example—only makes matters worse. The result: tight, tired muscles that store tension. "When your muscles contract and stay that way, your brain senses the discomfort," says

Charles Carlson, Ph.D., associate professor of psychology at the University of Kentucky in Lexington.

"Stretching reduces that tension," Dr. Carlson adds. "It produces a natural *ahhh*, which is what your body should really feel like." Also, it helps you avoid injury—a stressor in itself—by keeping your muscles and joints limber and loose.

DOING WHAT COMES NATURALLY

The act of stretching is very much instinctive. Even dogs and cats seem to understand how good it feels: Is there any Fido or Fluffy who doesn't conclude his nap by raising his rump, extending his front paws, and giving his body an all-over stretch?

Perhaps because stretching is so intuitive, so automatic, it hasn't received a whole lot of attention as a stress-relief tool. The research that has been done suggests that it is quite effective at relieving the general tension and pain associated with muscle tightness.

On a physical level, stretching teaches your muscles how to relax. "It's well-known that if you gently stretch and then release a muscle, it will slacken," says Dr. Carlson. What's more, after it has been stretched, a muscle is less likely to tense up for some time afterward. "It takes more sensory input (namely, stress) to make the muscle contract again," he notes.

Based on these principles, Dr. Carlson developed a program that he calls stretch-based relaxation. Originally conceived for people with too much pain to practice progressive muscle relaxation (PMR), stretch-based relaxation has become a de-stressing technique in its own right. Whereas PMR teaches you to systematically tense each muscle group in your body, "stretch-based relaxation focuses on stretching muscles," says Dr. Carlson.

EXTENDING WITH EASE

The complete program of stretch-based relaxation works all of the muscles in your body, from the tips of your toes to the top of your head. You begin with your lower legs, then move on to your upper legs, stomach, chest, forehead, eyes, jaw, neck, and lower and upper arms. "The hands, arms, and head are usually the hardest to relax," says Dr. Carlson. "So stretch-based relaxation starts with the muscles of the lower body to give people confidence."

The program is not only simple to learn but also proven to work. In one study people with moderate levels of muscle tightness or anxiety who did stretching had less tension in their jaw muscles than people who did PMR. The stretchers also reported feeling less anxious.

In another study 34 people with pain related to temporo-mandibular disorder (a condition that produces stiffness and pain in the jaw and temples) were asked to perform mental arithmetic—a task often used to induce stress in experiments. Some of the participants then practiced stretch-based relaxation, while others rested quietly. The stretchers showed less jaw tension and a quicker recovery from stress than the relaxers.

REACHING FOR RELIEF

The next time you're feeling tense, you might want to try the following stretching sequence designed by Dr. Carlson. When you've completed each step, pause for 60 seconds before moving on to the next one.

1. Push up your eyebrows with your index fingers and push down your cheeks with your thumbs. Hold for 10 seconds. Note the feeling of tension around your eyes. Release and feel your muscles relax.

2. Let your head drop toward your left shoulder and hold for 10 seconds. Do the same on your right side. Note any tension in your muscles as they stretch. Bring your head upright, releasing the tension.

3. Lace your fingers together and raise your arms over your head. Let them fall backward until you feel resistance. Hold for 10 seconds. Unlace your fingers and let your arms drop to your sides. Feel your muscles relax.

4. Press your palms together in front of your body at chest height, then lower them slowly until you feel resistance. Hold for 10 seconds. Let your hands drop to your sides and feel your muscles relax.

SUPPORT GROUPS
THERE'S STRENGTH IN NUMBERS

Sometimes a perfect stranger makes the perfect confidant. You can always count on your family and friends to nurture you emotionally and provide a network of comfort and compassion. But when you face a personal crisis—divorce, job loss, illness, or death in the family—the people closest to you, while they mean well, may not truly understand your anxiety, anguish, or anger.

You can try to tough it out or go it alone. But oftentimes this just compounds your stress. A better option may be to join a support group. Yes, you'll be amid total strangers. But these folks know what you're going through because they're in the exact same boat.

Support groups—also known as self-help groups or mutual-aid groups—are strong allies in the battle against stress, says Leslie Borck Jameson, Ph.D., clinical psychologist and associate director of the New York City Self-Help Center. They're effective, Dr. Jameson explains, because they foster the three key factors shown in repeated studies to reduce the impact of stress: social support, self-esteem, and coping skills.

SOUL SURVIVORS

A typical support group consists of ordinary people who meet regularly to talk about a mutual problem. Sometimes the group has a professional leader—a psychologist or a social worker, for example—but the goal isn't to provide therapy. Typically, no fee is charged, although you may be asked to make a small contribution to help pay for the meeting space.

The structure of the meetings can vary from one support group to the next. Some groups address a specific topic at each meeting, perhaps with a guest speaker and open discussion afterward. Other groups are less structured, with members bringing up whatever issues they find most pressing.

One characteristic that all support groups have in common: "They enhance your social support system the second you walk

221

into a meeting, even before you open your mouth," Dr. Jameson says. And this stabilizing, sustaining connection lasts well beyond the hour or two each week that you're all sitting in the same room together. "A lot goes on outside the meetings," Dr. Jameson notes. "People spend a good amount of time on the phone with each other. That's a unique aspect of mutual support."

And while you may join a support group because you need help, one of the benefits is that you end up helping others. "A support group gives regular people the opportunity to do something really special," says Dr. Jameson.

Let's say a woman who has had three miscarriages joins a support group to deal with her grief. Several months later, another woman who has had a similar experience joins the group. The "veteran" now has the knowledge and skills to offer comfort and guidance to the new member. "It's an incredible boost to self-esteem," Dr. Jameson notes.

THE BENEFITS OF BELONGING

A support group bolsters your ability to cope with a difficult situation in a way that no other antistress strategy does. You get the benefit of other people's real-world knowledge and experience in a caring, communal framework. What's more, your fellow group members are proof positive that no matter how you're feeling now, you can make it through your crisis.

The benefits of support groups aren't just theoretical. "There's infinite documentation that these groups can improve health and reduce stress," Dr. Jameson says. They do this by:

Reminding you that you're not alone. It's normal to feel abandoned and isolated in troubled times. A support group lets you know that there are lots of other folks who are in the same shoes as you and hurting just as much.

"In groups for widows, for example, a member may describe how she always seems to hear the car drive up or the front door open at just the time her husband used to get home from work. She may feel as though she's losing her mind," Dr. Jameson says. "But then other widows tell her that the same things happen to them, too. She'll realize that it's a quite common experience."

Restoring your self-image. In a study of recently widowed people, those who joined support groups demonstrated improved self-esteem and well-being over the course of a year. Those who didn't, on the other hand, experienced declines in their psychological health.

Offering practical advice. Support groups provide a unique forum for networking. Here's an example: One group member related how she was told by an architect that her house would require $40,000 worth of reconstruction to be accessible to her husband, who had a stroke. Another group member chimed in, "Let me tell you what I did"—and she proceeded to explain how she managed to get similar renovations done for one-fifth the cost.

Improving the symptoms of mental illness. It used to be thought that people with serious, chronic mental illness such as schizophrenia or manic-depressive disorder couldn't work together in a group setting. But research has shown that those who enroll in support groups after leaving the hospital are half as likely to be readmitted in the 10 months after they're discharged. They also are more likely to remain on the medications that keep them well.

Helping you to cope with illness. Perhaps the most widely cited example of the therapeutic power of support groups is the Arthritis Self-Help Course, a six-week program sponsored by the Arthritis Foundation and available throughout the United States. In one survey participants in the program reported 15 to 20 percent reductions in their pain. They led more active lives than people with arthritis who didn't enroll in the program. And they required less medical intervention—in fact, members of one group cut by half their number of doctor visits.

Other research has produced similar findings. For example, a study of people with severe emphysema and asthma found that those who joined support groups were less likely to be hospitalized than those who didn't. When people were admitted to hospitals, the support group members had stays that were less than one-fifth as long as those of nonmembers.

Another study of 86 women with advanced metastatic breast cancer found that support group members were less depressed and anxious than nonmembers. And they lived longer, too—18 months longer, on average.

BEFORE YOU SIGN ON

Whatever problem you're facing, you're almost certain to find a support group that you can join. "The range of these groups is amazing," Dr. Jameson says. "Every health situation recognized by the World Health Organization has a support group. There are also groups for bereavement, for victims of domestic violence, for every parenting situation, for anything requiring behavioral change—you name it."

To help you get the most benefit from your support group experience, you might want to keep these tips in mind.

Shop around. Not all groups are right for all comers. "We encourage people to try different groups to find the one that they feel will be most comfortable and useful," Dr. Jameson says.

Go to the source. The best single source of information on support groups is a self-help clearinghouse. These organizations, which are found throughout the country, keep exhaustive lists of all of the groups in a particular city or region.

In fact, there's even a clearinghouse that maintains lists of regional clearinghouses. It's called (appropriately enough) the Self-Help Clearinghouse, and it's a smart first step toward finding a group that will meet your needs. Call there at 1-800-777-5556.

Ask the experts. If you have a chronic illness, you can also get information about support groups by contacting the local chapter of the association or foundation that deals with your medical condition. Check the Health and Human Services listings in your phone book.

Don't delay. Most people turn to support groups in the midst of personal crisis. But don't feel you have to wait for a major upheaval in your life to join up. You can seek out a group whenever you feel the need for support, says Dr. Jameson.

Stay as long as you like. There's no time limit on being a member of a support group. Most groups are open-ended, and people stay in as long as they feel they can benefit.

"A lot of people attend a couple of meetings, get what they want, and leave," says Dr. Jameson. Other folks make the support group a part of their lives for years.

See also 12-Step Groups

T

TAI CHI

AN ANCIENT SOLUTION FOR MODERN-DAY STRESS

Your schedule demands that you go, go, go. But your body keeps begging you: "slow, slow, slow." It's kind of like speeding along the interstate with your gas gauge hovering around empty. How far do you think you can get before you replenish your energy supply?

You can put the breaks on your hectic pace and refill your body's fuel tank with regular practice of tai chi. This centuries-old Chinese discipline is actually a martial art. But it's quite different from the styles that we're most familiar with, such as karate and tae kwon do.

Tai chi is more like a combination of pantomime and ballet. Its fluid, graceful movements—bending arms, lifting legs, turning—are performed slowly and silently in what some have described as a moving meditation.

LOOKING EAST FOR RELIEF

Tai chi reduces stress by giving you a gentle but invigorating workout that triggers the release of endorphins, natural feel-good chemicals produced by the brain. Practitioners say that it also helps release energy that may be blocked by other negative forces in your body.

Blocked energy? To understand what that means, you need to know a little bit about the Eastern philosophy on which tai chi is based. It teaches that life force, or *chi*, flows through a series of pathways, or meridians, in the human body. "Stress comes from a blockage of chi," explains Robert Sohn, Ph.D., chairman of the board of the New Center College for Wholistic Health Education and Research in Syosset, New York, and author of *Tao and Tai Chi Kung*. Tai chi allows this life force to once again flow freely, because it requires you to keep your head and spine aligned as you move smoothly through a series of positions.

As in meditation, tai chi draws your attention to a single point. The difference is that instead of concentrating on a word or thought, you focus on your center of movement and balance, says Margaret Matsumoto, who teaches at the School of Tai Chi Chuan in New York City. It's this focusing that helps fend off stress. So as you do the movements of tai chi, "your mind becomes less cluttered with obsessive concerns and random distracting thoughts, such as money worries," Matsumoto explains.

CHOREOGRAPHED CALM

Tai chi fits naturally in our day-to-day lives, adds Matsumoto. "Instead of experiencing calm just when sitting down, you practice being in that state while on your feet and in motion, which is how we spend most of our time." Regular practice of this martial art also:

Keeps anxiety at bay. In an Australian study 96 students of tai chi completed difficult arithmetic tasks and watched a stressful film, then spent an hour practicing tai chi, walking briskly, meditating, or reading. Those who did tai chi recovered from stress-related anxiety as rapidly as those who walked or meditated and more quickly than those who read. The tai chi group received a cardiovascular bonus, too: The heart rates and blood pressure readings of the folks in this group were comparable to those of the walkers.

Promotes proper breathing. The motions of tai chi relax your abdomen, allowing your internal organs to drop down. This gives your diaphragm room to expand and leads to the kind of breathing that best aids relaxation, Dr. Sohn says.

The posture, breathing, and movements of tai chi combine to improve circulation and ship more oxygen throughout your body,

TOP-NOTCH TRAINING

To learn all of the intricacies of the movements of tai chi and to make sure you maintain proper body position at all times, you might want to sign up for a class. To locate one in your area, check with your local YMCA. Or inquire at a school of karate or kung fu; the instructor may know of someone local who teaches tai chi.

Before making a commitment, ask to sit in on a class or two to observe what's going on. And check out the instructor's credentials: He should have at least 10 years' experience in teaching tai chi.

Dr. Sohn adds. This leaves you feeling refreshed and heightens your alertness.

Maintains maneuverability. Those who practice tai chi report decreased tension in their lower backs and improved flexibility in their joints, according to Dr. Sohn.

Boosts immunity. Research has identified a link between tai chi and the body's disease-fighting ability. Participants in one study showed a 13 percent increase in the number of T-cell lymphocytes—the infection-fighting warriors of the immune system—20 minutes after a tai chi session.

Improves balance. Practicing tai chi can help senior citizens avoid debilitating falls. In one study 30 people with balance problems attended a tai chi class once a week for eight weeks. Those who completed this training showed, on average, a 10 percent improvement in their balance skills.

In the long run tai chi can make the difference between being able to get around unaided and needing support to walk as you get older. And keeping your balance becomes all the more important when you consider that 10 to 20 percent of women who fall and break their hips will die within the next year.

MASTERING THE MOTIONS

If you'd like to give tai chi a try, keep in mind that there are several different styles to choose from. Each style has its own distinct pattern of movements, called a form, that leads you through a series of postures, says William Phillips, president of the Patience Tai Chi Association in Brooklyn, New York. The rather fanciful-sounding names of these forms—Grasp the Sparrow's Tail, White Crane Spreads Its Wings—actually describe the motions involved.

One form in particular, called Reeling of Silk, conveys the fundamental flow of tai chi, says Dr. Sohn. "The name refers to slowly reeling silk from a cocoon. If there's the slightest jerk, the thread breaks," he explains. "Likewise, tai chi requires that the joints never lock, so energy flows continually."

You can get a taste of tai chi by trying the basic posture.

1. Sit or stand in an upright, but not stiff, position. Allow your lower abdomen to relax and expand.
2. Lower your shoulders and let your chest drop.
3. Keep your lower back straight and hold your neck in alignment. Make sure your body remains in a straight line.

That's all there is to it. "I've seen dramatic transformations in stress just by holding this posture," Dr. Sohn notes.

Tai chi instructors usually advise their students to practice twice a day, preferably morning and evening. In time, says Dr. Sohn, these slow, gentle movements will feel completely natural, and they'll carry over to your daily routine.

TIME MANAGEMENT
IT PAYS TO PLAN AHEAD

Among unhealthy habits that can fan the flames of stress, hurrying ranks right up there with worrying. Few things can get the old adrenaline flowing like the feeling that we have far too many things to do and way too little time to do them.

There's no question that time is our most precious commodity. Everybody gets the same amount: 24 hours in a day, seven days in a week. We can't beg, borrow, or steal any extra—not even a measly second. So instead, we tend to take on too many tasks, knowing full well we can't accomplish them all but determined to try just the same. Talk about a surefire formula for stress!

It would be a lot less stressful, and a lot more healthful, if we learned how to make the most of the time we do have—to use our hours, days, and weeks more efficiently. "Time management reduces stress not only by helping us get done what we need to but also by thwarting 'deadline paralysis,'" says Ronni Eisenberg, time-management consultant and co-author of *Organize Yourself*. "It gives us the all-important sense of control that is perhaps the most powerful antidote to stress."

PUTTING YOUR DUCKS IN A ROW

Many of us go through our days reacting to events. We wait until something happens, and then we try to fix it. We're like that little Dutch boy who sticks his finger in the dike. Except we can only stop so many of life's "leaks" this way. Eventually, we run out of fingers, or a leak develops that's simply too big for us to plug up.

A better plan of action is to shore up the dike so that it won't spring leaks in the first place. In time management terms, this means taking charge of how you spend your days. The following tips can help you do just that.

Know what's important. Your first step in taking charge is to decide what you most want to do with your time, so you can function in a proactive rather than a reactive way. Once you've done that, you can plan your day accordingly. "The key to using time to your advantage is to become aware of your priorities," says Eisenberg.

Get it on paper. Writing down what you want to do helps you see where you're headed and where you're supposed to be, says Eisenberg. Just don't make the mistake of jotting down lots of lists on lots of tiny scraps of paper. Keeping track of all those bits and pieces just becomes something else to worry about.

Make the Most of Every Minute

The human body has its own internal clock. It doesn't tick, nor does it have an alarm. But you can tell time by it—if you pay very close attention to how you're feeling.

This clock causes the body's systems and functions to ebb and flow throughout the day. As they fluctuate, so do your energy level, alertness, and strength.

"By being in touch with your body's natural rhythms, you can make much more productive use of your time," says Lynne Lamberg, a medical journalist and author of *Bodyrhythms*. She recommends scheduling high-demand activities for the times during the day when you'll do them best. For example:

Do the tough stuff in the early morning. Eighty percent of us are most alert and best able to think, organize, and plan in the A.M. That's why early morning is the right time to go about your toughest projects.

Don your thinking cap in late morning. Your short-term memory and your reasoning power peak around 11:00 A.M., which makes this a good time to schedule a meeting. Complex decision making, on the other hand, is strongest around noon.

Get creative in the early afternoon. Studies have shown

Instead, create a master notebook—a bound school notebook works well. Then use that to keep track of everything that you need to do.

Think big. To organize your list, ask yourself a few questions: What do you want to accomplish in the long run? Where do you want to be 5 or 10 years from now? "Fantasize about all your goals, both major and minor," says Cliff Mangan, Ph.D., former senior staff coordinator of counseling services at Temple University Counseling Service in Philadelphia. Then set intermediate that we do most of our daydreaming around 2:00 P.M. So while this isn't a great time for tasks that require vigilance, it's ideal for creative activities such as writing a letter or poetry.

Take a break in mid-afternoon. The so-called postlunch dip occurs around 3:00 P.M., when most of your bodily functions hit their low point. Don't schedule demanding tasks or meetings for this period. Return phone calls or run errands, or do routine tasks such as typing and filing.

While the rest of your body is in low gear, your long-term memory is shifting into overdrive. So you might want to use this time to bone up on new computer procedures or to study for that foreign language course you're taking.

Head for the gym before dinner. Your energy picks up at 5:00 P.M. That's when your reflexes are fastest and your coordination is best—so the time is just right for exercise.

There's also an evening peak in alertness, Lamberg observes. "Take advantage of it by doing household activities that require some concentration, such as balancing your checkbook," she advises.

and short-term goals that you can focus on now.

Let's say you want to redecorate your home. That's a long-term goal. Your intermediate goal might be to hang new curtains in your living room. Your short-term goal: going to a department store and selecting the curtains. Notice how much more doable that seems compared with refurbishing your entire house.

Get it over with. Plan to do important, self-contained tasks early in the day—especially things that you dread, such as paying bills or balancing your checkbook. Getting the unpleasantries out of the way alleviates the stress of anticipating them all day long. Plus, you'll get a feeling of accomplishment and satisfaction that will motivate you to take on your other to-do's.

There's another advantage to being an early bird. "Your brain is most receptive at two times of the day: as soon as you wake up and right before you go to sleep," says Dr. Mangan. He suggests making the most of the first and last 20 minutes that you're awake to get organized.

Leave room for error. One of the most common scheduling mistakes is not leaving enough time for interruptions. When you block out your day, Eisenberg urges, plan for only 75 percent of the available time.

Also, most of us tend to underestimate how long it will take us to accomplish a given task. Allow a little breathing room: It's a lot more realistic to overestimate rather than underestimate how much time you need.

Allow yourself some free time. We all need to leave a few blank spaces in our calendars. "Downtime can be very uplifting," says Dr. Mangan. "If you don't give yourself a few minutes to simply relax, you'll be tense, irritable, and anxious, which is bound to affect others. In that respect, I don't think it's selfish to be selfish."

MAKING UP FOR LOST TIME

Yes, you only have so many minutes in your day. But chances are you can free up a few of those minutes here and there and put them toward your high-priority tasks. It all comes down to knowing how to use your time wisely.

Keep track. How often do you say to yourself, "Where has the day gone?" Many of us really don't know how we spend our time. That's why it's a good idea to keep a diary for a week or two. "It can be very revealing," says Dr. Mangan. "You may not realize how much time you spend chatting with your neighbors or co-workers over coffee until you log it in."

Dr. Mangan suggests that you document your days in 15- or 30-

minute increments. Write down how much time you spend on various activities, including eating, sleeping, and getting dressed; cooking, grocery shopping, and household chores; and shuttling the kids around and other family obligations. Don't forget social and leisure activities as well as job-related tasks.

A diary is best for this kind of tracking, Dr. Mangan says. That way, you can carry it with you and write in it throughout the day, rather than waiting until day's end and then trying to recall everything you've done. "Pencil and paper are important tools in time management and, therefore, in stress management as well," Dr. Mangan observes.

Don't be disturbed. Let your answering machine pick up your telephone calls when you're in the midst of a project. Or tell a friend who tends to drop in for coffee every day at 11:00 A.M. that mornings are your work time. Then choose a time for these get-togethers that better suits your schedule.

Pass it on. Delegate to others those tasks that you absolutely can't do, that you don't want to do, or that they can do better. This is standard advice for business executives, but it applies equally well at home, Eisenberg says. "Bartering is a great solution," she adds. For example, if you have a teenager who's asking for a free ride to the mall, agree to the trip in exchange for some help cleaning the attic.

Aim for efficiency. There are lots of other ways that you can save time. The following suggestions may seem like no big deal. But in the long run, they'll reward you with lots of found hours.

- Lay out your clothes the night before. If your outfit is color-coordinated, pressed, and ready to wear, you'll be less apt to waste precious time rummaging for a clean shirt or the right belt in the morning.
- Shop by mail. It saves time—and it may save money, too.
- Stock up. Buy staple items in bulk to avoid repeated trips to the grocery store.
- Purchase Christmas and birthday presents anytime. See a good sale? Go for it!
- Put things away so that you always know where to find them.

DON'T PUT OFF UNTIL TOMORROW...

Among the biggest roadblocks to effective time management is procrastination. This habit does provide short-term relief from the tension of doing something that's difficult or unpleasant. But in the long term, it leads to even greater stress. When you finally get started on the task at hand, you have to rush to get it done.

Sometimes it makes sense to postpone a decision while you gather information or to delay starting a big project until you've cleared the decks for full concentration. But procrastination can easily become a habit that takes a needless toll on your efficiency and self-confidence. Here's what you can do to prevent the urge to put off.

Find the source. To overcome procrastination, you have to understand where it's coming from, says William J. Knaus, Ed.D., adjunct professor of psychology at Springfield College and American International College, both in Springfield, Massachusetts, and co-author of *Overcoming Procrastination*. He explains that it often has more to do with your perspective of the task rather than the difficulty of the task itself. For example, if you tell yourself "Writing reports makes me miserable—I can't stand doing it," you probably won't be able to start until you have no choice.

Don't expect perfection. Feeling that you have to do something flawlessly makes it that much harder to get started. When you're in the grip of perfectionism, "I'd like to do a good job on that report" becomes "I have to do a great job. If I don't, I'll be a failure." Who wouldn't wilt when faced with that kind of self-imposed pressure?

Just do it. A related symptom of procrastination is what Dr. Knaus calls the emotional resistance trap. This is the belief that you must wait until you feel right in order to do something—especially something important. You have to be in the mood. You have to be up for it.

Yes, it's great to feel inspired, at ease, and absolutely pumped up to start your novel, clean your boots, or shop for a new computer. But you may end up waiting a very long time for that to happen. "Usually, your feelings are a by-product of what you're doing, not a staging ground," says Dr. Knaus. In other words, just get started, and inspiration is likely to come of its own accord.

See also Organization

TOUCH

THE TACTILE TENSION TAMER

You probably remember the television commercial a few years back that urged people to "reach out and touch someone." It traded on a desire that every one of us has: to feel connected to family, to friends, to the world around us. We rely on such bonds for solace, stability, and strength when our lives are turned topsy-turvy by stressful situations.

We should take the ad's message seriously—not only by picking up the phone and dialing, but by literally reaching out and touching those we care about. The fact is, there's nothing quite like physical contact—an arm around the shoulders, a pat on the back, a genuine bear hug—to relax us and remind us that no matter what we're going through, we are not alone.

"You experience a physical reaction when someone touches you with affection," says Tiffany Field, Ph.D., professor of pediatrics, psychology, and psychiatry and founder and director of the Touch Research Institute, both at the University of Miami School of Medicine. Special touch receptors all over your body trigger the release of stress-relieving chemicals that slow down your internal functions and calm you.

GIVING STRESS RELIEF A HAND

Touch elicits a host of antistress messages, such as the comfort of the familiar, the presence of a bond, and simple brotherhood, explains Judith Hall, Ph.D., professor of psychology at Northeastern University in Boston and editor of the *Journal of Nonverbal*

Behavior. And touch sometimes serves to establish a symbolic connection that transcends time and space. "Touch leaves a trace of the other person," Dr. Hall says. "Something of that person rubs off on you when you connect."

Research suggests that the touch response is part of the body's basic engineering plan. Even the casual physical contact that we share with others in the course of daily life—hugs, handshakes, and brief touches—makes a difference. For example:

- The touch of a nurse's hand can lower blood pressure and slow heart rate, both signs of reduced stress.
- The casual touch of a waitress brings in better tips.
- The touch of a librarian while patrons are signing out books creates more positive feelings about the library, says Dr. Field.

The bottom line? "Physical contact really matters to people," says Dr. Hall. "Plain and simple, touch conveys love."

A TOUCHY SUBJECT

Of course, this all sounds good on paper. In reality, though, many of us are reluctant to initiate physical contact with others. And we tend to pull away when others attempt to make contact with us, an act that can earn them the label of "touchy-feely."

"People are somewhat touch-deprived in this country," acknowledges Dr. Field. "I don't know quite where that comes from. There are a lot of taboos in our culture, and they've become worse with concerns about sexual harassment and abuse."

Make no mistake: Improper touch is not acceptable and should never be tolerated. But as a result, we've become extremely cautious, even fearful, of casual physical contact. Dr. Field says it's unfortunate that teachers are forbidden to hug their young charges. "Kids don't grow or develop if they don't get touched," she explains. "They're more likely to have aggression problems."

Things can get even more complicated in adulthood. Whether a hug, a pat, or a hand on the knee is experienced as comforting or assaultive depends in part on the context. It's one thing to do it in a crowded room and quite another to do it in a closed office.

Subtleties of technique can make all the difference. A doctor who greets you with a hearty handshake, for example, can dispel the impersonality of the medical encounter. The wordless message, "You're a real person to me" puts you at ease in what is usually a stressful situation. But if the handshake seems rudimentary and automatic—you imagine he goes through the same flesh-pressing motion with everyone—it can be of little, if any, comfort to you.

"As wonderful as touch can be, its meaning can be ambiguous, and it's hard to predict the impact it will have on another person," concludes Dr. Hall. "It's not always stress-reducing."

FINGER TIPS

Always keep in mind that as relaxing and invigorating as touch can be, not everyone will respond to it in the same way. Introducing it into your relationships with family and friends requires sensitivity and tact (a word, incidentally, that comes from the Latin *tactus*, "to touch"). Here are some guidelines.

Turn pro. Like other communication skills, casual touching can be learned, Dr. Hall says. "You may feel stiff at first, but over time it will become more natural," she says.

Start with a small gesture. "You needn't begin by hugging people right and left," says Dr. Hall. Research has shown that minor, unobtrusive touches that people barely notice or don't notice at all—a hand on the arm, a comforting pat—also have a positive psychological impact.

Pay attention. Be sensitive to cues that touching is unwelcome. There's plenty a person can do short of screaming, "Hands off!" that will send you the message. For example, if the other person breaks off eye contact or stiffens his posture, regard it as a signal to restore distance, says Dr. Hall.

Make an offer that can't be refused. One of the best ways to boost the touch content of your personal relationships is to offer a massage. "This is a nonthreatening kind of touch," says Dr. Field. "It's soothing, and it's something most people adore."

See also Massage

12-STEP GROUPS
FIND COMFORT ON COMMON GROUND

Remember how your parents taught you to ride a bike? "It's just one foot in front of the other," they said. Life works that way, too. We best navigate the bumps, major and minor, by putting one foot in front of the other, taking one step at a time.

Except once in a while we stumble, or we wander off course. Before we know it, stress isn't just a part of our lives. It's nearly all-consuming. That's when we need someone to steady us and point us in the right direction. Who better to do that than a person who has already been down the same road?

This is the guiding principle for so-called 12-step groups. These organizations unite people who share the same problem, so they can discuss their experiences and find the strength and courage to cope.

Twelve-step groups offer a unique kind of support to individuals facing a crisis in their lives. A special bond naturally forms when one person can say to another, "I know your pain."

YOU'LL NEVER WALK ALONE

The original 12-step group, Alcoholics Anonymous, was founded more than a half century ago. These days, similarly structured organizations exist for families of alcoholics (Al-Anon), for people who abuse drugs (Narcotics Anonymous), for people who are addicted to gambling (Gamblers Anonymous)—and that's just the beginning. You'll find 12-step groups for problems ranging from overeating to smoking to chronic fatigue syndrome.

These are all big-ticket troubles. Dealing with any one of them isn't easy. Trying to do it alone is even harder. The 12-step group lightens the burden by acknowledging your struggle and letting you know that you're not a bad person because of what you're going through.

"The first function of a 12-step group is to combat demoralization," says James T. Marron, M.D., clinical associate professor of family medicine at the State University of New York Health Science Center at Syracuse College of Medicine. "People can go to Alcoholics Anonymous, for example, and be unconditionally accepted." And because of this acceptance, the shame and isolation brought on by a drinking problem begins to dissipate.

LAYING THE FOUNDATION FOR CHANGE

Lots of folks turn to 12-step groups for solace and strength. By one estimate, at least one of every eight Americans has attended a 12-step meeting. Participation in a group won't eliminate stress, of course. But by sharing your burden with others, you take some of the weight off your own shoulders.

While the problems they address vary, the groups themselves operate in much the same way. Among the characteristics they have in common:

They're voluntary. No one profits from a 12-step group. There may be a minimal charge to subsidize the cost of the meeting space, but members assist one another in goodwill. "Twelve-step programs perform therapeutic functions without being engaged in 'therapy,' " Dr. Marron says.

They teach self-acceptance. The 12-step concept acknowledges that individuals are often not capable of solving all of their problems on their own. Accepting this can provide a tremendous sense of relief. A common theme of 12-step groups is asking for help from a power greater than oneself.

They emphasize empathy. Group meetings are designed to allow members to bring up issues that are troubling them, so they can benefit from the insight and encouragement of others. Discussions at these meetings usually focus on topics such as anger, powerlessness, family conflicts, job troubles—the stresses that we all contend with in the course of ordinary life.

They foster coping skills. The problems that draw people to 12-step meetings—alcohol, drugs, compulsive overeating, gambling—can in part be seen as attempts to deal with stress. "Alcoholics Anonymous and similar groups substitute a positive coping mechanism for a negative one," Dr. Marron points out. Members of Alcoholics Anonymous, for example, learn that instead of taking a drink, they can experience more positive release by sharing their troubles with others.

They provide a sense of community. Members of 12-step groups are there for each other at all times, not just during meetings. They spend a lot of time on the phone together—in fact, they're encouraged to do so. This benefits both parties involved: The "receiver" gets the counsel he needs, while the "giver" gets the satisfaction of knowing that he has helped someone else.

They focus on the present. "Most people who act in self-destructive ways are living the past," Dr. Marron says. "In fact, that's true of depressed people in general. The idea is to get out of the past and to not worry about the future but to stay in the present. That's the message behind 12-step slogans such as 'One day at a time.' "

They offer a design for living. In addition to offering social support, 12-step groups provide a belief system—a model for coping, surviving, and thriving. For members of Alcoholics Anonymous, it's summed up in the words of the Serenity Prayer:

God grant me
Serenity to accept the things I cannot change,
Courage to change the things I can,
And wisdom to know the difference.

Taking the First Step

Locating a 12-step group is as easy as looking in your telephone directory. You should find a list of these organizations in the blue pages. You can also watch your local newspaper for announcements of group meetings. Or contact your local Alcoholics Anonymous office. They may be able to guide you to other programs such as Al-Anon and Gamblers Anonymous.

Perhaps the most comprehensive resource for information on 12-step groups is what's known as a self-help clearinghouse. These organizations are located throughout the country, and they maintain lists of all of the groups in a particular city or region. To find a clearinghouse that services your area, contact the U.S. Self-Help Clearinghouse at 1-800-777-5556.

See also Support Groups

V

VACATION
YOUR PASSPORT TO INNER PEACE

So long, stress. Ta-ta, tension. Your bags are packed, and you're heading out for one blissful week of absolute, uninterrupted relaxation.

Ahhh, vacation: It's a necessary escape from the hectic and humdrum, a rare chance to unwind and re-energize. Leaving behind your home and job to luxuriate in leisure suspends the stress cycle, that spiral of fears and worries that constantly nags at you during difficult times.

"A vacation is a diversion," says Matti Gershenfeld, Ed.D., a psychologist and president of Couples Learning Center in Jenkintown, Pennsylvania. "You stop doing stress-inducing stuff, and you start doing something else." The sense of escape can leave you feeling refreshed and invigorated—all ready to take on the world.

Of course, you don't have to hop a plane bound for the Bahamas or retreat to a lakeside cabin for the purpose of diversion. You can distract yourself just as well by digging in your garden, listening to music, or curling up with a good book. The advantage of a vacation, though, is that you literally remove yourself from your day-to-day routine and all of its stress-producing pressures and demands. "You talk to different people, do different things, and experience life in a different environment—perhaps in a different culture," notes Dr. Gershenfeld.

THE BEST-LAID PLANS . . .

Many of us can't wait to get away from it all. Once the plans are made, we count the weeks, the days, the hours until we finally depart for our little piece of paradise. But sometimes we expect too much from the experience. "Most people get two weeks of vacation a year," Dr. Gershenfeld points out. "So there's a lot riding on it."

And the higher our expectations, the greater the potential for disappointment. Our vacation fantasies rarely include rainy afternoons, traffic detours, or overbooked hotels. Airline commercials feature fun-loving families landing promptly in a sunny clime—not exhausted, irritated travelers wondering just when their silver bird will be released from its holding pattern.

The point is, things can happen during your vacation that are simply beyond your control. And if you let them get to you, your experience is just going to compound your stress instead of relieving it.

The key to a truly healing holiday is adopting the right attitude. It might help to incorporate the following three phrases into your vacation mantra.

- Be sensible.
- Be realistic.
- Be accepting.

PLOT THE PERFECT GETAWAY

Perhaps the most important part of your vacation is deciding how you want to spend it. While there is no one-size-fits-all formula for tension-taming travel, the following tips can help you choose the right destination—and ensure that your plans proceed as smoothly as possible.

Tickle your fancy. To be truly relaxing, your vacation has to suit your needs, your tastes, and your lifestyle. "Some people who work hard and put in lots of hours want to spend their time vegging out on the beach and doing absolutely nothing," says Dr. Gershenfeld. "Others like the stimulation of a different culture and derive aesthetic pleasure from, say, visiting churches in a foreign country."

RE-ENTERING THE REAL WORLD

The better your vacation, the more of a letdown you're likely to experience when it's over, and you have to return to the daily grind. "The knot in your stomach when you get back to real life—that's a sign of a good time," says Matti Gershenfeld, Ed.D., a psychologist and president of the Couples Learning Center in Jenkintown, Pennsylvania.

The best tonic for postvacation blues is to look to the future. Start thinking about your next excursion. Sure, you just got back. But planning another trip can help you hold on to all those good feelings that you just experienced.

One option is to schedule a three-day weekend—a mini-vacation that will give you a smaller but vital dose of relaxation. "Some people don't give themselves permission to take little vacations during the year," says Dr. Gershenfeld. Now that you know how good it feels, resolve to treat yourself right more often.

Decide for yourself. Well-meaning family and friends may try to influence you with tales of their travels—the lovely little islands, quaint hotels, and tremendous tours that brought them great pleasure. But what worked wonders for them may not do the same for you. While river rafting is perfect for thrill-seeking Joe, for example, it might leave couch potato Jane a nervous wreck.

"Your friends might have had a terrific time in Jamaica, but if you don't like snorkeling and sunbathing, don't go there," says Dr. Gershenfeld. "And above all, don't be guided by fashion."

Don't cut corners. You can't ignore the reality of your budget limitations, but neither should you compromise your heart's desire. Let's say you've always dreamed of visiting Europe, but you go to Turkey instead because there's a package tour that seems too much of a bargain to turn down. "You'll beat up on yourself," says Dr. Gershenfeld. "Don't get suckered into a 'good deal.'"

243

In fact, if anything, you should think big when planning your vacation. After all, what could be more satisfying—and more stress-reducing—than doing something you've always wanted to do, something that means a lot to you?

"I had a client who dreamed of captaining a luxury boat," recalls Dr. Gershenfeld. "He skipped vacations and saved for three years, and then he had a fabulous time. He even enjoyed all of the plans and preparations. He took lots of pictures, and now he has the trip to look back on."

Negotiate when necessary. Choosing a destination can become complicated when a significant other is involved. Suppose you want to head for the mountains, while your spouse longs for the beach. In this situation, what you shouldn't do is compromise by going to a place that's marginally acceptable to both of you. "You'll both end up dissatisfied," Dr. Gershenfeld says.

Instead, examine the deeper issues: What does each of you want out of your vacation? Activity? Peace and quiet? Luxury? Simplicity? List your preferences, then search creatively for places that meet both your and your spouse's requirements.

If your wants and needs are truly incompatible, consider taking turns every year. Opt for a time-share on the Florida coast this summer, a cottage in the Adirondacks the next. Whatever you ultimately agree to, it's essential that both of you accept the decision in a spirit of goodwill.

Both parties should be supportive, good-natured, and accommodating, no matter whose turn it is.

Expect the unexpected. High hopes are part of the joy of planning a vacation. An executive who devotes all of his energy to his job 50 weeks a year wants the two weeks he spends with his family to be a time of perfect harmony. A couple who have drifted apart hope to get reacquainted in a relaxed atmosphere and recapture the bloom of their honeymoon years. A single woman dreams of meeting her soul mate on a Caribbean cruise.

When your expectations become rigid, however, every setback turns stressful. "Be flexible," advises Dr. Gershenfeld. After all, it's only realistic to anticipate some bad moments—this is real life, after all. Don't jump to the conclusion that your vacation is ruined if something goes wrong. "If you yell at your kids, for example, just apologize and try to be more accommodating from then on," Dr. Gershenfeld suggests.

If you expect that things won't go smoothly, you might find your travel filled with lots of pleasant surprises. And if something does go wrong, notes Dr. Gershenfeld, you'll find it a lot easier to turn the negative into a positive.

VALUES
KNOW WHAT MATTERS MOST

Many of us have at least one prized possession—something we treasure, something we would never part with. It could be anything: a piece of jewelry handed down by a beloved grandmother, a baseball autographed by one of the game's greats, a souvenir from an especially memorable vacation. No matter what the item, it has meaning and importance to us.

We hold our values in equally high regard. We can't see them or touch them as we can our cherished chachkas. But we feel so strongly about them that they define who we are as individuals and influence virtually all of our life choices.

"We humans have a fundamental desire, a basic motivation, to discover meaning and purpose in our lives," says Robert Hutzell, Ph.D., a psychologist at the Veterans Administration Medical Center in Knoxville, Iowa. "We derive meaning from that which is valuable to us." Our values, in other words, serve as a barometer by which we measure life's joy, fulfillment, and success.

Contrary to what we so often hear these days, we all have values. The problem is that they're not always clearly defined. Modern life being as chaotic as it is, we seldom take the time to sit down and reflect on what matters most to us. Without the direction that values provide, we set ourselves up for stress.

THE GUIDE INSIDE

Being attuned to your values, on the other hand, can actually stave off stress by keeping you focused and reminding you what's really important in life. "Strong values are like a good road map," says Dr. Hutzell. "If you know where you're headed, you don't get lost." They can help you:

Choose wisely. When you're unsure of your values, you agonize over decisions time and again. How can you decide which road to take if you don't know where you want to go? If your values are clear and crystallized, it's easy to turn down temptations that don't mesh with them.

A promotion at work, for example, can boost your ego—not to mention your bank account. But if the new responsibilities will cut into family time, which you know to be a basic value in your life, you may find the strength to turn down the offer.

Weather minor setbacks. Sometimes we allow ourselves to dwell on problems that, in the grand scheme of things, don't amount to all that much. A strong sense of values keeps these problems in perspective and insulates you against the stress they generate. Petty setbacks, disagreements, and annoyances tend to melt away when you have a solid grip on what's important.

Beat boredom. When we lose sight of our values, we lose interest in life. We find ourselves constantly asking, "Why bother?" "When we're not focused on what's important to us, we find no meaning in life," explains Dr. Hutzell. "We experience this as boredom."

Give bad habits the boot. When we feel adrift or unsatisfied, it's tempting to adopt unhealthful—even dangerous—behaviors to fill the void. "If we don't find what's meaningful in life, we go for the quick fix," says Dr. Hutzell. Some people turn to drugs or alcohol, he says, while others are driven to compulsive workaholism, keeping themselves so busy that they don't have time to think about how they feel.

Eventually, though, a bad habit becomes a vicious circle. As the behavior intensifies, supportive relationships crumble, life becomes more unstable—and we seek more powerful diversions.

246

The point is, none of these substitutes for values can ease the chronic sense that something is wrong. They don't address the underlying need for purpose, direction, and fulfillment.

A MATTER OF PRINCIPLES

If you want to get in touch with your authentic values, the first thing you must do is forget the stuff you were taught by your parents and teachers.

Discovering what really matters to you means putting aside what should be important in favor of what is important. Don't worry, though: Discarding "proper" values won't transform you into a bad person. Rather, it will lead you to your very own deeply held convictions.

The following exercise will help you define your own value system. As you proceed through the four steps, just remember that values in themselves are neither good nor bad, says Dr. Hutzell. It's how you act on them that is good or bad.

"For example, power may be a value to you," Dr. Hutzell says. "You can actualize it by robbing a bank (which is bad) or by making a substantial gift to an organization that will cure a disease (which is good)."

Here's how to pinpoint your principles—and make them part of your stress-relieving repertoire.

1. Start with a list. Grab a sheet of paper and a pencil. On the left-hand side of the paper, list whatever values you can think of. These don't have to be values you adhere to—just the kinds of things that society holds dear. Some examples include accomplishment, affection, good appearance, competition, cooperation, creativity, excitement, family, friendship, honesty, leadership, loyalty, leisure, bravery, responsibility, self-confidence, spirituality, stability, and wisdom. Use these to start your list, if you like, but be sure to add a few more of your own.

2. Give them rank. Now that you have a nice long list, you can assess how important these values are to you. Rate each value on a scale of 1 to 10—1 being not at all important and 10 being highly important. Write your scores in a second column.

247

3. Evaluate your success. Now comes the hard part. Again using a scale of 1 to 10, rate how you feel you're doing at achieving each value in your life. Write these scores in a third column. Then for each value, subtract the number in the third column from the number in the second column. Write the results in a fourth column on the right-hand side of the page.

4. Do some fact-finding. Now that you've completed your very own value chart, you can use it in two ways. First, take a look at the high-scoring items in the first column. These are the values that are authentically important to you. In a sense, they define your place in the world.

Then shift your attention to the fourth column. High numbers here indicate major discrepancies between what you want from life and what you're actually getting. You can use this information as inspiration in developing an action plan that will help you shape a less-stressed lifestyle that is more in sync with your value system. Now that's a value in itself!

VOLUNTEERING
HELP OTHERS TO HELP YOURSELF

Something magical happens around the holidays. Maybe it's the spirit of the season that moves us. Or maybe it's a last-ditch effort to make Santa's "good" list. Whatever the reason, we seem just a little more willing to reach out to those less fortunate and in need. For our compassion, we're rewarded with a profound sense of satisfaction that makes us feel a whole lot better about ourselves and the world around us.

That's a pretty good argument for making the simple act of giving a year-round activity. And it's backed up by some very convincing scientific proof that lending a hand does indeed lighten life's load—for those who give as well as those who receive.

"Volunteering is a very real buffer to stress," says Allan Luks, executive director of Big Brothers/Big Sisters in New York City, an organization that pairs adult volunteers with inner-city youths in a variety of educational and relationship-building activities. He cites the tension-taming feelings of warmth, energy, and euphoria that people typically experience when they volunteer—a phenomenon that has been dubbed helper's high.

In a study Luks conducted of 3,296 volunteers—from those who assist AIDS patients to those who help feed the homeless—an astounding 95 percent reported immediate, positive physical benefits from their time spent helping others. According to Luks, the study suggests that doing a good deed causes the brain to release endorphins, natural feel-good chemicals that melt away stress.

GOOD VIBRATIONS

You get much more from volunteering than just a fleeting flush of good feelings, Luks says. More than half of the people in his study reported long-lasting psychological benefits, including increases in self-worth, happiness, and optimism—and reductions in depression and feelings of helplessness. You'd be hard-pressed to find a better formula for stress reduction.

Volunteering supports your stress self-defense in other ways, too. For example, it can:

Deliver distraction. When you help others, you forget about your own troubles. Just like meditation, volunteering focuses your attention and short-circuits everyday stress triggers, says Luks.

Supply support. "People talk of being connected when they help others," says Luks. "The feelings you get from volunteering are the direct opposite of negative emotions such as loneliness."

Build self-esteem. It's impossible to feel rotten about yourself when you spend a part of your time helping others, says Phyllis Moen, Ph.D., professor of human development and sociology at Cornell University in Ithaca, New York. "If you've ever volunteered, you see yourself as someone who does something worthwhile," she notes.

Cultivate control. Many studies have shown that we handle stress best when we feel that we're in the driver's seat. Volunteer work fulfills this need for a sense of control.

LEND A HAND AND LIVE LONGER

The benefits of volunteering aren't "all in your head," either. There are plenty of physical perks as well. Research has shown that the act of giving can:

Add years to your life. In 1956 Dr. Moen began a long-term study of 1,000 women—all residents of upstate New York. At the start of the study, the women were interviewed about their roles as mothers, wives, friends, workers, and members of volunteer organizations. They were then followed for three decades. Of all of the women's life roles, "volunteering seemed to make the most difference in their physical health," says Dr. Moen.

Some of the participants passed away during the course of the study. Interestingly, the women's levels of social involvement in 1956 proved to be an accurate predictor of who would survive. But not just any social involvement: Membership in volunteer organizations—in which the women engaged in activities such as helping in hospitals and community libraries—made the greatest difference in longevity.

Dr. Moen also found that regular paid employment had none of the life-lengthening benefits of volunteering. "In what we do to earn a living, most of us don't have much control over the hours and aspects of our work," she says. "As a volunteer, we do productive work that we choose. And if we don't like it, we can do something else."

Diminish depression. In Dr. Moen's study women who engaged in volunteer work were less likely to be depressed but more likely to have higher self-esteem and to find greater satisfaction in life. Even those who, at the start of the study, were judged to be lacking in self-esteem and at high risk for depression showed significant gains in the intervening years if they spent time helping others.

"Seeing these improvements was really striking," says Dr. Moen. "Ordinarily, risk factors for depression tend to go up with age."

Ease aches and pains. For physical ailments caused or aggravated by stress, volunteer work may be the perfect prescription. Among the participants in Luks's study, for example, those who suffered from chronic headaches reported relief that lasted for

OPPORTUNITY KNOCKS

Choosing the right activity can make all the difference in whether your volunteer experience is a positive one. To find out what your options are, perhaps the best place to start is your telephone directory, says Allan Luks, executive director of Big Brothers/Big Sisters in New York City, an organization that pairs adult volunteers with inner-city youths in a variety of educational and relationship-building activities.

Check the blue pages for the heading "Volunteer Services." Or just browse through the various categories of listings to see if anything catches your attention.

Another option: Think of key words for volunteer opportunities that you'd be interested in, then look them up in the white pages of the phone book. For example, if you or a loved one has struggled against serious illness, you may find it especially rewarding to help others with the same health problem. Look up the condition—say, arthritis or cancer—in the white pages. There's bound to be an organization or foundation that can hook you up to volunteer opportunities.

Many cities operate volunteer action centers, which coordinate a broad spectrum of volunteer opportunities. You can find out if there's one serving your area by contacting your local government office or a national organization called Points of Light Foundation, 1737 H Street NW, Washington, DC 20006.

hours after volunteering. Others said that arthritis, back pain, and asthma became less troublesome.

It's not that any of these conditions were "cured," Luks explains. Rather, it's that the positive feelings associated with volunteering pushed pain sensitivity into the background—both while folks were helping others and afterward. "This allowed many of these people to function in ways they otherwise could not," Luks says.

CHOOSE YOUR CAUSE

No matter where you live, you'll likely discover that volunteer opportunities abound. Nonprofit organizations and other community groups are constantly in search of helping hands, and they'll welcome your offer of assistance. The following tips will help you maximize the stress-busting benefits of volunteering.

Follow your heart's desire. The most important criterion for a positive volunteer experience is choosing an activity that you genuinely enjoy. If what you're doing makes you uncomfortable or unhappy, it won't offer you much in the way of stress reduction. In fact, a very small proportion of the people Luks surveyed—1 percent—reported that their volunteer work actually increased their stress. This reaction was most common in people who felt that they had to help but that the situation was beyond their control.

As an example, Luks describes two women who volunteered in the same nursing home in the same city. One called it "the best thing that ever happened to her. She talked about walking into a room and holding a patient's hand—how much the person appreciated it and how good it felt," Luks recalls. "The other woman couldn't think about anything but the smell and her feeling that no matter what she did, she could never help the person.

"If you're not getting a good feeling, explore other volunteer situations," adds Luks. "Don't assume that you can't help someone in some other way."

Take the hands-on approach. "Helpers whose volunteer work includes personal contact—tutoring, helping the elderly, reading to the blind—are much more likely to report good feelings," says Luks. "Stuffing envelopes or baking cakes and cookies for fundraisers may be just as important, but people who do these types of tasks don't report the same benefits."

Talk to strangers. The most healthful volunteer activities involve working with people you don't know, says Luks. Helping family and friends is certainly a wonderful thing to do, but it rarely includes the element of choice and control that makes volunteering therapeutic.

Get real. A realistic, positive attitude makes helping others . . . well, helpful. If you set your sights on changing the person you're assisting—propelling a failing student onto the honor roll, for example, or bringing an AIDS patient back to health—you're liable to feel frustrated, depressed, and even more stressed. Instead, focus on the process: You're providing vital human support to someone who really wants it.

Make a commitment. Volunteering should be a regular activity. Like exercise, it's something you must keep on doing for maximum benefit. "If you volunteer just once in a while, it won't have much of a buffer effect against stress," says Luks.

In his study, those who participated in volunteer activities weekly were 10 times more likely to be in good health than those who did it annually. "The more frequently they helped, the greater the benefit," Luks says. His prescription for volunteering: at least two hours a week.

Don't feel obligated. "I'd hate for people to view volunteering as just another thing they should do," says Dr. Moen. For a woman with small children or a man whose job requires long hours, adding a volunteer commitment may just contribute to stress overload. "Take a good, hard look at your life," suggests Dr. Moen. "Volunteering may be something you can't do now but will do later."

Make helping a habit. You needn't join an organization to reap the benefits of volunteering. You'll find plenty of opportunities to help others in the course of your day-to-day routine. So-called random acts of kindness—opening a door for someone who has trouble doing it himself, shopping for a housebound neighbor—give you good feelings, too.

Interestingly, Luks found in his study that people who engage in "formal" volunteer work are more likely to pitch in off-the-cuff. "It's as if once you experience how good it feels to help others, you'll find ways to do it everywhere," he says.

WALKING

STAY ONE STEP AHEAD OF STRESS

Feeling like life is pummeling you with one sucker punch after another? Just remember: When the going gets tough, the tough get going.

Okay, so it's a cliché. But it's also smart advice. Believe it or not, moving your body can mend your mood and undo the physical effects of stress.

Best of all, you don't have to run marathons or hoist dumbbells to experience the stress-stomping benefits of exercise. In fact, all you really have to do is put one foot in front of the other.

That's right: Walking, the easiest and most natural of workouts, may also be the most therapeutic. Not only does it reinforce your resistance to stress, it also tones your muscles, strengthens your heart, and improves your circulation. And few things can clear those mental cobwebs and leave you feeling refreshed and invigorated like walking can.

THE POWER OF PERAMBULATION

We aren't accustomed to thinking of walking as exercise. After all, we've been hoofing it since we took our first tentative steps as toddlers. It's something we do automatically, without a whole lot of thought.

Yet research has demonstrated that when it comes to combating stress, walking can keep pace with more vigorous activities such as

TWO'S A CROWD?

Many people have discovered the pleasure of walking in the company of others. Couples use the time to reconnect with each other. Families enjoy Sunday afternoon strolls. And walking clubs, formal and informal, have spread across the land.

Walking en masse does have its downside, however. Finding a mutually pleasing pace may take some experimentation and compromise. And then there's the chatter factor: A perambulating gabfest may be a nice interpersonal interaction, but you're likely to miss out on the unique satisfaction that comes from feeling yourself in rhythmic motion.

"It's hard to be attuned to the rhythm of your walk if it has become a social encounter and your body is just being pulled along," says Deena Balboa, a psychotherapist who directs the Walking Center in New York City. "You should differentiate between walking as a stress reliever and walking as a social activity." If your goal is the former, then she suggests that you try being "alone together" as you walk in companionable silence.

Music is another sometimes mixed blessing. Many people enjoy a tuneful accompaniment to their walks, and for some, a soundtrack makes the minutes flow more easily. "But for others, music is an irritating distraction," says Balboa. What's worse, music that urges you to step more quickly than is comfortable can actually detract from your relaxation. Experiment with slower rhythms to find one that lends itself to a dancelike natural pace, she suggests.

running. One study found that people experienced significant improvements in feelings of self-esteem after a session of walking—not hip-swinging racewalking but a moderate stroll. In another study people enrolled in a walking program showed reductions in anxiety, while those enrolled in a more demanding running program did not.

"Walking has terrific mental health benefits," says Alan Miller, Ed.D., instructor at the Children and Families Professional Development Center of Florida International University in Miami. "And unlike running, it's injury-free, so you don't have to worry about setbacks."

WORK OFF THOSE WORKPLACE BLUES

Dr. Miller has witnessed firsthand just how effective walking can be in defusing job-related stress. His work began when he was asked to design a stress-relief program for people at real risk for burnout: staffers at a mental health institution.

His original program was a strenuous, continuous aerobic workout. There was only one problem: Few people stuck with it. "As the year unfolded, there were a lot of dropouts," Dr. Miller recalls. "It appealed only to people who were already fit and who looked good in fitness gear . . . it was like a fashion show."

An assistant suggested walking as an alternative. "People really took to it," says Dr. Miller. Intrigued, he set up a study to see just what walking could do. Of a group of 90 employees, 30 enrolled in a regular walking program, 30 participated in regular relaxation training, and 30 did nothing. "By far, the walkers had significantly greater reductions in work-related stress and anxiety," he says.

Interestingly, many of the successful walkers were not what you'd consider athletic types. In fact, this was the same bunch who had given a resounding thumbs-down to the aerobics program. These folks ranged in age from late thirties to fifties. Most hadn't exercised in years, and some were overweight. But at least three times a week, they walked around the grounds of the hospital for distances ranging from 1½ to 3 miles. After eight weeks virtually all had lost weight and lowered their heart rates—and they were walking faster to boot.

Even more impressive was the fact that walking seemed to make these people immune to work-related stress. Not that their jobs had changed. They still reported the same stressors: too much work, not enough support from their supervisors, and so on. "But the stressors didn't affect them as much," says Dr. Miller. "If their boss was a jerk when they started the program, he was still a jerk. They just didn't let it bother them."

STRAIGHTEN UP AND STRIDE RIGHT

Walking for stress relief doesn't require any fancy footwork—that's part of its appeal. But you can maximize the therapeutic benefits of your constitutionals with these tips from Deena Balboa, a psychotherapist who directs the Walking Center in New York City.

Don't emphasize exercise. Walking to relieve stress doesn't necessarily entail a strenuous so-many-miles-in-so-many-minutes workout. "From our point of view, walking is not exercise per se," Balboa says. "It can be used as exercise, but stress reduction isn't contingent on that."

Go natural. Forcing your body into fitness-walking mode, with its exaggerated arm and hip movements, is "a contradiction to your natural athletic grace," Balboa says. You may boost your heart rate, but you'll be tensing and contracting your body—certainly not what you want when you're trying to de-stress.

Don't weight. You'll also want to forgo the hand, wrist, and leg weights, Balboa says, since these devices can throw off your natural rhythm and gait. Even if you're walking for fitness, there's little evidence that using weights gives you a better workout.

Mind your movement. Practicing the technique known as mindfulness while you walk can enhance the calm and relaxation you experience. Simply stroll very slowly and open your mind to the sensations that arise as your feet make contact with the ground, flex, and lift off. Become aware of your breathing. Try to keep your rear foot in contact with the ground a shade longer than you're used to, just to see how it feels.

Center your stride. Ordinarily, we think of walking as starting from the hips. Instead, imagine a point in the area of your navel, or slightly higher, and envision your legs beginning their motion there. This actually corresponds to the anatomical structure of the muscle system involved in walking, and keeping the image in mind may help you adopt a more open, relaxing stride.

Get in the swing. "Artificially pumping your arms creates stress," says Balboa. "Let your arms adjust themselves to the speed at which you walk."

257

Feel like you're floating. Some people find that imagining a floating, skating kind of movement adds a graceful ease to their walking and reduces pounding on their joints. But don't take this as a prescription: If it feels uncomfortable, don't try to force it.

Find your rhythm. Each of us has a particular pace that is most soothing and energizing. It's a very individual matter. No one can tell you what yours is, but you'll know it when you find it. It just feels natural and right. At this speed, you're neither pushing yourself forward nor holding yourself back.

Make it routine. Balboa doesn't advocate walking so many times a week, so many minutes at a time. Instead, she suggests that you find ways to accommodate it in the structure of your life. "Once you discover that walking is appealing to you, you'll factor it into your day with enough consistency that it has a rewarding effect," Balboa says. "What works for you" is the only rule.

See also Exercise, Mindfulness

WRITING

PUT YOUR PROBLEMS ON PAPER

We devoted the better part of our grade-school years to honing our penmanship, and for what? These days we reserve our perfectly scribed Ps and Qs for signing checks, making to-do lists, and jotting reminders for family members. The last time many of us did anything more creative, it was to compose a masterwork on how we spent summer vacation.

If you're looking for a good reason to give your writing skills a workout, this might be it. Research has shown that putting pen to paper can help you release all of those powerful pent-up emotions that accompany stress. This not only enhances your ability to cope with a stressful situation but also produces measurable benefits such as better immune function and improved physical health.

When we keep our feelings bottled up inside, they allow stress to fester, which is a tremendous drain on our energy stores. Talking helps us get things off our chests—but many of us aren't all that comfortable revealing ourselves to others. Writing, on the other hand, enables us to purge in complete privacy.

What's more, "putting our feelings into writing structures the experience and creates meaning," says James Pennebaker, Ph.D., professor of psychology at Southern Methodist University in Dallas. It transforms a churning mass of painful emotions into a coherent story, with a beginning, a middle, and an end. "Once the event is organized, it can more readily be assimilated and set aside," Dr. Pennebaker says.

FEELING TENSE? THEN TAKE NOTE

People who keep diaries and journals derive tremendous release and satisfaction from the writing process. They know they have an outlet where they can unburden themselves and let their feelings flow in confidence, much as they might to a most empathetic, trusted friend or therapist. And they know they have somewhere to turn, in good times and bad.

Because it is such an effective stress-reducing tool, writing can:

Bolster physical health. In one of Dr. Pennebaker's experiments 23 university employees were instructed to write about some current or past trauma or upheaval in their lives. "I want you to just let go and express yourself and write about your deepest thoughts and feelings related to this issue," Dr. Pennebaker told the group. Meanwhile, another 18 employees were assigned to write about trivial topics such as their morning's activities or the room in which they were seated. These people were specifically told not to discuss their thoughts and feelings. Each group wrote for 20 minutes once a week.

After four weeks, all of the participants were given medical exams. The people who wrote about their personal problems showed significant improvement in liver function, along with lower levels of stress hormones in the blood. The folks in the other group didn't experience these benefits.

Reduce sick days. The people who wrote about their personal problems also lost notably fewer workdays to illness after the experiment was completed. Nearly three-quarters of these folks showed a decline in absenteeism between one month before and one month after the study. By comparison, less than half of the people in the control group had reductions in the number of sick days.

Boost immune function. In another study, this one involving college students, those asked to write about personal traumas for four consecutive days showed improvement in their disease-fighting immune function at the conclusion of the assignment. What's more, this improvement was still discernible six weeks later. By comparison, a control group who wrote about superficial topics demonstrated none of these benefits.

Help you handle adversity. Yet another of Dr. Pennebaker's studies featured 41 middle-age people who had recently been laid off. They were assigned to one of two groups: one that wrote about their feelings surrounding the loss of their jobs, the other that wrote about nontraumatic topics. A third group of 22 unemployed people didn't write at all.

Eight months later, more than half of the people who wrote about their layoffs had found jobs—more than twice the number of people who wrote about nontraumatic topics and four times the number of nonwriters. "I think that writing helped these folks come to terms with their hostility and anger at being laid off," Dr. Pennebaker says. The groups had the same number of interviews, but the writers were the ones who got jobs. "For the others, some of their hostility probably came through during their interviews," Dr. Pennebaker suggests.

Make change easier. Starting college is incredibly stressful: a new environment, new people, a more demanding workload— and all at once. You'd think that a writing assignment would simply compound a student's stress. But freshmen who sat down and put into words their deepest thoughts and feelings achieved better grade point averages in their first semester than those who wrote about inconsequential things. "Having the students write helped them get past the problems of adjustment," says Dr. Pennebaker.

SIGN OFF ON STRESS

You can reduce stress in your own life by applying the same writing process that Dr. Pennebaker uses in his studies. "It works best for people who find themselves thinking or worrying too much about something," he says. This could be a painful event from the past, a current crisis (such as a troubled relationship), or just more everyday hassles. Here are his guidelines.

Be regular. Commit yourself to writing for at least 20 minutes every day for four consecutive days. Find a place where you won't be disturbed—ideally, one that's separate from your familiar environment, such as a library.

Don't stop. The important thing is to write continually. Once you put pen to paper, keep the words flowing. Don't worry about grammar, sentence structure, spelling, or penmanship. Neatness doesn't count.

Let your mind wander. It's natural to ask, "What should I write about?"

"You have to be loose," Dr. Pennebaker says. You might start with the issue that seems to be bothering you, but if your writing takes an unexpected direction, just go with it. Some people stay with the same subject day after day, while others delve into different areas of their lives.

Go deep. Whatever your theme, allow yourself to explore your deepest thoughts and emotions. Remember, no one has to see what you're writing. "You can begin with how the events at hand relate to your childhood," says Dr. Pennebaker. "You can focus on your current situation or on the future. Some people explore who they are and who they'd like to be."

Choose what's comfortable. Many people prefer to do their writing in a diary or journal. But if you're more at home with a computer, that's fine, too. In his earliest studies Dr. Pennebaker's subjects wrote longhand with a pen. These days, he has them typing on computer keyboards. Even a typewriter or a quill pen will do.

Don't set limits. Though 20 minutes a day for four days is the recommended minimum for writing, you don't have to stop there.

If you feel that you can write longer on any given day, or if you have more to say after four days, give yourself free rein.

Expect a little sadness at first. When you start writing, you may not feel great right away. Many, but not all, of the people in Dr. Pennebaker's experiments reported that they felt a bit anxious or down for an hour or two after writing. This normal reaction to confronting feelings that you've kept hidden almost always dissipates within four days. If negative feelings persist beyond that period, you might do better with some personal support. "Consider talking things over with a close friend or a therapist," Dr. Pennebaker suggests.

Y

YOGA

THE POSE THAT REFRESHES

When we hear the word *yoga*, most of us conjure an image of exceptionally limber people stretching and bending their bodies in amazing ways. It hardly looks like the sort of thing you'd want to do when you're trying to unwind.

So it may come as a surprise that yoga has a long and rich history as a highly effective relaxation technique. This centuries-old healing art counteracts stress by helping you regain control of your body processes, your emotions, and your spiritual life. These are "your inner resources," according to Phil Nuernberger, Ph.D., psychologist and president of Mind Resource Technologies and a faculty member at the Himalayan International Institute of Yoga Science and Philosophy in Honesdale, Pennsylvania.

What's more, the unusual body positions that we're familiar with—they're called asanas—are actually only one part of yoga. Its teachings also emphasize controlled breathing, meditation, and diet. In fact, the multiple facets of yoga make it as much a science as a philosophy, Dr. Nuernberger says.

HEALING MIND AND BODY

Yoga is believed to have originated thousands of years ago, with the earliest known references to it dating back to around 3000 B.C. Even though it has been around a long time, it has proved that it

BREATHING EASY

Yoga features a number of different breathing techniques that by themselves can calm and relax you. For fast relief from stress, try one of the following exercises, recommended by Phil Nuernberger, Ph.D., psychologist and president of Mind Resource Technologies and a faculty member at the Himalayan International Institute of Yoga Science and Philosophy in Honesdale, Pennsylvania.

Alternate nostril breathing. "This technique quiets the mind," says Dr. Neurnberger. "And by controlling the breathing muscles, you also control your autonomic nervous system."

1. Determine which is your dominant nostril—it's the one through which most of your breath is passing. Close off the other nostril (the passive one) by gently pressing against it with a finger. Exhale for a count of four to six.

2. Now close off the dominant nostril and inhale through the passive one for the same count. Follow this pattern—exhaling through the dominant nostril and inhaling through the passive nostril—for three cycles.

3. Reverse the pattern: Exhale through the passive nostril and inhale through the dominant nostril for three cycles.

4. Breathe smoothly, evenly, and steadily throughout the exercise. Keep your inhalations and exhalations equal in length.

5. Do one complete set three times a day.

Complete breathing. This energizing exercise is a souped-up version of the diaphragmatic breathing that is at the heart of yoga.

1. After you've filled your lungs by pushing out your abdomen, expand your chest cavity still farther by raising your rib cage. Continue the inhalation as you slightly elevate your collarbones.

2. Now exhale fully, reversing the order: First lower your collarbones, then let your chest drop, then push the air out by drawing in your abdomen.

3. Repeat five or six times whenever you're feeling tired and sluggish. The oxygen boost will restore alertness.

can hold its own against the most modern of stressors. Study after study has turned up convincing evidence that yoga can help defuse stress by:

Enhancing alertness and energy levels. Researchers at Oxford University compared the effects of yoga breathing and stretching with those of other relaxation techniques. After 30 minutes of the yoga exercises the participants showed "a marked increase in perceptions of mental and physical energy, alertness, and enthusiasm," the researchers wrote. Yoga proved to be "significantly superior" to the other techniques in terms of its ability to boost energy and improve mood.

Reducing anxiety. In a study at Brooklyn College of the City University of New York, students who attended a hatha yoga class reported "significant reductions in stress from the first day of class. Lengthy training did not seem necessary to enjoy the stress-reducing benefits," the study's authors wrote. The students said that they felt less anxious, tense, depressed, angry, confused, and fatigued after their yoga sessions.

Boosting brain wave activity. Another study had participants engage in a more intense yoga program: a daily 50-minute session of yoga breathing and relaxation techniques. Over the course of a month, the participants showed a gradual but significant increase in the activity of alpha brain waves, which are associated with relaxation. What's more, their breathing rates slowed significantly— and their body weight gradually dropped.

FOCUSING ON THE FUNDAMENTALS

There are many different styles of yoga. In the United States most classes teach what is known as hatha yoga. But even within hatha yoga there are different "schools," or philosophies. Generally, though, they all feature the following components.

Breathing. Proper breathing technique is essential to the practice of yoga. "Breathing is the flywheel mechanism for the body," says Dr. Nuernberger. "If you don't breathe properly, you'll still have stress in your system, no matter how many relaxation exercises you do."

Yoga emphasizes diaphragmatic breathing. This means that instead of expanding your chest and sucking in your stomach when you inhale—which is what most of us do habitually—you push out your abdomen and lower your diaphragm muscle on the floor of your chest cavity. This allows air to flow deep into your lungs. Then when you exhale, you pull in your abdomen to raise your diaphragm and push air out.

Incidentally, this is how we breathe as infants. But as we grow up, we shift to chest breathing as we learn "good posture," says Dr. Nuernberger. Diaphragmatic breathing "is a matter of retraining your body to do what's natural," he says.

Poses. Yoga poses may look hard to do, but most are really nothing more than slow stretching—an activity that in itself is known to relax muscles and relieve stress. Their names—cobra, tree, mountain, and dancer, for example—are symbolic of the movements they entail. Synchronizing your inhalations and exhalations with each movement deepens relaxation, which in turn makes the pose more effective, Dr. Nuernberger says.

Mindfulness. Yoga calms your mind by focusing your awareness. "It's an exercise in mindfulness," Dr. Nuernberger says. As you slowly and smoothly assume each pose, your attention is held by the physical sensations it creates as well as by the emotions that accompany it. "Focusing on the mental associations that arise helps you discover what's really going on in your head," Dr. Nuernberger notes.

And as you gradually learn to hold a pose for 30 seconds, a minute, or even longer, your awareness deepens. "This allows you to really study your mind as it experiences the mental, emotional, and physical effects of the pose," Dr. Nuernberger explains.

Meditation. Sitting meditation, where you develop the ability to focus your awareness while remaining still, is another integral part of yoga. The simplest meditation is a breathing exercise in which you keep your attention on the sensation of your breath as it passes through a point between the nostrils at the bridge of your nose.

A Lesson in Relaxation

While you can practice yoga on your own, it's best to learn proper technique from an expert. Yoga classes can be found virtually everywhere. If possible, Dr. Nuernberger suggests, check out several different classes to find a knowledgeable instructor whom you'll feel comfortable working with. Inquire about the instructor's credentials—whom he has trained with and for how long, for example. Talk to his students as well. You want someone with a good understanding of breathing, not just a fitness trainer, Dr. Nuernberger says.

If you have lower back problems or arthritis, you have a lot to gain from yoga. But it is especially important to find the right teacher. "You need someone who has the training, experience, and skill to help you learn to work your body gently and carefully," Dr. Nuernberger says. The same applies for older folks.

Above all, you want an instructor who can inspire and guide you, Dr. Nuernberger says. Yoga is less a belief system than a discipline mastered through personal experimentation. "The teacher helps you learn but doesn't tell you what to do," he says.

See also Deep Breathing, Meditation, Mindfulness, Relaxation Response

INDEX

Boldface page references indicate main discussions of topic. Underscored references indicate boxed text. Prescription drugs are denoted with the symbol Rx.

Brain waves, 129–30, 265
Breathing, **76–79**
   alternate nostril, <u>264</u>
   with asthma, 42
   belly, <u>77</u>
   chest, <u>77</u>
   complete, <u>264</u>
   deep, 76–79, <u>77</u>
   facial massage and, 134
   hyperventilation, 78
   during imagery, 125
   in tai chi, 226–27
   in yoga, <u>264</u>, 265–66
B vitamins, 161, 163

C

Cabin fever, <u>157</u>
Caffeine, 163–64
Career change, **23–24**
Chamomile, 109
Children, parents' stress levels and, **50–52**
Cholesterol levels, effect of stress on, 145
Choline, 161
Cinnamon oil, in aromatherapy, 35
Circulation, increasing, 134
Claustrophobia, preventing, 33
Coffee, 163–64
Communication, **52–57**
   with family, 86–88
   health benefit of, with chronic illness, 12
   intimate, 102, 126–28, 215
   in lovemaking, 215
   during massage, 134–35
   pros and cons of, 52–53
   during relocation, 26
   during unemployment, 16
   wedding plans and, 13
Community services, therapeutic, 60–61
Competition, healthy, <u>180</u>

Compromise in marriage, 14
Concentration, affected by noise, 192
Confidence, 72–75, 112
Confrontation, handling, 37–40
Coping skills
   for divorce, 7
   family and, 85
   improving, with
     religion, 207
     12-step groups, 239
     writing, 260
Cortisol, 134
Counseling, **57–62**
   divorce and, 8–9
   goals of, understanding, 61–62
   group therapy, 8
   intimate talk and, 128
   professionals, 59–60
     selecting, 60–61
   purpose of, 58–59
   support groups, 8–10, 17, 221–24
   12-step groups, 238–40
Cucumber fragrance, to promote relaxation, 34

D

Dancing, **63–67**
Daydreaming, **67–71**. *See also* Visualization
Death in family, **9–11**, 85, <u>139</u>
Decision making, stress-free, **72–75**
Dental discomfort, relieving, with music, 151
Depression
   medication for, <u>139</u>
   postpartum, <u>21</u>
   postvacation, <u>243</u>
   remedies for
     aromatherapy, 35
     exercise, 82
     herbs, 108

Index

Index

Index

Water therapy, **118–21**, <u>119</u>. *See also*
 Flotation tanks
Weight loss, 33
Work-related stress
 career change, 23–24
 meditation for, 144
 unemployment, 15–17, <u>139</u>
 walking to relieve, 256
Worry
 Bach flower remedies, use in relieving,
 46
 confronting, <u>70</u>
 pets' effect on, 175

sex and, 213
sharing, with children, 52
Writing, 12, **258–62**

Y

Ylang-ylang fragrance, to relieve depression, 35
Yoga, **263–67**, <u>264</u>

Z

Zoloft (Rx), 108, <u>139</u>